The Rape of the Turin Shroud

How Christianity's most precious relic was wrongly condemned, and violated

William Meacham

LULU.COM

© 2005 William Meacham

All Rights Reserved. Fair use of text under copyright law allows limited free citation. For permission to quote larger texts please contact the author at wmeacham@hkucc.hku.hk

Cataloging-in-Publication Data

Meacham, William.
   The rape of the Turin Shroud : how Christianity's most precious relic was wrongly condemned, and violated / William Meacham.
         p.   cm.
   Includes bibliographical references and index.
   ISBN 1-4116-5769-1
   1. Holy shroud.
   BT587.S4
      232.966—dc22

Contents

Preface i

PART I: THE PINNACLE

1. The Shroud of Turin 1
2. Critique and Reply 32

PART II: THE FALL

3. The Ultimate Test? 52
4. Maneuvering and the Grand Council 60
5. The Dating 87
6. Grappling with the Result 99
7. Three Scenarios 120
8. Where Do We Stand with "the Date?" 136

PART III: THE DESECRATION

9. Road to Disaster 147
10. The "Restoration" and its Aftermath 171
11. Altered Shroud Unveiled 186
12. Impact on the Relic 201
13. Reactions 228

PART IV: WHAT NEXT FOR THE TURIN SHROUD?

14. New Research Proposals 237
15. A Final Effort 251

Epilogue 260
References 264
Index 276

The Author

William Meacham is an archaeologist specializing in South China. He has written or edited 7 books on archaeology (including *Archaeology in Hong Kong* published by Heinemann in 1981) and two books on English teaching. He has attended 18 international conferences, and published 51 articles (15 in peer-reviewed international journals) on various aspects of South China archaeology. Besides the Turin Shroud, other research interests are the origins of the Austronesians, and genealogy. Born in Nashville, Tennessee, Meacham was educated at Tulane University in New Orleans, the Sorbonne in Paris and the Gregorian University of Rome. He has lived in Hong Kong since 1970, holding positions at the Hong Kong Museum of History and the Christian Study Centre on Chinese Religion and Culture. Since 1980 he has been Hon. Research Fellow at the Centre of Asian Studies, University of Hong Kong. He has directed more than 30 archaeological excavations on government or private contract. The largest of these was the 16-month survey and salvage excavation of Chek Lap Kok island, site of Hong Kong's new airport.

His main involvements in the Turin Shroud are:

1983 – wrote the most comprehensive study of the Shroud ever published in a peer-reviewed academic journal, *Current Anthropology* published by the University of Chicago Press

1986 – member of the conference convened by the Pontifical Academy of Sciences and the Archbishop of Turin to advise on carbon dating the Shroud, by invitation of the conveners

2000 – delegate to the "world congress of experts" in Turin, by invitation of the Turin Archdiocese

2002 – attended the preview of the Shroud after "restoration," by invitation of the Turin Archdiocese.

Preface

This Book Arose Out Of The Fascination I have had for the last 24 years with the object known as the Shroud of Turin, *la Santa Sindone* or "Holy Shroud" as it is called in Italy. It has been a great honor for me to get to know most of the leading Shroud researchers of the late 20th century, especially some members of the American scientific team STURP. It was one of their reports that provoked my curiosity and consuming interest in the relic. Although I had heard of the Turin Shroud before, I had, probably like millions of non-Catholics around the world, dismissed out of hand the notion that a sheet now in Italy could, by some miraculous means, have the actual image of Christ's body imprinted on it. Although I had seen occasional references to the relic on TV, the whole notion seemed so far-fetched as not to merit serious consideration.

What brought me "face-to-face" with the great unresolved mystery of the Shroud, and changed the course of my life, was an article in *Archaeology* magazine in 1981. Leafing through it as usual when it arrived, I stopped on an article entitled "The Shroud of Turin through the microscope" and read the first few paragraphs. It was compelling stuff, not overly dramatized or sensational, just the findings of a photographer and a microscopist who were baffled by what they had just spent a few weeks investigating. I found it hard to believe that after such intense scrutiny there was no explanation for the image, not even a plausible theory about how it was made. As one might expect, the relic correlated well with the Biblical accounts of Christ's torture and execution, yet it had features that no forger would ever think of. And the realism of the anatomy and blood flows seemed to indicate that it was the imprint of a real corpse. These considerations led me to a long study over several months, reading everything about the Shroud that I could get my hands on, corresponding with the researchers I could contact, and finally writing a major article on the subject. It was published in 1983 in the journal *Current Anthropology* and forms Part I of this book.

The 1980s constitute a veritable peak in the history of the Shroud, on several accounts. It was afforded the greatest scientific attention during this time, as the results of the STURP team were being published in scientific journals. And it had undoubtedly attracted the widest following and popular interest of any relic in the world. I was fortunate to become involved at the precise moment that I did, as the Shroud was coming to the so-called "ultimate test," namely C-14 dating. This was a topic that I knew well, having made use of C-14 many times as an archaeologist. The culmination of my involvement came in 1986, when I was invited by the Pontifical Academy of Sciences to attend a conference it was organizing to consult with scholars on the carbon dating of the Shroud. From there it was all downhill. It soon became clear that the project to date the Shroud was marked by petty rivalries, arrogance, secrecy, influence-peddling and incompetent planning.

What followed was, predictably in many ways, a disaster. Not only was the Shroud denied the proper carbon dating it deserved, but it then suffered the most unwarranted universal condemnation as a fraud. In one dramatic announcement in October 1988, the Shroud was knocked from its lofty position as the possible burial cloth of Jesus Christ bearing His blood and image, to that of a medieval fake that someone had done up with a bit of linen. A second and even worse disaster would follow in 2002 when, in the name of conservation, the cloth was subjected to what has to be called unintentional vandalism. The authorities in Turin allowed an aggressive and unnecessary "restoration" that removed an important part of the relic's historical heritage, destroyed valuable scientific data and altered the cloth and its study forever. This operation was planned and executed in total secrecy, but when news leaked out it caused an uproar.

These things should not have happened. Even worse, the carbon dating is still, amazingly almost two decades later, unconfirmed by follow-up measurements, and its accuracy is disputed on solid grounds. The "restoration" has been roundly condemned by most scholars, who see it as a conservation and scientific disaster. The reasons why these events happened are complicated, and I have tried to put them under the microscope and sort out the various strands. One finds a mélange of stubborn, arrogant and/or abrasive personalities, cronyism, opportunism, all sorts of intrigues, a political situation inherited from Machiavelli, and a pinch of anti-Americanism thrown in for good measure. And that is only considering the pro-Shroud factions!

I had the opportunity to meet the main players in both dramas, and was able to observe how they thought and worked. The person mainly responsible for the C-14 debacle was the scientific adviser to the archbishop of Turin, Luigi Gonella. He was an animated pipe-smoking lecturer whom I got to know fairly well; we spent hours in conversation on numerous occasions, and had lengthy correspondence right down to the wire. I have tried to demonstrate in these pages what the basic mistakes were, and how easily they might have been avoided. Ironically, maddeningly, the same sorts of mistakes were made again in the "restoration," for many of the same reasons, by a new set of advisers appointed by a new archbishop. I met Cardinal Poletto in 2000, not long after he was installed as archbishop of Turin. We seemed to hit it off immediately, partly due to the fact that I was the only Italian-speaking foreigner at a conference his archdiocese was hosting. I saw him again, at his invitation, at the unveiling of the "new-look" Shroud and we had several exchanges of correspondence after that. It did not take long to realize that my first, rather positive impression of him could not have been more wrong.

This book focuses on these two major events. It is not intended to be a complete and up-to-date survey of research on the Shroud, though the reader is given a broad introduction, and brought right up to the present on major issues. Part I is a general overview of how the study of the relic stood in 1983, and what the principal areas of contention were. Part II describes the lead-up to the carbon-dating of 1988 and its aftermath, which continues to the present day. Part III deals with the disastrous intervention wrongly called a "restoration" that took place in 2002. Part IV reviews the current situation, new initiatives and the prospects for future research.

As the reader will learn from Part I, there are literally hundreds of research nooks and crannies under the general rubric of the study of the Shroud. Since the 1980s, there have been a few advances in our understanding of the body image and the bloodstains, particularly in exactly what constitutes the image, but no major breakthroughs. There have been new and outrageous theories, as always, such as the claim that Leonardo da Vinci created the Shroud (pity that it was first recorded a hundred years before he was born), or that the image is a proto-photograph (centuries before the discovery of photography) on cloth of all things. There have been wild Rorschach-like "discoveries" of a multitude of objects supposedly present in the image, including the crucifixion nails, the lance, the scourge, a host of flowers, cryptic inscriptions, and all sorts of other stuff. And there have been serious doubts cast on the reliability of the pollen evidence, notably the fact that most types were not identified down to species level, and so cannot be definitively said to have come from the Middle East.

But far and away the greatest focus in Shroud writing of the last 17 years has been on the C-14 dating, especially how it might be incorrect. This has become by far the most important and over-riding issue, as the Shroud cannot be authentic if the C-14 date is correct. The editor of a major New York publishing house said he felt this book did not deal with the main question that most people would want to know – did the Shroud wrap the body of Christ or not? He clearly had not read much of what I sent him, as everything hinges on the carbon dating issue. In a very real way it has become **the** crucial question for the Shroud: could the cloth possibly be 2000 years old in the light of the carbon dates?

Since September 2002 much attention has also been devoted to the damage done by the "restoration" – a tragedy if the cloth is indeed the real burial shroud of Christ. I have tried to tell the stories of these two historic events in the saga of the Shroud, as far as I can reconstruct them from my own memories and notes, plus the accounts of others. It is the terribly depressing story of a most unwarranted fall from grace, and an inexcusable desecration. Or one might say that, like the One Whose image it bears, the cloth was unjustly condemned, and then defiled. The damage from the "restoration" is permanent, while that of the carbon dating is merely to the Shroud's reputation. Another New York editor commented that the book had a most unsatisfactory conclusion. Alas, this is true. Neither story has a happy ending. But sometime in the not-too-distant future, the dating of the Shroud just might.

PART I. THE PINNACLE

1. The Shroud of Turin

Of All Religious Relics, the reputed burial cloth of Christ held since 1578 in Turin has generated the greatest controversy. Centuries before science cast the issue in a totally new perspective, disputes over the authenticity of the Shroud involved eminent prelates and provoked a minor ecclesiastical power struggle. From its first recorded exhibition in France in the 1350s, this cloth has been the object of mass veneration, on the one hand, and scorn from a number of learned clerics and freethinkers, on the other. Appearing as it did in an age of unparalleled relic-mongering and forgery and, if genuine, lacking documentation of its whereabouts for 1,300 years, the Shroud would certainly have long ago been consigned to the ranks of spurious relics (along with several other shrouds with similar claims) were it not for the extraordinary image it bears.

Sepia-yellow in color, the apparent frontal and dorsal imprints of a man's body may be discerned on this 4.3 x 1.1-m linen cloth. Stains of a slightly darker carmine or rust color, with the appearance of blood, are seen in areas consistent with the biblical account of the scourging and crucifixion of Christ. The image lacks the sharp outline and vivid color of a painting and is described as "melting away" as the viewer approaches the cloth. Yet the consensus of skeptical opinion up to the 1930s (with a few surviving remnants today) was that the image was indeed a medieval painting of Jesus that had through time taken on the appearance of a truly ancient relic.

Modern technology served as a catalyst to renewed controversy when the Shroud was first photographed, during a rare exhibition in 1898. Black-and-white photography had the fortuitous effect of considerably heightening the contrast of the image, thus bringing out details not readily discernible to the naked eye. Remarkably, its negative image was found to be an altogether more lifelike portrait of the body and, especially, of the face. From the rather grotesque and murky facial imprint visible on the cloth, reversal of light and dark revealed a harmonious and properly proportioned visage. This discovery of course created a sensation in the media, with claims of miraculous intervention and accusations of darkroom hoax.

Photography made another and far more important contribution in making available copies and enlargements of the Shroud image for detailed study by anatomists and art historians. By the time of its next exhibition in 1931, the Shroud had attracted a considerable following among scholars; it was inspected at that time by experts in various fields, and a vastly superior set of photographs was taken. The scientific inquiry into this object, whether medieval fraud or "the holiest icon upon the holiest relic" (Stacpoole 1978), had begun, culminating by 1980 in what must be the most intensive and varied scrutiny by scientific means of any archaeological or art object in history.

In a statement that may not be as hyperbolic as it seems, Walsh (1963:8) observed: "The Shroud of Turin is either the most awesome and instructive relic of Jesus Christ in existence ... or it is one of the most ingenious, most unbelievably clever, products of the human mind and hand on record. It is one or the other; there is no middle ground." However, as in almost every complex issue, there is indeed a middle ground (albeit rather weak) in this case, but it has not to my knowledge been investigated in other writings on the Shroud. Clearly, every remote possibility of forgery, hoax, accident, or combination thereof must be examined before a firm archaeological/historical judgement on this artifact can be proffered.

Of the three interrelated areas of interest in this relic – authenticity, mechanism of image formation, and religious significance – we shall be concerned here mainly with the first. While high technology and theology contend respectively with the other aspects of the relic, determination of its origin and place in history is an archaeological issue. The cloth is an unprovenanced artifact purporting to be associated with events in recorded history and encoded with considerable information about its past. Direct study and testing of the relic since 1900 have yielded a wealth of data, and here I attempt to review and summarize the major empirical data and other relevant research. Further, and unlike the authors of the most recent broad reviews on Shroud studies (e.g. Wilson 1978, Sox 1981, Schwalbe and Rogers 1982), I address the question of authenticity in historical/ archaeological terms.

Authentication of the Shroud differs from that of manuscripts, sculptures, and other materials only in the wide range of data from many disciplines – anatomy, scientific analyses, history, archaeology, art history, exegesis – which has a bearing on the issue. The fact that it is a religious relic associated with supernatural claims is of no consequence here; certainly there is no justification for employing different or stricter criteria than for any other important artifact, except perhaps in according greater consideration to the possibility of forgery. Considerations of the Shroud have frequently been marred by an intense desire to believe and an imprecise use of data among the overzealous and by an insistence on impossible standards of proof among the skeptics. Clearly, authenticity should be judged on criteria no more and no less stringent than those applied in the usual identification of ancient city sites, royal tombs, manuscripts, etc.

The body imprint

Scientific scrutiny of the Shroud image began in 1900 at the Sorbonne. Under the direction of Yves Delage, professor of comparative anatomy, a study was undertaken of the physiology and pathology of the apparent body imprint and of the possible manner of its formation. The image was found to be anatomically flawless down to minor details: the characteristic features of rigor mortis, wounds, and blood flows provided conclusive evidence to the anatomists that the image was formed by direct or indirect contact with a corpse, not painted onto the cloth or scorched thereon by a hot statue (two of the current theories). On this point all medical opinion since the time of Delage has been unanimous (notably Hynek 1936; Vignon 1939; Moedder 1949; Caselli 1950; La Cava 1953; Sava 1957; Judica-Cordiglia 1961; Barbet 1963; Bucklin 1970; Willis, in Wilson 1978; Cameron 1978; Zugibe, in Murphy 1981). This line of evidence is of great importance in the question of authenticity and is briefly reviewed below.

The body was that of an adult male, nude, with beard, mustache, and long hair falling to the shoulders and drawn at the back into a pigtail. Height is estimated at between 5 ft. 9 in. and 5 ft. 11 in. (175-180 cm), weight at 165-180 lb. (75-81 kg), and age at 30 to 45 years. Carleton Coon (quoted in Wilcox 1977:133) describes the man as "of a physical type found in modern times among Sephardic Jews and noble Arabs." Curto (quoted in Sox 1981:70, 131), however, describes the physiognomy as more Iranian than Semitic. The body is well proportioned and muscular, with no observable defects.

Death had occurred several hours before the deposition of the corpse, which was laid out on half of the Shroud, the other half then being drawn over the head to cover the body. It is clear that the cloth was in contact with the body for at least a few hours, but not more than two to three days, assuming that decomposition was progressing at the normal rate. Both frontal and dorsal images have the marks of many small drops of a postmortem serous fluid exuded from the pores. There is, however, no evidence of initial decomposition of the body, no issue of fluids from the orifices, and no decline of rigor mortis leading to flattening of the back and blurred or double imprints.

Rigor mortis is seen in the stiffness of the extremities, the retraction of the thumbs (discussed below), and the distention of the feet. It has frozen an attitude of death while hanging by the arms; the rib cage is abnormally expanded, the large pectoral muscles are in an attitude of extreme inspiration (enlarged and drawn up toward the collarbone and arms), the lower abdomen is distended, and the epigastric hollow is drawn in sharply. The protrusion of the femoral quadriceps and hip muscles is consistent with slow death by hanging, during which the victim must raise his body by exertion of the legs in order to exhale.

The evidence of death in a position of suspension by the arms coupled with the characteristic wounds and blood flows indicate that the individual had been crucified. The rigor mortis position of outstretched arms would have had to be broken in order to cross the hands at the pelvis for burial, and a probable result is seen in the slight dislocation of the right elbow and shoulder. The feet indicate something of their original positioning on the cross, the left being placed on the instep of the right with a single nail impaling both. Apparently there was some flexion of the left knee to achieve this position, leaving the left foot somewhat higher than the right. Two theories, each supported by experimental or wartime observations, contend as regards cause of death: asphyxiation due to muscular spasm, progressive rigidity, and inability to exhale (Barbet, Hynek, Bucklin) or circulatory failure from lowering of blood pressure and pooling of blood in the lower extremities (Moedder, Willis).

Of greatest interest and importance are the wounds. As with the general anatomy of the image, the wounds, blood flows, and the stains themselves appear to forensic pathologists flawless and unfakeable. "Each of the different wounds acted in a characteristic fashion. Each bled in a manner, which corresponded to the nature of the injury. The blood followed gravity in every instance" (Bucklin 1961:5). The bloodstains are perfect, bordered pictures of blood clots, with a concentration of red corpuscles around the edge of the clot and a tiny area of serum inside. Also discernible are a number of facial wounds, listed by Willis (cited in Wilson 1978:23) as swelling of both eyebrows, torn right eyelid, large swelling below right eye, swollen nose, bruise on right cheek, swelling in left cheek and left side of chin.

The body is peppered with marks of a severe flogging estimated at between 60 and 120 lashes of a whip with two or three studs at the thong end. Each contusion is about 3.7 cm long, and these are found on both sides of the body from the shoulders to the calves, with only the arms spared. Superimposed on the marks of flogging on the right shoulder and left scapular region are two broad excoriated areas, generally considered to have resulted from friction or pressure from a flat surface, as from carrying the crossbar or writhing on the cross. There are also contusions on both knees and cuts on the left kneecap, as from repeated falls.

The wounds of the crucifixion itself are seen in the blood flows from the wrists and feet. One of the most interesting features of the Shroud is that the nail wounds are in the wrists, not in the palm as traditionally depicted in art. Experimenting with cadavers and amputated arms, Barbet (1953:102-20) demonstrated that nailing at the point indicated on the Shroud image, the so-called space of Destot between the bones of the wrist, allowed the body weight to be supported, whereas the palm would tear away from the nail under a fraction of the body weight. Sava (1957:440) holds that the wristbones and tendons would be severely damaged by nailing and that the Shroud figure was nailed through the wrist end of the forearm, but most medical opinion concurs in siting the nailing at the wrist. Barbet also observed that the median nerve was invariably injured by the nail, causing the thumb to retract into the palm. Neither thumb is visible on the Shroud, their position in the palm presumably being retained by rigor mortis.

The blood flow from the wrists trails down the forearms at two angles, roughly 55° and 65° from the axis of the arm, thus allowing the crucifixion position of the arms to be reconstructed. It is generally agreed that the separate flows from the left wrist and the interrupted streams along the length of the arm are due to slightly different positions assumed by the body on the cross. This seesaw motion is interpreted as necessary simply in order to breathe or as an attempt to relieve the pain in the wrists (the median nerve is also sensory and pain from injuries to it excruciating). A postmortem blood flow with separation of serum is seen around the left wrist and more copiously at the feet, presumably from the removal of the nails.

The pathology described thus far may well have characterized any number of crucifixion victims, since beating, scourging, carrying the crossbar, and nailing were common traits of a Roman execution. The lacerations about the upper head and the wound in the side are unusual and thus crucial in the identification of the Shroud figure. The exact nature of these wounds, especially whether they were inflicted on a living body and whether they could have been faked, is highly significant. Around the upper scalp and extending to its vertex are at least 30 blood flows from spike punctures. These wounds exhibit the same realism as those of the hand and feet: the bleeding is highly characteristic of scalp wounds with the retraction of torn vessels, the blood meets obstructions as it flows and pools on the forehead and hair, and there appears to be swelling around the points of laceration (though Bucklin [personal communication, 1982] doubts that swelling can be discerned). Several clots have the distinctive characteristics of either venous or arterial blood, as seen in the density, uniformity, or modality of coagulation (Rodante 1982). One writer (Freeland, cited in Sox 1981) questions the highly visible nature of the wounds and clots, as if the Shroud man had been bald or the stains painted over the body image.

Between the fifth and sixth ribs on the right side is an oval puncture about 4.4 x 1.1 cm. Blood has flowed down from this wound and also onto the lower back, indicating a second outflow when the body was moved to a horizontal position. All authorities agree that this wound was inflicted after death, judging from the small quantity of blood issued, the separation of clot and serum, the lack of swelling, and the deeper color and more viscous consistency of the blood. Stains of a body fluid are intermingled with the blood, and numerous theories have been offered as to its origin: pericardial fluid (Judica, Barbet), fluid from the pleural sac (Moedder), or serous fluid from settled blood in the pleural cavity (Saval, Bucklin).

So convincing was the realism of these wounds and their association with the biblical accounts that Delage, an agnostic, declared them "a bundle of imposing probabilities" and concluded that the Shroud figure was indeed Christ. His assistant, Vignon (1937), declared the Shroud's identification to be "as sure as a photograph or set of fingerprints." Ironically, the most vehement opposition was to come from two of Europe's most learned clerics.

The history of the Shroud

While medical studies of the body image were providing strong evidence for genuineness, inquiries into the Shroud's history showed its case to be extremely weak. In 1900, the distinguished scholar Canon Ulisse Chevalier published a series of historical documents shedding light on the early years of the Shroud in France and casting seemingly insurmountable doubts on its authenticity. An English Jesuit, Herbert Thurston, condemned the relic in a persuasive and powerful style "that muted and almost stifled the controversy in the English-speaking world" (Walsh 1963:69).

With rivals at Besançon, Cadouin, Champiegne, and elsewhere, this purported "Shroud of Christ" appeared in 1353 in Lirey, France, under mysterious circumstances and with no documentation whatever. It immediately began to draw large numbers of pilgrims to a modest wooden church founded by the Shroud's owner and tended by six clergy but in financial difficulties. Its exhibition was condemned by the resident bishop, Henri de Poitiers. His successor, Pierre d'Arcis, compiled a memorandum in 1389 urging the pope to prohibit further exhibitions of the relic because its fraudulent nature had been discovered by de Poitiers and an unnamed artist had confessed to painting the image. To d'Arcis, the absence of historical reference was equally damning; he considered it "quite unlikely that the Holy Evangelists would have omitted to record an imprint on Christ's burial linens, or that the fact should have remained hidden until the present time" (quoted in Thurston 1903). In all the recorded veneration of countless relics down to the 13th century, there had been no mention of Christ's shroud's bearing an imprint of his body. This silence of history together with the suspicious circumstances of the Shroud's appearance and the confession of the artist seemed sufficient to settle the matter. Thurston concluded confidently, "The case is here so strong that ... the probability of an error in the verdict of history must be accounted, it seems to me, as almost infinitesimal." However, this historical argumentum ex silencio must be considered as an open verdict, as we shall see.

In 1203, a French soldier with the Crusaders camped in Constantinople (who were responsible for the sack of the city the following year) noted that a church there exhibited every Friday the cloth in which Christ was buried, and "his figure could be plainly seen there" (de Clari 1936:112). It is likely that this cloth and the Turin Shroud are the same, especially in view of the pollen evidence (discussed below) and the fact that these are the only known "Shrouds of Christ" with a body imprint. It now seems virtually certain that the Turin Shroud was among the spoils of the Crusades, along with many other relics looted from churches and monasteries in the East and brought back to Europe. Another shroud, now at Cadouin, was found by the Crusaders at Antioch in 1098, brought back to France, and venerated down to the present. (Unfortunately for its cult, the Cadouin Shroud was discovered to have ornamental bands in Kufic carrying 11th century Moslem prayers [Francez 1935:7].) Wilson (1978:200-215) argues that the Turin Shroud was held and secretly worshipped by the Knights Templars between 1204 and 1314, passing later into history in the possession of a knight with the same name as the earlier Templar master of Normandy (Geoffrey de Charny). Others (e.g.Rinaldi 1972:18) identify the Turin Shroud with the "Burial Sheet of the Redeemer" brought to Besançon from Constantinople, according to unsubstantiated tradition, by a Crusader captain in 1207.

The enigma of the Shroud's history prior to the Crusades will probably never be resolved, but certain points of departure for hypothesis can be established. Pollen samples taken from it reveal that it has been in Turkey and Palestine, and the medical evidence seems to place it in the era of crucifixion. These data strongly suggest that the Shroud is a relic from the early church period. Whether forgery, accident, or genuine, however, the cloth has escaped the gaze of history through a long period in which a relic purporting to be Christ's burial linen and actually bearing his image would have attracted enormous attention and pilgrimage. Whereas other important relics acquired by the Byzantine capital were received with much fanfare and ample recording, there is no mention of when or from what quarter this shroud was obtained. It first appears in the lists of relics held at Constantinople in 1093 as "the linens found in the tomb after the resurrection."

Of the many relics which "came to light" during the first great cult of relics in the 4th century, there is no mention of a shroud. However, history is not totally silent on the possible preservation of Christ's burial cloth. In a pilgrim's account dated ca. 570 there occurs a reference to "the cloth which was over the head of Jesus" kept in a cave convent on the Jordan River. In 670, another pilgrim described having seen the 8-ft.-long shroud of Christ exhibited in a church in Jerusalem (cited in Green 1969). Earlier references to the preservation of the burial linens are more legendary. A passage in the apocryphal 2nd century "Gospel of the Hebrews" relating that Jesus gave his shroud to the servant of the priest and a statement by St. Nino of the 4th century that the burial linen was held first by Pilate's wife and then by Luke the evangelist, "who put it in a place known only to himself."

It is of course impossible to establish whether any of these early references actually describe the Turin Shroud, and we may conclude only that it was possibly lost or kept in relative obscurity during the early centuries, eventually being taken to Constantinople. If genuine, the most difficult time for which to construct a plausible scenario is the earliest period. How might such an important relic of Christ's burial have been preserved by persons and in circumstances unknown to the early church at large? And, whether genuine or forged, what is to account for the 700 to 1,000 years during which the image on the cloth is not mentioned?

The actual shroud of Christ may well have been kept in obscurity by 1st century Christians, perhaps for political reasons and/or out of aversion to an "unclean" object of the dead. By A.D. 66 the Judaeo-Christians had migrated east of the Jordan, and thereafter little is known of them apart from their increasing isolation from the early church and their heretical tendencies. If the Shroud had been taken from Jerusalem by this group, its obscurity in the early centuries would be understandable. Justin Martyr, writing in mid-2nd century, observed that Christians who still kept the practices of orthodox Judaism were a rarity regarded with much suspicion.

Other factors which may have played a role in the Shroud's early history and absence of documentation are (1) a very gradual emergence of a visible image on the cloth, (2) folding or wrapping of the cloth so that none or only a portion of the image was visible, and (3) storage, oblivion, and re-discovery of the relic. In times of prosperity as in turmoil and persecution, valued relics were customarily placed in various parts of church structures, homes, and catacombs; it often happened that these objects were forgotten, only coming to light in later construction or warfare. The looting of Edessa (Urfa, Turkey) by 12th century Turkish Moslems, for example, yielded "many treasures hidden in secret places, foundations, roofs from the earliest times of the fathers and elders ... of which the citizens knew nothing" (Segal 1970:253). Similarly, it was not uncommon for manuscripts, works of art, and relics kept in monasteries gradually to drift out of the collective memory; the most notable example is the Codex Sinaiticus, which reposed in a Sinai monastery for over 1,000 years, its importance totally unknown to its keepers.

Wilson (1978:109-93) has offered an elaborate and ingenious identification of the Shroud, folded four times to show only the face, with the Mandylion, a cloth said to have received the miraculous imprint of Christ's face and to have been taken to Edessa in ca. A.D. 40 by the disciple Thaddeus. This semi-legendary account of the "Image of Edessa" describes it as having been hidden in a wall during a persecution in A.D. 57 and forgotten until its discovery during a siege of the city ca. 525. The history of the Mandylion is well documented thereafter; it was held at Edessa until 944 and then at Constantinople until its disappearance in 1204. There are, however, numerous problems with a Shroud/Mandylion link (Cameron 1980), notably the difference in size, separate mention on relic lists, and the silence on its eventual "revelation" as a burial cloth.

The tradition of the miraculous imprint of Christ's face developed first in the Byzantine empire. Gibbon (1776-78: chap. 49) records that "before the end of the sixth century, these images made without hands were propagated in the camps and cities of the Eastern empire." In the 7th and 8th centuries in the West arises a similar tradition, that of Veronica, who wiped the brow of Christ with her veil and found a facial imprint remaining. It is quite possible that these traditions have an ultimate basis in the Shroud and its figure, transformed into an image of the living Christ to accord with early Byzantine iconographic conventions. On the other hand, the flourishing of these traditions represents a most likely impetus and context for a forged burial cloth with body imprint.

In sum, although the Shroud's history prior to 1353 is a matter of much rich conjecture and little firm evidence, there are numerous possible avenues by which the Shroud could have come down to us from the Jerusalem of A.D. 30. Genuine or forged, the absence of references to it in the 1st millennium is equally enigmatic. It must be admitted, however, that even if the Shroud's history could be extended back to the early Byzantine era, the case for its authenticity would not be significantly improved.

The Shroud and the Biblical record

The fact that the Shroud is not easily harmonized with the Gospel accounts has been taken as evidence both for and against authenticity. A number of biblical scholars (discussed in Bulst 1957 and O'Rahilley 1941) have rejected the Shroud because of a perceived conflict on two points: the washing of the body and the type of linen cloths used in wrapping it. Robinson (1978:69), on the other hand, suggests that "no forger starting, as he inevitably would, from the Gospel narratives, and especially that of the fourth, would have created the Shroud we have." The Shroud could of course be genuine and not necessarily agree in every detail with the biblical account: it could also have been forged by persons who were close to the early burial traditions and therefore based their work on a better understanding of the Johannine Gospel account than is possible today.

The wounds seen in the Shroud image correspond perfectly with those of Christ recorded in the Gospel accounts: beating with fists and blow to the face with a club, flogging, crown of thorns, nailing in hands (Aramaic *yad*, including wrists and base of forearm) and feet, lance thrust to the side (the right side, according to tradition) after death, issue of "blood and water" from the side wound, legs unbroken, McNair (1978:23) contends that such an exact concordance could hardly be coincidental: "it seems to me otiose, if not ridiculous, to spend time arguing ... about the identity of the man represented in the Turin Shroud. Whether genuine or fake, the representation is obviously Jesus Christ."

The apparent bloodstains on the Shroud conflict with the long-established tradition in biblical exegesis that Christ's body was washed before burial, which was carried out "following the Jewish burial custom" (John 19:40). The phrase, however, refers directly to the deposition of the body in a linen cloth together with spices. All of the Gospels convey the information that Christ's burial was hasty and incomplete because of the approaching Sabbath. In the earlier accounts of Mark and Luke, the women are said to be returning on Sunday morning to anoint the body with ointments prepared over the Sabbath, when washing a body for burial was effectively forbidden by the ritual proscription of moving or lifting a corpse.

Greater difficulties are encountered in John's descriptions of the burial linens. The synoptic Gospels record that the body was wrapped or folded in a fine linen *sindon* or sheet. Although the traditional idea is that this sheet was wound around the body, there is no difficulty in reconciling it with the Shroud. John (20:5-8) describes the body as "bound" with *othonia*, a word of uncertain meaning generally taken as "cloth" or "cloths." In the empty tomb he relates seeing "the *othonia* lying there, but the napkin (*soudarion*) which had been over the head not lying with the *othonia* but folded [or rolled up] in a place by itself." To elucidate this passage, almost as many theories as there are possibilities have been put forward; one which would exclude the Shroud is that the linen sheet was cut up into bands to wrap around the corpse, but most exegetes reject this notion. The fact that Luke describes the body as wrapped in a *sindon* and then relates that the *othonia* were seen in the empty tomb is taken by some as an equation of the two, by others as a distinction. Most commentators identify the Shroud with the *sindon* and offer one of the following interpretations:

(1) The *othonia* is the Shroud, the *soudarion* is a chin band tied around the head to hold up the lower jaw, and the hands and feet were bound with linen strips. In the account of Lazarus, a *soudarion* is mentioned "around his face," and his hands and feet are bound with *keiriai* (twisted rushes). Three-dimensional projections of the Shroud face have indicated a retraction of beard and hair where a chin band would have been tied. The Greek *soudarion* is clearly a kerchief or napkin.

(2) The *soudarion* is the Shroud, and the *othonia* are bands used to tie up the body. In the vernacular Aramaic, *soudara* included larger cloths, and the phrases "over his head" and "rolled up in a place by itself" suggest an item more substantial than a mere kerchief.

Clearly, the Shroud as a "fifth gospel" is difficult to harmonize with the others. Although it can be worked into the biblical accounts of the burial linen, no evidence for its authenticity can be gleaned therefrom. On the other hand, the exact correspondence of the wounds of Christ with those of the Shroud man is of supreme importance; if genuine, the Shroud would provide a most extraordinary archaeological reflection of the crucifixion accounts rendered by the evangelists. But upon this ultimate question, the verdict of history and exegesis must be recorded as open.

Scientific analyses

Direct examination of the Shroud by scientific means began in 1969-73 with the appointment of an 11-member Turin Commission (1976) to advise on the preservation of the relic and on specific testing which might be undertaken. Five of its members were scientists, and preliminary studies of samples of the cloth were conducted by them in 1973. A much more detailed examination of the Shroud was carried out in 1978-81 by a group of American scientists known as the Shroud of Turin Research Project (Culliton 1978, Bortin 1980, Stevenson and Habermas 1981, Schwalbe and Rogers 1982).

Samples of pollen collected from the Shroud by commission member Frei (1978) yielded identifications of 49 species of plants, representative of specific phytogeographical regions. In addition to 16 species of plants found in northern Europe, Frei identified 13 species of halophyte and desert plants "very characteristic of or exclusive to the Negev and Dead Sea area." A further 20 plant types were assigned to the Anatolian steppes, particularly the region of southwestern Turkey-northern Syria, and the Istanbul area. Frei concluded that the Shroud must have been exposed to air in the past in Palestine, Turkey, and Europe. Suggestions that the Shroud pollen derives from long-distance wind-borne deposits or from dust from the Crusaders' boots do not merit serious discussion.

The cloth itself has been described (Raes 1976) as a three-to-one herringbone twill, a common weave in antiquity but generally used in silks of the first centuries A.D. rather than linen. The thread was hand-spun and hand-loomed; after ca. 1200, most European thread was spun on the wheel. Minute traces of cotton fibers were discovered, an indication that the Shroud was woven on a loom also used for weaving cotton. (The use of equipment for working both cotton and linen would have been permitted by the ancient Jewish ritual code whereas wool and linen would have been worked on different looms to avoid the prohibited "mixing of kinds.") The cotton was of the Asian *Gossypum herbaceum*, and some commentators have construed its presence as conclusive evidence of a Middle Eastern origin. While not common in Europe until much later, cotton was being woven in Spain as early as the 8th century and in Holland by the 12th.

The Turin Commission conducted a series of tests aimed at clarifying the nature of the image. Thread samples were removed from the "blood" and image areas for laboratory investigation. Conventional and electron microscopic examination revealed an absence of heterogeneous coloring material or pigment. The image and "blood" stains were reported to have penetrated only the top fibrils; there had been no capillary action, and no material was caught in the crevices between threads. Both paint and blood seemed to be ruled out, and magnification up to 50,000 times showed the image to consist of fine yellow-red granules seemingly forming part of the fibers themselves and defying identification. Finally, standard forensic tests for haematic residues of blood yielded negative results.

The Shroud of Turin Research Project (STURP) formed around a nucleus of scientists studying the Shroud by means of computer enhancement and image analysis. Jackson et al. (1977) scanned the image with a microdensitometer to record lightness variations in the image intensity and found a correlation with probable cloth-to-body distance, assuming that the Shroud was draped loosely over the corpse. They concluded that the image contains three-dimensional information, and confirmation was obtained by the use of a VP-8 Image Analyzer to convert shades of image intensity into vertical relief. Unlike ordinary photographs or paintings, the Shroud image converted into an undistorted three-dimensional figure, a phenomenon which suggested that the image-forming process acted uniformly through space over the body, front and back, and did not depend on contact of cloth with body at every point. Computer analysis (Tamburelli 1981) of the body image also revealed that it was formed nondirectionally, whereas the scourge marks exhibited a radiation from two centers to the left and right of the body, the former being somewhat higher than the latter. Enlargements of the scourge marks revealed an extraordinary detail consisting of minute scratches.

The Shroud face is also highly detailed, and the relief figure constructed therefrom had an extraordinary clarity and lifelike appearance. Retraction of the hair and beard where a chin band might have been tied has been noted. Flat, button-like objects interpreted as coins appear on both eyes; the protuberances stand out prominently when processed by isodensity enhancement (Stevenson and Habermas 1981:fig.17). Independently of STURP, another researcher (Filas 1980), working with third-generation enlargements of the 1931 photographs, noted the presence of a design over the right eye, apparently containing the letters UCAI. Filter photographs and enhancements done by STURP also show UC and AI shapes, but somewhat askew (Weaver 1980:753). Whanger (quoted in a United Press International report, April 8, 1982) found exact agreement between the shape and motif of a coin of Roman Palestine and the image over the right eye, when superimposed in polarized light. There is, however, no general agreement on the inscription or on the identification of the protuberances as coins.

The blood areas were the subject of special attention from STURP, employing analytical methods of much greater sensitivity than those used by the Turin Commission. Even during cursory inspection, however, it was discovered that, contrary to the Commission's findings, the stains do penetrate to the reverse side of the cloth. Color photomicroscopy (Pellicori and Evans 1981:41) showed the stains to consist of red-orange amorphous encrustations caught in the fibrils and in the crevices. Unlike body image areas, the blood regions exhibit the capillary and meniscus characteristics of viscous liquids, viz., penetration, matting, and cementing of the fibers – a phenomenon consistent with blood, paint, or other staining agents. Ultraviolet fluorescence photographs (Gilbert and Gilbert 1980) revealed a pale aura around the stains at the wrist, side wound, and feet, with a fluorescence similar to that of serum, X-ray fluorescence measurements (Morris, Schwalbe, and London 1980) showed significant concentrations of iron only in the blood areas. Both transmission and reflection spectroscopy yielded an absorption pattern characteristic of hemoglobin, and chemical conversion of the suspected heme to a porphyrin was accomplished (Heller and Adler 1980). Blood constituents other than heme derivatives – protein, bilirubin, and albumin – were also identified chemically (Heller and Adler 1981:87-91). A total of 12 tests confirming the presence of whole blood on the Shroud are described by Heller and Adler (1981:92). Finally, fluorescent antigen-antibody reactions (Bollone, Jorio, and Massaro 1981) indicated that the blood is human blood.

The presence of traces of whole blood must be considered as firmly established, with the probability that the blood is human. It is possible, of course, that an artist or forger worked with blood to touch up a body image obtained by other means. Attempts to ascertain how the image came to be imprinted on the cloth have not yielded definitive results. An impressive array of optical and microscopic examinations was conducted, including most of those used in testing for blood constituents, infrared thermography and radiography, micro-Raman analysis, and examination by ion microprobe and electron scanning microscope (Jumper and Mottern 1980). There was general agreement among researchers on the nature of the image – degradation and/or dehydration of the cellulose in superficial fibers resulting in a faint reflection of light in the visible range (Pellicori 1980). Only the topmost fibrils of each thread are dehydrated, even in the darkest areas of the image, and no significant traces of pigments, dyes, stains, chemicals, or organic or inorganic substances were found in the image. It was thus determined that the image was not painted, printed, or otherwise artificially imposed on the cloth, nor was it the result of any known reaction of the cloth to spices, oils, or biochemicals produced by the body in life or death. STURP concluded that "there are no chemical or physical methods ... and no combination of physical, chemical, biological or medical circumstances which explain the image adequately" (Joan Janney, quoted in an Associated Press report, October 11, 1981). Two theories currently contend among STURP researchers: a "photolysis effect" (heat or radiation scorch) and a "latent image process" whereby the cloth was sensitized by materials absorbed by direct contact with a corpse. Wags were quick to label these "the first Polaroid from Palestine" and "a Christ contact print."

Much publicity has been generated by the assertions of McCrone (1980), a former STURP consultant, that the image is a painting, judging from the microscopic identification of traces of iron oxide and a protein (i.e., possible pigment and binder) in image areas. The STURP analysis of the Shroud's surface yielded much particulate matter of possible artists' pigments such as alizarin, charcoal, and ultramarine, as well as iron, calcium, strontium (possibly from the soaking process for early linen), tiny bits of wire, insect remains, wax droplets, a thread of lady's pantyhose, etc. (Wilson 1981). However, this matter was distributed randomly or inconsistently over the cloth and had no relationship to the image, which was found to be substanceless, according to the combined results of photomicroscopy, X-radiography, electron microscopy, chemical analyses, and mass spectrometry. McCrone's claims have been convincingly refuted in several STURP technical reports (Pellicori and Evans 1980:42; Pellicori 1980:1918; Heller and Adler 1981:91-94; Schwalbe and Rogers 1982:11-24). The results of previous work by the Italian commission also run totally counter to those claims (Filogamo and Zina 1976:35-37; Brandone and Borroni 1978:205-14; Frei 1982:5). Undaunted, McCrone (personal communication, 1982) continues to stake his reputation on the interpretation of the Shroud image as "an easel painting ... as a very dilute water color in a tempera medium."

More promising for future research was the identification by microanalyst Giovanni Riggi of a substance chemically resembling natron, a powder used in ancient Egypt to dehydrate the corpse prior to embalming. An accelerated dehydration process producing a form of Volckringer (1942) print similar to those left by plants pressed in paper is a possibility now under investigation. While further research may shed new light on the origins of the image, the possibility must be recognized that the precise mechanism of image formation may never be known. Scientific testing of the Shroud has not, however, reached a dead end; autoradiography of the entire cloth, thread-by-thread microscopic search, a complete vacuuming of the cloth for pollen and other particles, and of course C-14 dating have been suggested.

Proposals for radiocarbon dating of samples from the Shroud are still under consideration by the Catholic church, although approval has been given in principle. The result eventually obtained will undoubtedly have an enormous and, I would submit, unwarranted impact on the general view of the Shroud's authenticity. A C-14 age of 2,000 years would not appreciably tilt the scales toward genuineness, as only the cloth, not the image, would be so dated. A more recent date of whatever magnitude would also fail to settle the matter in view of the many possibilities of exchange and contamination over the centuries (variations in ambient atmosphere, boiling in oil and water, exposure to smoke and fire, contact with other organic materials) and the still unknown conditions of image formation, which affected the very cellulose of the linen. The antiquity of the Shroud can, however, be established from archaeological data now available, employing criteria commonly accepted for the dating of manuscripts, ceramics, and stone and metal artifacts not subjected to radiometric measurements.

The fact that the exact manner of image formation is not and may never be known does not pose a serious obstacle to establishing the Shroud's authenticity. The absence of a satisfactory explanation of the image formation does not, as Mueller (1982:27) argues rather curiously, rule out natural processes and leave only human artifice or the supernatural. Rather, the information obtained from medical studies and direct scientific testing establishes the framework for the issue: the Shroud was used to enshroud a corpse, and the image is the result of some form of interaction between body and cloth and does not derive from the use of paint, powder, acid, or other materials which could have been used to create an image on cloth. Whatever process gave rise to the image, the necessary conditions may have prevailed accidentally during a forger's attempted use of a corpse to stain the cloth in an actual burial. It is virtually unimaginable that a forger of any period would have known of a secret "dry" method (as proposed by Nickell 1979) to produce such an image, a method apparently used only once and evasive of the most sophisticated modern means of detection. The evidence certainly points very strongly toward a natural though extremely unusual process, possibly aided by substances placed with the body and linen at the time of contact.

Anthropological, archaeological, and art historical issues

There is evidence that the body once folded in the Shroud was the victim of a Roman crucifixion. Though used as a method of execution by the Persians, the Phoenicians, the Greeks, and other societies of antiquity, crucifixion in the Roman world was distinctive in a number of ways. Flogging invariably preceded execution and was usually carried out as the condemned proceeded to the crucifixion site; the victim was made to carry his own crossbar and was tied or nailed thereto and then hoisted onto a cross; or a T-shaped frame. Evidence in the Shroud image attests to each of these traits, except that the Shroud man was stationary with arms above the head or outstretched during the flogging. Further, both the whip marks and the side wound appear to have been inflicted with Roman implements. Unlike the depictions of medieval artists, the dumbbell shape of the scourge wounds and their occurrence in groups of two or three match exactly the *plumbatae* (pellets) affixed to each end of the multithonged Roman *flagrum* (whip), a specimen of which was excavated at Herculaneum. The side wound is an ellipse corresponding exactly to excavated examples of the leaf-shaped point of the *lancea* (lance) likely to have been used by the militia: it does not match the typical points of the *hasta* (spear), *hasta veliaris* (short spear), or *pilum* (javelin) used by the infantry. The lance thrust to the side of Christ was, according to Origen of the 4th century, administered, following the Roman military custom, *sub alas* (below the armpits), where the wound of the Shroud image is located.

The wrist-nailing of the Shroud image is highly significant, as it contradicts the entire tradition in Christian art from the first crucifixion and crucifixion scenes of the early 6th century (hardly 200 years after crucifixion was abolished) down to the 17th century, of placing the nails in the palms (McNair 1978:35). The few portrayals thereafter (Van Dyck, Rubens) of nailing in the wrist have been considered influenced by the Shroud or chronological markers for dating it. Similarly, the impaling of both feet with a single nail occurs in art only in the 11th century and after. Again, the Shroud is construed by some as the origin of the trend, by others as influenced by it. The style of nailing of wrist and feet was confirmed as Roman by a recent archaeological discovery. The first human remains with evidence of crucifixion were unearthed by bulldozers at Giv'at ha-Mivtar, near Jerusalem, in 1968. Among the stone ossuaries of 35 persons deceased ca. A.D. 50-70, one marked with the name Johanan held the remains of a young adult male whose heel bones were riveted by a single nail with traces of wood adhering to it (Tzaferis 1970). At the wrist end of the forearm, a scratch mark as if from a nail was identified on the radial bone; parts of the scratch had been worn smooth from "friction, grating and grinding between the radial bone and the nail towards the end of the crucifixion" (Haas 1970:58), a grim confirmation of the seesaw motion deduced by Barbet to have characterized the final agonies of the Shroud man.

In several important respects, however, the Shroud evidence varies from the usual crucifixion and burial practices of 1st century Palestine. Prior to crucifixion, a wide range of tortures might be inflicted: gouging of the eyes, mutilations, burning of the hair, etc. (Hengel 1977). The choice of torments apparently depended on the inclinations of the execution party and was bounded only by a concern to avoid the premature death of the condemned. The crown of thorns devised for Christ and the mocking and beatings appear to derive from the judicially sanctioned subjection of the condemned to the caprice of his guards. The Shroud man, like Christ, was flogged in a stationary position rather than on the way to the execution ground. In deference to strong Jewish feeling against leaving a corpse exposed after sunset, the Roman administration in Palestine allowed the breaking of the legs (*crurifragium*) to hasten death. John's Gospel (19:32) specifically records that the thieves crucified with Christ had their legs broken in order that the bodies could be taken down before nightfall. The right tibia, left tibia, and fibula of the Johanan remains were also broken, but the legs of the Shroud man were not. There is no historical mention of any other method of hastening death or coup de grace, and indeed crucifixion elsewhere in the empire was mandated to be a slow and agonizing death, usually lasting 24-36 hours. The lance thrust to the side of Christ thus appears as a capricious and unique act by one of the guards.

Again out of consideration for local custom, the Romans allowed the bodies of crucified Jews to be buried in a common pit instead of being left on the cross or thrown on a heap for scavenging animals as was the general practice. Certainly the use of a sheet of fine linen cloth such as the Shroud would indicate a degree of wealth, respect, family ties, or ranking not normally pertaining to common criminals. In general burial practice, the body would have been washed and anointed with oils, and the linen would not have been removed from the body. In other respects, the Shroud does accord with burial customs known or surmised of 1st century Jews. The account by Maimonides, a 12th century Jewish scholar at Cordova, parallels what can be constructed from the 4th century Palestinian Talmud, 2nd century Mishna, and biblical accounts: "After the eyes and mouth are closed, the body is washed; it is then anointed with perfumes and rolled up in a sheet of white linen, in which aromatic spices are placed." The possible presence of a chin band and coins over the eyes has been noted; the failure to wash the body may be explained by the Sabbath prohibition or by the existence of early injunctions, similar to those later incorporated in the medieval codes of Rabbinical law, against washing of the body or cutting of the hair, beard, and fingernails of victims of capital punishment or violent death (Lavoie et al. 1981). Finally, the burial posture of the Shroud figure is seen in a number of skeletons excavated at the ca. 200 B.C.-A.D. 70 cemetery of the Essene sect at Qumran (Wilson 1955:60), which were laid flat, facing upwards, elbows bent and hands crossed over the chest or pelvis. Sox (1981:134), however, sees the position as a reflection of medieval modesty.

The placing of coins or shards over the eyes of the corpse was known among medieval Jews and believed to be an ancient tradition (Bender 1895:101-3) to prevent the eyes from opening before glimpsing the next world; in the pagan tradition, coins were placed on the body as payment to Charon for crossing the River Styx. Recent excavations (Hachlili 1979:34) at Jewish tombs of the 1st century A.D. near Jericho have yielded the first evidence of this practice; two coins (A.D. 41-44) were found inside a skull, undoubtedly having fallen through the eye sockets. On the Shroud, the pattern over the right eye exactly matches the size and shape of some of the cruder coins (leptons) of the procuratorial series in Judea, especially those of Gratus (A.D. 15-26) and Pilate (26-36). The UCAI "inscription" was suggested to be a misspelling of the Greek TIBERIOU KAICAROC ("Tiberius Caesar," A.D. 14-37); in 1981 an unpublished coin bearing the letters IOUCAI was discovered in a collection (F. Filas, news release, September 1, 1981). Although the letter-like shapes on the Shroud are not clear enough to be distinguished with certainty from vagaries of the image and the weave, their location in the correct position on the coin shape when seen in relief would seem to give the inscription a small measure of credibility. One cannot, however, go very far with this evidence, for even if the imprint could be confirmed as a Pilate coin, such coins were circulating for at least several decades after minting and were probably obtainable for a considerable time thereafter, the coins of Pilate having gained a certain notoriety in Judea for their use of pagan symbols (Kanael 1963).

Coon's description, noted above, of the Shroud face as Semitic in appearance is supported by Stewart (cited in Stevenson and Habermas 1081:35), who points out other features of the image which suggest a Middle Eastern origin. The beard, hair parted in the middle and falling to the shoulders, and pigtail indicate that the man was not Greek or Roman. The unbound pigtail has been described as "perhaps the most strikingly Jewish feature" of the Shroud (Wilson 1978:54) and has been shown to have been a very common hairstyle for Jewish men in antiquity. The estimated height of the Shroud man at around 175-180 cm corresponds with the average height (178 cm) of adult male skeletons excavated in the 1st century cemetery near Jerusalem (Haas 1970) and with the ideal male height of 4 ells (176 cm) according to an interpretation of the Talmud (Kraus 1910-11).

Some of the earliest representations of Christ from the 2nd to 4th centuries portray him as youthful, clean-shaven, and Greco-Roman; others depict a bearded, Semitic face much more akin to that of the Shroud. Beginning in the 6th century, the face of Christ in Byzantine art became highly conventionalized, with a certain resemblance to the Shroud figure.

Vignon (1939) noted 20 peculiarities in the Shroud face (e.g. a transverse streak across the forehead, a V shape at the bridge of the nose, a fork in the beard, etc.) that are common in Byzantine iconography. He suggested that the Shroud might have been the source of this artistic tradition. Whanger and Whanger, using a system of polarized light to superimpose images, found 46 points of congruence between details of the Shroud face and the face of Christ in a 6th century Mt. Sinai mosaic and 63 points of agreement between the Shroud face and the face of Christ on a 7th century Byzantine coin. In other respects, however, the Shroud image differs markedly from Byzantine art of the early centuries in revealing a dead Christ, covered with wounds and blood, nude, lacking any indication of majesty or divinity. The crucifixes and crucifixion scenes of the 5th to 8th centuries invariably show a nonsuffering, glorified Christ, eyes open, clad in a tunic, with no bleeding or signs of physical agony. Again, the evidence indicates very strongly that the Shroud image does not derive from the art of this or any era, but may be the source of certain features.

In summary, the evidence from anthropology, archaeology, and art history corroborates in a compelling manner that of medical and scientific analyses. It should now be considered well-established that the Shroud is indeed an archaeological document of crucifixion – a conclusion reached by STURP and most serious students of the Shroud since the 1930s. Attempts to interpret it as a painting (McCrone), a wood-block print (Curto 1976), a bas-relief rubbing (Nickell 1979), a scorch from a hot statue (Papini 1982), or a colored "clay press" (Gabrielli 1976) are untenable, derive from consideration of only a small portion of the evidence, ignore the vast array of data to the contrary, and need not be discussed further. The confirmation by archaeology of numerous details found in the image and of hypotheses deduced therefrom – nailing of the wrist, single nailing of both feet together, seesaw motion on the cross, coins on the eyes, burial posture, and Middle Eastern origin, even the UCAI "misspelling" – give the Shroud an undeniable ring of authenticity as an archaeological object.

The pollen, the Semitic appearance of the figure, and other anthropological evidence combine to indicate an origin of the Shroud in Palestine or possibly Asia Minor; the pathological data coupled with the evidence of Roman implements and style allow it to be assigned with confidence to the period of Roman crucifixion, thus from the Roman conquest of Turkey and Palestine in 133-66 B.C. to Constantine's banning of this form of execution ca. A.D. 315. The "obvious" representation of Christ in the image further narrows the dating of the Shroud to A.D. 30-315. On this final point of identity we arrive at the "crux" of the issue, for there were thousands of crucifixions during this period in Palestine and Asia Minor.

Forgery/accident hypotheses

The identification of the Shroud figure may be approached by testing the uniqueness of the set of traits it shares with the historical description of the death of Christ. That is, the question may be posed whether these shared details can be established to a reasonable degree as historically specific, in the same manner that, for example, the singular characteristics of the tomb of Tutankhamen or the Shang-dynasty kings mentioned in oracle texts allow a definite identification. Such an archaeological/historical identification may be initiated by endeavoring to generate alternative hypotheses, derived from the known historical context, which might account for the configuration of features characterizing the Shroud. Calculations of cumulative probabilities (e.g. Donovan 1980; Stevenson and Habermas 1981:124-29) based on mere historical guesswork (legs not broken: 1 chance in 3; lance thrust to side: 1 in 27; etc.) are of no scientific validity whatever.

In order to be as definitive as possible, we shall examine a wide range of scenarios – some little more credible in ancient history than the notion that Hitler is alive in Brazil is in the present. And yet, any conceivable scenario which could be successfully superimposed on the Shroud's particular pattern of data would have to be taken seriously. In considering the Shroud as a possible forgery, an unwarranted emphasis on intentionality creeps into the discussion. Between deliberate hoax and true relic are various shades of accident, mistaken identity, excessive reverence for an inspirational "visual aid," and/or exaggerated claims. The ultimately important question is, of course, not how this image on cloth came to be taken as Christ's, but how it acquired such an extraordinary accuracy in the details of Christ's historically known life and anthropologically known times.

Painting

The interpretation of the Shroud as a painting by an unknown medieval artist emerged from its suspicious history as highly likely and has persisted with unusual stubbornness down to the present. Its prominence as the main forgery theory is such that virtually all commentators expend great effort in disproving it, believing the authenticity of the relic to be established thereby. The notion has indeed been disproved so thoroughly and absolutely that it should be permanently buried. I shall simply list yet again the numerous items of evidence, many of which would be sufficient singly to establish that the image is not a medieval painting, rubbing, scorch, or other work of art: anatomical detail, realism of the wounds, presence of blood, absence of pigment or binder, reversal of light and dark, diffuseness of the image at close range, three-dimensional information, absence of outline or shading, lack of directionality in the colored areas, lack of change in color from light to dark tones, color not affected by heat or water, detail and twin radiation of scourge marks, nailing of wrists, single nailing of both feet together, characteristic wounds of the Roman flagrum and lancea, Oriental cap rather than Western circlet crown, accuracy in Semitic appearance and Jewish burial posture, pollen from Turkey and Palestine, difficulty in reconciling the Shroud with biblical accounts, nudity of the figure. Each of these features could be explained by invoking extraordinary circumstance, e.g. absence of pigment due to the use of a thin solution and frequent washings of the relic, real blood used by the artist, pathological exactitude from the artist's genius, scourge marks and wrist nailing from intuition, a cloth of Middle Eastern origin, etc. Clearly, however, the cumulative effect is to place the painting hypothesis somewhat lower in credibility than notions of the Marlowe authorship of Shakespeare's plays or an Egyptian influence on the Mayas.

Unknown crucifixion victim

Guilty of McNair's charge of otiosity, a number of commentators, including the STURP team, have suggested that the Shroud could be the gravecloth of a person who suffered injuries in the same manner as Christ. We shall examine here the possibility of such an occurrence without obvious intent to imitate the experiences of Christ. This hypothesis thus hinges on the degree to which features now interpreted as "clearly representing Jesus Christ" should be considered unique.

The major characteristics of the Shroud figure which seem to identify him as Christ are the lacerations of the head and the wound in the side; of lesser importance are the evidence of stationary flogging: and absence of *crurifragium*. Certainly, the methods of capital punishment did not always follow a rigid procedure; an example is the occasional lifting of prohibitions on the use of the *flagrum* or crucifixion to punish Roman citizens. Political prisoners in Palestine may well have received harsher penalties than common criminals in the form of more severe flogging and prolonged sufferings on the cross. On the other hand, the bodies of rebels and subversives were not normally released for burial, according to a 6th century digest of Roman law (Ulpian, cited in Barbet 1963:51). In the

Matthew account (28:62-64), the Sanhedrin were clearly unprepared when the request for Christ's body was granted.

The crowning with thorns is described in John's Gospel as a spontaneous and capricious invention of the guards in response to absurd claims of kingship associated with their prisoner. Ricci (1977:67) and others contend that this trait is a singular and identifying mark of Christ; among the recorded tortures of the condemned prior to crucifixion there is no such crowning or spiking of the scalp. It must be allowed, however, that similar injuries might have been sustained by other crucified men, perhaps palace intriguers or leaders of rebellion. An instance is recorded by Philo of a mock crowning in ca. A.D. 40 during a visit of the Jewish King Agrippa to Alexandria; a mock procession was staged with an idiot dressed in ragged royal purple and crowned with the base of a basket. Preexecution tortures might also have caused punctures of the scalp resulting, if credulity is strained, in a pattern similar to an Oriental crown (mitre or cap) of thorns. Therefore, while the parallel between the head wounds of the Shroud man and those of Christ is striking, it is not sufficient of itself to establish the identification.

The postmortem nature of the side wound also exactly parallels the biblical account, and again there is no historical mention of a practice of this or any method of coup de grace during crucifixion, other than the *crurifragium* in Palestine. Bulst (1957:121) interprets an ambiguous phrase in Quintilian (1st century) as suggesting that piercing the corpse may have preceded its release for burial. However, an exhaustive search by Vignon (1939) and Wuenschel (1953) turned up only one slightly dubious reference to such a practice: the martyrs Marcellus and Marcellinus were dispatched with a spear during their crucifixion ca. 290 because their constant praising of God annoyed the sentries. In this instance, as in that of Christ, the spearing appears as a spontaneous act by the guards. One might conclude that similar transfixions may have occurred occasionally, were it not for the universal attitude in the early church toward the issuance of blood and water from Christ's side. Christian apologists of the 2nd and 3rd centuries – a period of frequent crucifixions – believed the flow to be a miracle, Origen, who had witnessed crucifixion, could write: "I know well that neither blood nor water flows from a corpse, but in the case of Jesus it was miraculous." Certainly such a belief could not have prevailed if piercing the corpse sub alas had been other than a very rare happening indeed.

The omission of normal washing and anointing of the body may possibly be explained by the onset of the Sabbath, since ritual differential treatment of execution victims does not seem to have been practiced in 1st century Palestine. The individual burial and quality of linen suggest that the Shroud man was not a criminal, slave, or rebel. Finally, the lack of decomposition staining of the cloth indicates that, barring highly unusual preserving conditions arresting the normal bodily decay, the Shroud was removed from the corpse after 24-72 hours. It would have been kept in spite of the deep-seated aversion of the Jews (and most peoples of antiquity) to anything which had been in contact with the dead, not to mention bearing the actual stain of a corpse. Eventually, the similarity of its imprint with the body of Christ would have been noticed.

Clearly, this scenario requires the most improbable combination of many fortuitous and highly improbable events. For each detail, an explanation of sorts can be concocted, but that all of them could have been strung together accidentally into a configuration corresponding exactly to the biblical account of Christ's crucifixion is, quite simply, inconceivable. The order present in the Shroud data reveals, just as surely as does the workmanship of an artifact, an intentionality in its composition. If it is not the actual Shroud of Christ, it must be the result of a deliberate attempt to duplicate the experiences of his death and burial.

Early forgery

The first centuries of Christianity afforded ample possibility and motivation for the forgery of a relic such as the Shroud. A widespread cult of relics developed in the 4th century following the conversion of Constantine and was intensified by the discovery of the True Cross during an expedition to Jerusalem of Constantine's mother in 326 and the distribution of shavings of the wood throughout the empire. Similar "discoveries" soon followed, of the nails, lance, crown of thorns, clothing, and other material items from the life of Christ, the apostles, Old Testament figures, saints, and martyrs. As noted above, a Shroud of Christ was claimed by a convent on the Jordan in 570, and cloths believed to bear his facial imprint were current by ca. A.D. 500. Early ecclesiastical writers frequently denounced spurious relics created for reasons of rivalry, reverence, or profit, and relic forgery was especially rife in Egypt and Syria in the 4th century. It may be suggested, then, that forgers obtained the corpse of a crucifixion victim, marked it to resemble Christ, and attempted to imprint an image on cloth, achieving by accident a remarkable result.

The objections to this scenario are manifold and insurmountable. Of greatest importance is the medical interpretation of the head wounds as inflicted on a living body; spiking the scalp of a corpse or marking it with blood could not approach the pathological exactitude of the wounds and blood flows on the Shroud man. Straining credulity, one might escape this difficulty by postulating a collusion between forgers and executioners for preparation of a victim with suitable head wounds. The postmortem side wound presents equal if not greater difficulties: it was inflicted on an upright corpse, resulting in a copious flow of blood and clear fluid (matching the biblical account); a second flow issued when the body was horizontal, not simply laid out but being moved, as indicated by the collection of blood across the small of the back. There can be no doubt that early forgers could not have attained such precision and that it was unnecessary in any case for the simple production of a bloodstained cloth for a gullible public.

There are numerous other difficulties with this hypothesis: (1) The major demand for relics came after the state establishment of Christianity, by which time crucifixion had been abolished. (2) Stains, dyes, oils, or other materials likely to have been used by early forgers in an attempt to imprint the cloth are completely lacking on the Shroud. (3) The victim appears to have been Jewish, with the correct burial posture, chin band tied and eyes covered, yet the legs were not broken as was the practice in Palestine. (4) A successful imprint of Christ's likeness made in this era would have been trumpeted as another great relic "come to light." (5) An image of the nude and unwashed body of Christ would have been considered offensive, lessening or destroying its economic and ceremonial value. Based on the already shaky premise that forgers accidentally and spectacularly succeeded in their task, this hypothesis is hopelessly fraught with difficulties. It can be unequivocally rejected, and with it any possibility that the Shroud is the product of a forgery attempt. As Donald Lynn (quoted in Rinaldi 1979:14) of STURP concluded, "it would be miraculous if it were a forgery."

Imitation of Christ

Finally, the possibility may be considered that the Shroud man was literally a "little Christ" – that, out of fanaticism, extreme asceticism or desire for martyrdom, someone was able to inflict or have inflicted the exact wounds of Christ on his own person. There is ample evidence of asceticism and self-denial carried to extremes in the early monastic-anchorite movements of the late 3rd and 4th centuries. Hermits isolated themselves in the deserts, in cave cells, on pillars, there to indulge in all manner of bizarre vilifications of the flesh: wearing of chains for years, self-flagellation, dietary privations, exposure to heat and cold, etc. The above-cited theological writer Origen in his youth committed self-castration; the first monk ascete, Paul of Egypt, was reportedly found dead in his cell in a kneeling position of prayer.

The 4th century anchorites of Egypt retained practices of mummification of the dead; the body was wrapped in bandages and the outer surface sometimes painted with a mask or Christian symbols. As this custom fell out of use, the dead were simply wrapped in a winding sheet and carried into the desert, to be buried after three days of wailing. The Shroud might thus be the burial sheet of an unknown but charismatic figure in the early anchorite communities of Egypt or Syria, crucified by followers in a manner exactly imitating that of Christ. The presence of natron on the Shroud takes on a special relevance here, and several other details may be fitted into this hypothesis: the wrist and foot nailing of Roman crucifixion would have been known; the victim might have been "Semitic," the crown of thorns conceived of as a cap, the cloth preserved in the desert conditions; and the areas were rife with relic-mongering.

The hypothesis requires, on the other hand, a virtually impossible double occurrence of freakish events: a self-styled crucifixion and a body imprint by unknown mechanism. There are other difficulties: the matching of the wounds with Roman implements, the Jewish burial customs (most unlikely to have been known), the linen itself (luxurious and urban), and of course the silence of the historical record on the entire proceedings. The coup de grace for this wildest of hypotheses is, appropriately, the lance wound in the side. It would have been well nigh impossible to draw forth intentionally from a corpse a flow of blood and fluid at a single thrust. The presence of pericardial or pleural fluid in sufficient quantity and the exact site, angle, and depth of piercing would have to be carefully determined before such a feat could be performed by a modern surgeon, as Barbet discovered in experiments on corpses.

A similar set of historical circumstances can be cited in attributing the Shroud to a crucified martyr eager to imitate the "Way of the Cross." That early Christians sometimes exhibited a fanatical desire for physical suffering and martyrdom is well documented; it is reflected in the remark of Antonius, 3rd century proconsul of Asia, when confronted with mass confessions and volunteers for martyrdom: "Miserable people, if you are so weary of life, is it not easy to find ropes or precipices?" Hagiographies overflow with accounts of martyrs' showing contempt for the exertions of their torturers, and a situation may be imagined in which the condemned entreated or goaded their guards into "glorifying" them with a crown of spikes and a spear wound in the side.

By the 3rd century, linen *brandea* or "second-class relics" were being created by touching them to the body or blood of a martyr. At the beheading of Bishop Cyprian of Carthage in 258, a linen sheet was spread on the ground to collect his blood, and the body was then carried through the streets in the cloth. Is it possible that the Shroud is a similar relic in linen intended to absorb the blood and holiness of an exceptional martyr who bore all of the wounds of Christ? The answer again must be a definite negative. The scenario posits the concurrence of no fewer than four extremely rare and improbable phenomena – a martyr's crown of thorns, a postmortem side wound, blood and fluid issuing therefrom, and the imprint. If a spear thrust to the corpse on the cross had been a common practice, eventually a repetition of the blood and fluid flow from the wound would have occurred, but to attach this extremely unlikely event to the other wounds and features of the Shroud and to the accident of body imprint, all in total historical obscurity, is clearly to enter the world of fantasy.

It is unnecessary to extend this exploration of extremely farfetched and improbable hypotheses to the limits of the imagination, e.g. to concoct a massive conspiracy such as might be formulated to challenge any historical document or fact. Suffice it to note that even the most preposterous notions – e.g. mass crucifixions conducted during the persecutions to replicate in every detail Christ's sufferings (Gramaglia, in Sox 1981:69) – would founder on many of the Shroud's details and on the accidental image formation. Neither should any consideration be given to the ludicrous suggestions of the "paranormal," that the Shroud man was a stigmatist bearing in exact detail all the wounds of Christ, or that the Shroud is a satanic ploy to focus attention on the dead rather than the spiritual Christ.

Conclusions

The question of authenticity may be readily divided into two stages: (1) the Shroud as a genuine burial cloth recovered from a grave or removed from a corpse and (2) the Shroud as the gravecloth of Christ. The first stage may be established from direct examination of the object and comparison with relevant data from other disciplines. The second stage relies heavily but not entirely on the historical record and, ironically, at certain points on the silence in that record. In the foregoing discussion, we have reviewed the evidence related to each stage of the authentication process. The final judgement generally depends on whether one is inclined to stress the positive or the negative evidence.

As early as 1902, the basic cleavage of opinion on the Shroud was already apparent. For the anatomists, scrutiny of the image yielded positive evidence that it was the imprint of a corpse bearing wounds exactly corresponding to those described of Christ. For historians, the silence of history and the sudden appearance of the relic in suspicious circumstances constituted an equally convincing negative indication. It has been my contention here that, while the lack of historical documentation and the claimed confession of the artist are difficulties, the evidence from the medical studies must be treated as empirical data of a higher order. The dead body always represents a cold, hard fact, regardless of a lack of witnesses or a freely offered confession of murder. With anatomists and forensic pathologists of the highest caliber in Europe and America (many of whom are also well versed in the history of art) of one mind for 80 years about the image as a body imprint, one is on firm ground in characterizing the Shroud as the real shroud of a real corpse. The direct testing of the last 20 years goes farther in demonstrating that the relic is a genuine gravecloth from antiquity rather than the result of a medieval forger's attempt to imprint the cloth with a smeared corpse. Fleming (1978:64) concurs, with the conclusion that "it is the medical evidence that we are certainly looking at a gruesome document of crucifixion which satisfies me that the Shroud is not medieval in origin."

Current opinion on the Shroud's authenticity ranges generally from "probable" to "proven" for Stage 1 and from "possible" to "probable" for Stage 2. For a variety of reasons, not the least of which is the fact that the object is a religious relic, these opinions seem to err on the side of the cautious, place undue emphasis on the negative evidence, and are often based on an assumption that the identity of the Shroud man is "unprovable." Rather, the second stage of authentication may well be more easily demonstrable than the first, as even the arch-skeptic Schafersman (1982a:41) admits. That is to say, if the Shroud image is truly a body imprint (as the evidence overwhelmingly indicates), and if the wounds seen in the imprint are real (on which point there is little room for doubt), then surely we must conclude that the imprint must be from the body of Christ.

Therefore, applying standards of proof no more stringent than those employed in other archaeological/historical identifications, one is led, I submit, to an almost inescapable conclusion about the Shroud of Turin: it is the very piece of linen described in the biblical accounts as being used to enfold the body of Christ. The pattern of data revealed by the Shroud is unquestionably unique, it concurs in every detail with the record of Christ's death and burial, and it is unfakeable. The combination of premortem, postmortem, and postentombment information cannot be matched with any other known or hypothetical series of events. In eliminating other explanations of the Shroud's origin, I have put greatest weight on the most firmly established evidence – the uniqueness of the body image phenomenon and the pathology of the wounds. The former has defied the most sophisticated technological investigation, while on the latter there has been unanimous agreement and such force of medical opinion that it cannot be questioned without dramatic new revelations. But every detail of the Shroud, from the pollen to the scourge marks, accords with or does not run counter to authenticity, which may be considered as "reasonably well established," at least in the same sense that many other facts of history or archaeology are established by the interpretation of documents and material evidence. Its authenticity should be accorded a degree of certainty comparable, for example, to the identification of ancient city sites such as Troy, Ur, etc., to the dating of the Lascaux cave paintings, or to the description of the death of Nero – all of which rely on a complex and seemingly unfakeable pattern of data. The Shroud's authenticity is a matter for expert rather than personal opinion and certainty not a matter of faith; it involves a "judgement of fact" rather than a "judgement of value" (after Mandelbaum 1938).

Delage, to his eternal credit as a scholar, perceived all this of the Shroud in 1902, working with the poorer 1898 photographs and in a milieu of militant agnosticism. The anatomical realism of the body imprint and the accuracy of the wounds led him to conclude, "The man of the Shroud is Christ ... if instead of Christ, there was a question of some person such as a Sargon, an Achilles or one of the Pharaohs, no one would have thought of making an objection" (quoted in Walsh 1963:66). I have here examined the remotest possibilities of forgery or imitation precisely because of the religious nature of the relic and the spurious character of many similar objects ascribed by tradition and popular veneration to holy men, religious leaders, or miraculous events. Most such relics would not allow of a positive identification in any case; nor would the Shroud were it merely a piece of ancient linen. But encoded in the image are data of such specificity that the relic can be fixed in time and place, used to generate hypotheses to be tested in the laboratory and in the field, and finally attributed to a single, historical person.

There is, however, a disturbing current (now reaching cliché status) in Shroud studies, expressed both by scientists and those with a religious interest, that the Shroud's identification with Christ is beyond the scope of science or proof and requires a leap of faith. Sox (1978.56), for example, contends that, even after exhaustive testing, "it can never be said that this is Jesus' burial cloth ... this conviction, as always, must come through the eyes of faith." Cameron (1978:59) believes that "we shall only be able to prove that the Turin Shroud might be the burial cloth of Jesus Christ, not that it actually is." Weaver (1980:752) asks, "Is it the Shroud of Christ himself? That, say both scientists and theologians, will remain forever outside the bounds of proof."

This line of thought must be rejected as verging on obscurantist and lacking any solid basis in historical/archaeological assessment of the object and the relevant data. To my knowledge no writer on the Shroud has examined the various hypotheses presented above (unknown crucifixion victim, early forgery, imitation of Christ) or seriously attempted to probe the uniqueness of the Shroud data other than in unscientific probability calculations. To suggest that science (in the form of direct testing of the cloth) can attain only a certain point, beyond which lies subjective opinion or faith, is to ignore the essentially scientific character of historical knowledge. This attitude is reflected even in the much more reasonable conclusion of STURP member Bucklin (1981:189) that identification of the Shroud man "is not within the realm of science, but may be decided by careful historical inquiry." Unfortunately, STURP spokesman Janney (in the Associated Press report quoted earlier) confuses the matter with the claim that "the classical scientific method cannot prove who it was" beyond establishing that the Shroud figure was "a scourged, crucified man." In truth, it is merely obvious, not scientifically proven *sensu stricto*, that the body was male. But in the same scientific manner in which complex patterns of data are interpreted in the natural and social sciences, alternative explanations may be rejected with a reasonable degree of certainty, and a firm association of the Shroud man with the historical phenomenon of crucifixion and with the historical person of Christ may be established. The fact that these relationships are not subject to irrefutable laboratory confirmation does not place them "outside the bounds of proof," except on the philosophical level that no knowledge of the past derived from the study of history, social science, geology, paleontology, or astronomy can be proven beyond any possibility of doubt.

The genuineness of the Shroud must have a considerable impact on biblical exegesis, especially on the allegorical school which has emphasized the symbolic and spiritual rather than the historical content of the Gospels. As noted above, a genuine Shroud provides a striking confirmation of the recorded detail of the torture and execution of Christ. The crown of thorns was not a poetic embroidery of the basic story. The flow of blood and water from the side, seen by tradition as miraculous and by modern demythologizing as symbolic (of atonement through suffering and of purification by baptism), must now be seen as at least a real, natural physiological occurrence. The removal of the cloth from the body after a brief contact period is also indicated, demolishing what little remained of the theory that the empty tomb of Christ was an invention of the early church.

On the Shroud as evidence of Christ's resurrection, those with "eyes of faith" have seized upon the inability of scientists to arrive at a technologically credible mechanism of image formation and asserted that the Shroud might constitute empirical evidence for some moment of regeneration or "transmaterialization." Clearly, the data can be taken no farther than to indicate a separation of body and cloth before the onset of decomposition and the prevalence of rare conditions in the tomb which resulted in the image. These conditions may reasonably be assumed to derive in some as yet unknown manner from the 40 kg "mixture of myrrh and aloes" which, according to John (19:39), was placed with the body in the linen as a preservative and aromatic. An alternative but perhaps less likely theory is that the imprint resulted from a "Kirlian effect" or other unknown quality of Christ's body; the aura of light and the rare condition of haematidrosis (bloody sweat) recorded of Christ may be cited in this regard.

The Turin Shroud is without doubt one of the most mystifying and instructive archaeological objects in existence. Although its first thousand years are a total blank, intention and accident combined to preserve it, however unceremoniously, from discovery in the tomb to eventual transfer to Constantinople. Although the image-forming process is not known, the image itself is an important document of Christ's crucifixion and has appropriately been termed "the fifth gospel." And whereas the scholarly consensus a mere 60 years ago deemed the Shroud a medieval fraud, the present evidence allows a firm archaeological judgement for authenticity.

The Shroud has been probed by virtually every appropriate element of high technology; science, like Thomas, has verified for itself the reality of the wounds. The verdict on this awesome cloth must be that, remarkably, it is exactly what it appears to be. As a unique specimen of material evidence relating to one of mankind's great religious teachers and major historical events, this icon-relic, this strange 1st century photograph of Christ, has tremendous anthropological significance and enduring fascination for a wide range of people of differing beliefs.

2. Critique and Reply

Publication Of My Article Unleashed a new round of strident and often vicious debate on the Shroud. Major articles in *Current Anthropology* are normally sent to 20-30 scholars and their replies are published in the journal. In this case, the editors made a point of seeking out the most vocal of Shroud opponents and publishing their comments, along with others more moderate or sympathetic. A long-time reader of the journal told me that the debate was among the fiercest he could recall in recent years. The comments are summarized here, followed by my reply, in order to give the reader an idea of the intensity of the debate and the issues that were being raised in the controversy over the Shroud.

James E. Alcock, York University, Toronto, Canada – said that Meacham correctly points out that if carbon-dating were to indicate that the cloth is about 2,000 years old or older, one could still argue that a medieval artist painted the image on an old piece of linen. But Alcock maintained that a carbon-date indicating that the cloth is much younger would be compelling evidence against authenticity. The possibility that contamination might be a factor struck him as "sheer whimsy." He felt that Meacham had given a very one-sided view of the evidence, and noted that "science does not proceed by pronouncements of authenticity. It requires free and open inquiry and debate."

Robert Bucklin, Los Angeles, Calif. U.S.A. – "From the point of view of a physician-pathologist, with more than 30 years' experience in the study of the Shroud of Turin, I find the report by Meacham extremely satisfying. His approach is thoughtful, scientific, and rational, and he has objectively combined known results of highly technical research findings with his comprehensive review of historical events and biblical references. The conclusions that he has drawn are wholly realistic."

K.O.L. Burridge, University of British Columbia, Vancouver, B.C., Canada – noted that scientists share with most of the lay population a proper scepticism towards relics and other unlikely phenomena, but "they will also take a leap beyond the evidence if need be." However, "faith in a negative is as good as faith in an affirmative. If Jesus Christ was not a historical figure, then of course the Shroud, if it is a shroud, cannot be his. If Christ actually lived, then it would seem that the Shroud might have been his. So many of our supposed certainties are actually possibilities or probabilities that now and again we need, as a basis for our faith in the rest, something that is without doubt either precisely what it appears or seems to be – authentic – or a fraud."

John R. Cole, University of Northern Iowa, Cedar Falls, Iowa, U.S.A. – "This is more religious apologetic than analysis. Meacham claims to discuss his topic from a strictly scientific viewpoint, however, and I will adopt the conceit here, raising technical objections to a patently religious argument. Tacked-on references to skeptical views do not disguise a credulous bias and hope." Further, he maintained that extraordinary claims demand extraordinary proof "in part because they are liable to extraordinary incentives for fraud, wishful thinking, and unconscious bias, and attempts to prove the Shroud of Turin 'authentic' have to be attempts to prove it 'supernatural' and thus supposedly beyond scientific proof." He said that Meacham was attempting to prove a religious claim scientifically, but failed to do so. Instead, Meacham had violated the "sleeping-dog" rule – stirring up an issue, which redounds to the detriment of his religious viewpoint when examined in detail. Cole cited the lack of distortion of the image that should have been caused by folds and wrinkles; he asked "why a vivid 14th century image would have faded radically over the next five or six centuries when it had supposedly remained bright and clear until its 14th century 'discovery'?" He claimed that the details of crucifixion recorded on the Shroud "echo only the Book of John, which is generally regarded as nonhistorical."

Richard J. Dent, University of Maryland, College Park, Md. U.S.A. – claimed that "this relic is an authentic artifact not of the event in question, but of ourselves and our society." He called the Shroud an "ideotechnic" artifact, i.e. an artifact that is a material representation of society conceptualizing itself. He affirmed that "ideology and, by extension, ideotechnic artifacts are products of the imaginary relation of individuals in society to the real relations in which they live. Ideology is a mask. To begin to understand and to pierce this mask, and thus understand the significance of Meacham's paper, we must first recognize the Shroud and this particular documentation as an artifact of ourselves. Once we have done this, the paper has a lesson of value for anthropological archeology." He maintained that the overall goal of this paper was "to suppress or lessen the conflict that arises when an event is mythologically real but materialistically and empirically unreal. If one can suppress the conflict of believing in the crucifixion yet not having any direct evidence to substantiate it, the mythology is more believable. And if one can achieve this goal with the opposition's methodology (scientific method), so much the better. ... We must at least give him high marks for an attempt at documenting one of the great ideotechnic artifacts of our time. However ... we should not lose sight of what Meacham is up to: he is creating an ideotechnic artifact, albeit a grand one, nothing more."

John P. Jackson, University of Colorado, Colorado Springs, Colo. U.S.A. – pointed out that "although the case for the Shroud's authenticity is rather good, in my opinion, the authentication question is still open." He pointed out two major holes in authentication: the 13 centuries of lack of documented history of the Shroud, and the mechanism of image formation. "Without this critical determination, it seems to me that the authentication question will be open to dispute." He noted however, that in view of the large array of data already collected concerning the Shroud, "one cannot but be impressed at the resistance of the hypothesis that the Shroud is the burial cloth of Jesus to scientific rejection."

Walter C. McCrone, McCrone Research Institute, Chicago, Ill. U.S.A. – said that Meacham's attempt to provide a balanced approach to the discussion of the Turin Shroud "succeeds well in all areas except one – inclusion of the only direct physical data on the image particles from the 'Shroud.' ... Nowhere does he present or discuss my work: what I did, how I did it, or why he considers my conclusions invalid. He does not even reference one of my detailed papers (McCrone 1981). I feel like Hughes Mearns's 'little man who wasn't there': 'He wasn't there again today/Oh! How I wish he'd go away.'"

McCrone staked his reputation on his interpretation of the Shroud samples: "It is based on sound microscopical examination carefully done by an experienced microscopist who has studied many dozens of paintings over many years by the same procedures. Whatever reputation I may have rests confidently on the conclusion that the 'Shroud' is entirely an artist's work. ... No one has spent anything like the time and effort I have put into study of these 32 tapes with their thousands of 'Shroud' linen fibers and millions of pigment particles. No one in STURP has this specialized background in small-particle identification, trace analysis, or the study of paintings by microanalytical methods. Substantially all of the image on the 'Shroud' fibers consists of common and well-known pigments and a stain on the fibers due to ageing of the paint medium."

Paul C. Maloney, Ancient Near Eastern Researches, Quakertown, Pa., U.S.A. – claimed that both antagonists and protagonists are premature in their conclusions. "While STURP seems to have made a good case for the Shroud cloth's having wrapped a dead body, we still have no undisputed evidence that the Shroud is older than 1357. If we conclude, with STURP, that the cloth does not appear to have been faked, we might simply suppose that it wrapped a crucified victim in the 14th century. However, crucifixion had been outlawed 1,000 years before. Clearly, the cloth must first be subjected to C-14 tests before there can be any advance in understanding the historical background of the Shroud and bridging the gap between the 1st and the 14th century. This is one of those 'standards of proof' mandatory for any interpretation of this cloth. Meacham dismisses C-14 dating by appealing to contamination problems, but sophisticated techniques clean a sample before testing to remove most contaminants. Margins of error are supplied with each date given, providing a measure of accuracy."

"Secondly, since STURP has not completely published the details of its techniques, instrumentation, laboratory experimentation, and scientific findings, lack of information remains a problem. For example, while Meacham is well versed in Heller and Adler's work analyzing the bloodstains on the Shroud, he states: 'It is possible ... that an artist or forger worked with blood to touch up a body image obtained by other means.' He makes no mention of the very intriguing suggestion that the bloodstains might have been there before the image was. The full critical details of this observation have not yet been published (see, provisionally Schwalbe and Rogers [1982:40]). If it should prove correct, it would bode ill for the artist hypothesis."

Regarding the criteria for establishing authenticity, Maloney wanted "a distinction to be made "between 'proof' as the term is often loosely employed in the human sciences and 'proof' in the exact sciences. ... History and archaeology are not capable of 'proof' in the strictest sense."

Marvin M. Mueller, Los Alamos National Laboratory, Los Alamos, N.M., U.S.A. – characterized the article as "a thorough and impassioned presentation of the case for authenticity but [it] should not be considered a work of balanced scholarship." He claimed that powerful arguments against authenticity were not covered adequately, and that these arguments have not been refuted by the work of STURP. He cites "a leading forensic pathologist (Michael Baden, deputy chief medical examiner of New York for Suffolk County) who stated that the blood flows did not appear realistic, and disputed inferences of rigor mortis and wound pathology. Mueller claimed that "there is **no way** that an image of the quality and beauty of the Shroud image could have been produced by contact of the cloth with a full relief (body or statue) – projection distortion in mapping a full relief onto a plane alone guarantees that, as has been made manifest in several experiments. To cite an extreme example: A sheepskin laid out flat does not much resemble a sheep. Only human intervention (leaving aside the supernatural) can produce a quality image of a full relief."

Joe Nickell, Lexington, Ky., U.S.A. – cited "forensic expert John Fischer" who found the conclusions of the STURP chemists regarding blood to be untenable. Fisher claimed that similar results can be obtained with a tempera paint. And "in light of the Commission's forensic experts' impressive analyses" there were grave doubts about the identification of the "bloodstains" as blood. He added: "Authenticity advocates still need to show a similarly old (600-2,000 years) bloodstain which has remained **red** and to explain how **dried** blood (as on the arms) was transferred to cloth. A forger, of course, could have used some real blood."

Countering Meacham's assertion that "the evidence from the medical studies must be treated as empirical data of a higher order," Nickell stated that "the pathologists he cites have all been religious devotees of the 'relic,' and two serve on the Executive Council of the Holy Shroud Guild (as do STURP's leaders)." He cited instead the remarks of Michael M. Baden, "one of America's foremost medico-legal experts, [who] doubts that the Shroud ever contained a corpse and that, even if it did, any qualified pathologist would reach the kind of conclusions being touted as expert medical opinion."

Nickell claimed that with a bas-relief sculpture, "the wet-mold, dry-pigment technique automatically produces monochromatic negative images with minimal distortion and visually proper tonal gradations. Such images are superficial, 'directionless,' highly resolved, fire-stable, and characterized by blank spaces surrounding the forms. There is no cementing of fibers." Thus it is a technique that closely replicates the image found on the Shroud.

Adam J. Otterbein, Holy Shroud Guild, Ephrata, Pa. U.S.A. –
"Meacham makes an excellent point in saying that, although chemistry and physics alone will never be able to prove that the Turin cloth is the burial cloth of Christ, a broad archaeological assessment which includes

all relevant data can lead not to a 'leap of faith,' but to a logical conclusion based on the total evidence. Not all archaeological conclusions can be proven by a microscope or reproduced in a laboratory."

"He correctly divides the question of authenticity into two sections: (1) Is the Shroud a genuine burial cloth? and (2) Is the Shroud the burial cloth of Christ? Although science is still unable to explain the chemistry of the image formation process, recent investigation has reinforced the arguments that the Shroud did enclose a human corpse. In previous centuries those who claimed fraud never denied that the image was intended to represent Christ. Today science denies fraud and says that the image could be Christ. In treating the Shroud's relation to the biblical record, Meacham mentions some objections that suggest an apparent conflict between the Shroud and the Gospels. His position could be strengthened by reference to two articles by Wuenschel (1945, 1946), who has shown that the original Greek text admit of interpretations compatible with the Shroud and Jewish burial customs."

S. F. Pellicori, Santa Barbara Research Center, Goleta, Calif. U.S.A. –
"The foundation for Meacham's conclusion rests heavily on some pieces of 'evidence' which have not been adequately substantiated. Much weight is given to pollen studies; however, Frei does not provide data that would permit the statistical significance of his findings to be assessed. For example, from the sample as a whole, what is the true percentage of positive identifications? What is the predicted probability of occurrence? etc."

"Much heat and emotion have been generated over the 'findings' of inscriptions, coins, etc., by some people. The methodologies of these people are in themselves suspect, a problem often encountered when nonscientists attempt to apply scientific techniques. Regardless of that observation, examination of high-quality STURP photos failed to reveal unambiguous letter forms. The technique of preexposing a pattern to the retina (Whanger) assists the eye in seeing this pattern in a subsequent field of dots which are unrelated (except for a preferred linear trend due to the weave structure)."

Steven Schafersman, Rice University, Houston, Tex. U.S.A. – said that Meacham's conclusions were "a blatant example of human credulity [that] rarely finds its way into the professional scholarly literature." Instead, he believed that "all empirical and logical evidence to date demonstrates that the Shroud is the product of a clever medieval artist, a forged relic with no other purpose than to awe and deceive an ignorant and credulous stream of pilgrims willing to pay to view it. The major difference between the

Shroud of Turin and other medieval relics is that it is a far more cunning and convincing artifact than the others. Another difference is that the other relics are not today believed to be genuine by intelligent and educated adults."

He disputed Meacham's assertion that a 14th century C-14 date would fail to settle the matter "of the age of the Shroud because of exchange and contamination over the centuries," claiming that other artifacts susceptible to C-14 dating much older and more exposed than the Shroud have been dated with great reliability. He defended McCrone's interpretation but clarified that "the image on the Shroud **today** is due primarily to the dehydrated cellulose of the linen (the alteration or recrystallization of the cellulose was effected by some component, still undetermined, of the pigment or binder) and hardly at all to the iron oxide pigment, which explains STURP's spectroscopic results."

He concluded: "I have no quarrel with the notion that the image on the Shroud is supposed to represent Jesus Christ. And as a religious relic, why shouldn't it? From the moment of the Shroud's first appearance to the present, no one has suggested otherwise, except rhetorically as a prelude to documenting the evidence for the true identity of the man on the Shroud. Meacham's painstaking rendition of this ritual is therefore characteristic and serves only to reveal his dogged belief in the authenticity of the Shroud of Turin and of Jesus Christ, a personage best considered by available evidence to be mythical [and] all investigations to date demonstrate that the Turin Shroud is an artifact connected with the mythical crucified and resurrected Christ only as a religious relic, and certainly not in any material sense."

<u>Giovanni Tamburelli, Centro Studi e Laboratori Telecomunicazioni, Turin, Italy</u> – "This paper is an interesting and all but exhaustive analysis of the problems concerning the authentication of the Turin Shroud. Only the results obtained by computer (see Tamburelli 1981, cited by Meacham, and also Tamburelli 1979) have not sufficiently been taken into account. In fact, almost the whole Passion of the Man of the Shroud according to the Gospel could be read in the data supplied by the computer. Obviously, this is only a probable "reading," because, after 2,000 years, very clear details can be interpreted in terms of hypotheses or, at most, probabilities. […] The striking similarities of these facts with Gospel are a clear contribution in favor of the Shroud's authenticity. Hence, the probability that the Man of the Shroud was Jesus Christ is greatly increased by the results obtained with the aid of the computer."

CRITIQUE AND REPLY

<u>Alan D. Whanger, Duke University Medical Center, Durham, N.C., U.S.A.</u> – cited work done by himself and his wife "showing that the Shroud image was well known in the early part of the 6th century and, being presumed to be an authentic image of Christ, was scrupulously copied in many media. Our image-overlay technique allows minute and detailed comparison of various images." He describes an encaustic icon of Christ in St. Catherine's monastery at Mt. Sinai and a solidus of Justinian II, struck between A.D. 692 and 695, both of which show similarities to the Shroud image. He also described his image overlay technique and his conclusion that both eyes had coins placed on them and the inscriptions on each coin could be partially read.

Reply

The skeptics are certainly out in full array among the commentators – out of all proportion, I might add, to either their real numbers or the force of their case. If only the latter were as strong as their rhetoric! It is surprising to find their arguments directed almost entirely to the discredited notion of medieval "clever artistry." Mueller and Cole allege that my treatment of the Shroud is "not a work of balanced scholarship" because it does not consider this hypothesis in a substantial manner. I chose not to convey the impression that "general and powerful arguments" have been advanced for clever artistry precisely because none have. I have informed the reader that there are skeptics (and arch-skeptics), that there are difficulties, major and minor unresolved questions, many divergences of opinion among Shroud researchers, and a number of options short of accepting full authenticity, but I have relegated the idea that a clever medieval artist could have created the Shroud to the level of a footnote, in the same way that reputable scholarship would dismiss questions of Shakespeare's authorship, Hitler's escape from Berlin, and outer-space contributions to ancient civilization. Akin in many ways to these notions, the skeptical case for medieval artistry is based in part on the denial of empirical data, is built on a postulated complex of exceptional circumstance, and is quite untenable.

When Delage's 1902 lecture on the Shroud's authenticity provoked a storm of controversy, he wrote (1902:683): "If our proofs have not been received by certain persons as they deserve to be, it is only because a religious question has been injected into a problem which in itself is purely scientific." Unfortunately, little has changed in the intervening 80 years, and Delage's remark certainly applies to the comments of Dent, Nickell,

Schafersman, and above all Cole, who even claims that ordinary standards of evidence do not apply to the Shroud and that I have presented a "religious apologetic." One can only wonder if Cole has ever heard or read a "patently religious argument." I categorically reject the implication that a religious viewpoint can be discerned in the article or that any argument is constructed on a theological base. Cole and Mueller do attempt to press the supernatural into any argument for authenticity, in spite of the fact that crude approximations of the Shroud image have been produced by the use of a corpse and spices, oils, etc., as Cole himself points out. Injecting the religious/supernatural element into the issue only distracts from the scientific evaluation, which is not, as Dent maintains, the use of science to serve "the opposite camp," but rather the proper investigation of a material object. The skeptics have not, I submit, advanced their arguments or camouflaged their highly vulnerable position by this distraction.

The historical existence of Christ and an object possibly associated with him are not "intrinsically religious questions" as Cole mistakenly believes. Emotional issues abound in science, certainly in the pages of *Current Anthropology*, yet would Cole have exceptional standards applied to them for this reason? Further, to accept Cole's "sleeping-dog rule" would excise many legitimate areas of scientific interest. He violates his own rule in pronouncing the Book of John "non-historical"; it is generally regarded as a highly theological eyewitness account. Similar, Schafersman must be applying extraordinary standards indeed to reject all reputable scholarship and consider Christ by "all available evidence to be mythical," whereas only last year this same evidence made him "think it probable that Jesus was an authentic person" (1982a:45). Most of Schafersman's comments are equally in conflict with empirical data, yet he labels my conclusion on the Shroud as a "blatant example of human credulity."

Dent seems to be on his own peculiar crusade. Even without following Binford, Leone, et al., one does not lose sight of what he is up to – making the Shroud an ideotechnic artifact so as to dismiss it. The Shroud would be in very good company, however, as all the material of history, archaeology, and evolution could also be so described, following Croce. In Dent's highly ideological comment, he points out that ideology is a mask and genuinely appears to believe that, armed with his own particular one, he is able to "pierce this mask" and perceive that the crucifixion is "mythologically real but materialistically [sic] and empirically unreal." Regardless of what mask he adopts, I do not see how on earth Dent can know the latter. Perhaps he really intends to refer to the resurrection. If not, for Dent there is no history, only ideotechnic constructions. He would presumably use the same terms to describe the assassination of Gandhi or the reconstruction of *Australopithecus*.

For one major misunderstanding that has crept into some comments I admit responsibility by omission. In concluding that the case for authenticity is very strong, I had no intention to imply that further study is not necessary or desirable. The work done thus far does indicate the direction of future research projects, as I stated, and there is a sense in which studies of the Shroud will always be incomplete. Similarly, in pointing out the limitations of C-14 dating I would not for a moment argue that it need not be done. To the contrary radiometric dating ranks as the highest priority at present.

Beyond misunderstanding lies invective, and the comments of Cole, Nickell, Schafersman, and Mueller are phrased in an emotive tone not conducive to reasoned discussion. They bristle with intemperate rhetoric: "gullibility," "credulous bias," "notoriously subjective," "sheer whimsy," "blatant example of human credulity," "conceit," and "so-called evidence," to mention but a few examples. Doubts about personal competence or expertise emanate from Schafersman (graduate student) and Nickell (English instructor) like stones from inside a glass house: Frei's work is "questionable," STURP members may be pseudo-scientists, Heller and Adler are "nonforensic scientists," Filas and Whanger "nonexperts," and Bucklin and Gambescia "religious devotees of the 'relic'." Those with views supporting the skeptics are *mirabile dictu* described in lavish terms: the Turin Commission consisted of "forensic experts;" McCrone is "probably the best-known forensic microbiologist in the world" and "a distinguished expert"; Baden is not only "one of America's foremost medico-legal experts," but "one of the world's most distinguished pathologists." Naturally, the former group is subject to a pro-authenticity bias, make "subjective inferences," and find "artifacts of their own hopes," whereas the latter conduct "impressive analyses" and make discoveries and "positive identifications." I leave it to the reader to decide whether this is the type of rhetoric usually associated with a carefully reasoned argument, not to mention a "powerful case."

Turning to some of the disputed points of data, the latest summary of STURP findings (Dinegar 1982:7) does give credence to both the pollen and the chin band. Pellicori's doubt on the pigtail has not to my knowledge been published. I did not intend to give the impression that STURP was monolithic in its thinking, and several divergences were noted; I did attempt to relate what appears to be a solid STURP consensus. The Turin Commission did not report that blood penetrated the cloth (Frache, Rizzatti, and Mari 1976:50-51; Fleming 1978:62). The three-dimensional effect indicates that the image has **correct** tonal gradations, i.e., contour information of a type not seen in medieval paintings, rubbings, or black prints. The Shroud image may have faded slightly since 1357, but it is incorrect to state as a fact that it has faded radically. My suggestion of a possible "Kirlian effect" was rather speculative, but the Volckringer phenomenon should have definite applicability, being essentially a cellulose dehydration process producing exact, negative images.

The Mandylion's semilegendary history (Wilson 1978:158, 322) puts its discovery at the time of a Persian siege of Edessa in 544. I find the Mandylion/Shroud equation extremely difficult, for the reasons Cameron (1980) cites, especially the absence of mention of its revelation as a full-length body image and the lack of discoloration of the exposed portion of the cloth. On the other hand, the case made by Whanger, Wilson, and Vignon (1938) before them for the Shroud image's having been known and copied in early Byzantine times is quite compelling. I would suggest, therefore, that the Mandylion was a very early copy of the Shroud face, perhaps as early as the 1st or 2nd century if the Abgar legend contains a grain of truth, and that the concept of images miraculously imprinted on cloth by Christ's face derives from a residual folk memory of the Shroud and the Mandylion copy of it.

The presence of coins or flat objects on the eyes seems well established by the three-dimensional reconstructions of Jumper and Tamburelli. The letter-like shapes are discernible in the earlier Enrie photographs, and several numismatists see the possible imprint of a Pilate coin. This is certainly not a baseless claim or a Rorschach effect, but it may be the result of a peculiarity of the Enrie film and technique, not replicated by STURP. Whanger (personal communication, 1983) points out that there are discrepancies between the 1931 and 1978 photographs which are not explained by STURP) and which may be the result of minor damage to the image in the interval. I fully agree with Pellicori that, until new strategies are devised, the point is moot.

Several comments are directed toward my caution with regard to C-14 dating. It is **not** an infallible technique, and, as any field archaeologist knows, contamination either *in situ* or after excavation is always a possibility to be taken seriously. Maloney is correct to point out that pretesting cleansing will remove most of the normal contaminants (humic acids and lignins), but he errs in assuming that the quoted margin of error reflects in any way the possibility of contamination. One can never be certain that material of more recent age has not been trapped in the structure of the cellulose, that hydrocarbons have not formed, that ion exchange has not taken place, etc. Stuckenrath (1965:280) notes that the result is often more recent than expected and cites the wide divergence – from 1750 to 800 B.C. – of a series of 16 contemporaneous wood and charcoal samples; Peacock (1979:212) and Codegone (1976:40) cite same-sample inconsistencies; Hamilton (1965:43) cites conflicts between the C-

14 results and known historical ages. Alcock, McCrone, and Schafersman may find my lack of absolute faith in the method "sheer whimsy," "invalid," or "absurd," but it is based on experience: more than 50 samples excavated and prepared and submitted for dating and liaison with major C-14 laboratories at Oxford, Canberra, and Teledyne. I believe that most archaeologists and radiocarbon scientists would agree that to trust the method to produce an "absolute date" for a single artifact is what is absurd. It may, however, be comforting to Alcock to believe that an ancient date can easily be accommodated by the skeptics' position while a recent date would settle the matter. The truth is that no serious question in archaeology can be settled by a single date, especially on an artifact subjected to so many contamination possibilities. I would reject the claim that there are dated objects "more exposed" than the Shroud. In any event, what archaeologist worth his salt would give any credence to a date on an excavated sample which had been handled by hundreds of workers, kept in CO_2-rich and high-humidity atmospheres, remained missing for a long while, been boiled in oil (mentioned in a 16th century text), washed, burnt and repaired, and touched to the sick and to fresh paintings, had wax dribbled onto it, etc.? Unless, of course, the result was to his liking after all! Backward contamination is so rare that it may be dismissed, and the eventual dating of the Shroud will at least provide a minimum age.

The evidence for blood is a point of empirical data on which the skeptics reveal the weakness of their position and methods. Nickell quotes the unpublished opinion of "forensic expert" Fisher to the effect that the chemical tests were not specific for blood; McCrone claims that his work (published in his own magazine) shows no blood. But according to the work of Heller (Professor of Life Sciences at the New England Institute), Adler (Professor of Chemistry at Western Connecticut) and Baima (Professor of Legal Medicine at Turin University) – all published in peer-reviewed scientific journals – "there is **nothing** else on earth which could give this battery of positive criteria other than blood" (Heller, personal communication, 1982). Claims that false positives could be obtained from a tempera paint are undemonstrated and incorrect. Nickell counterposes the Commission's "highly sophisticated tests" – really quite standard forensic tests, apart from neutron activation, which Nickell wrongly assumes to have a bearing on the identification of blood. In his use of their data, Nickell ignores the conclusions of the Commission experts that "generic and specific diagnoses of blood on material of a very ancient date ... can have a real probative value only with a positive result" and that their negative finding "does **not** allow us to make an **absolute** judgement on the exclusion of haematic remains" (Frache, Rizzatti, and Mari 1976:51, 54, emphasis in the original, translation mine). In view of the positive microchemical evidence for blood and the positive identification of the blood as primate by both Baima Bollone and Adler (personal communication, 1983), the presence of blood traces on the Shroud must be considered as proven. And, as Maloney points out, there is now strong evidence (Jumper et al. 1983) that the bloodstains were on the cloth prior to the body image. Finally ultraviolet fluorescence and microchemical identification of serum albumin in the clear areas within the blood flows provide conclusive evidence that the bloodstains on the Shroud derive from direct contact with a corpse and not from an artist's brush.

The pollen is another case of empirical data subjected to unreasonable doubt. Frei's pollen evidence does indicate a Middle Eastern origin for the cloth, which is not too surprising, as several other linen "shrouds" were brought back from the Crusades as relics. Pellicori misses the significance of the pollen as a marker, percentages would be useful in determining the immediate environment represented by a deposit but not at all in proving that certain types are intrusive. The presence on the Shroud of a wide variety of Palestinian and Anatolian species is ipso facto evidence of an exposure to air in those regions, unless a similar presence can be documented in Holocene pollen deposits or on other medieval artifacts in France or Italy. It may be, as Mueller contends, that few STURP members give the pollen data any credence, but this does not detract in the least from the hard evidence Frei's work has revealed, especially in the identification of halophytes found almost exclusively around the Dead Sea. Riggi (1981), a member of STURP, has reported preliminary findings of Shroud pollen and minute animal forms "extremely similar in their aspects and dimensions" to those from Egyptian burial fabrics.

Cole and Mueller challenge my statement on the unanimity of medical opinion. Obviously, this was not intended to include every doctor or biologist who has seen a snapshot of the Shroud and formed an opinion. Baden's remarks are repeated in no fewer than four comments, but he is a lone sniper laying siege to a fortified city. Regardless of his prestige, his opinions appear off the cuff. He has not seen the Shroud, nor does he appear to be familiar with the vast medical literature or to have been in contact with other scholars; he has not published on the subject; he is said to be "something of an iconoclast" (Bucklin in Rhein 1980:50); his opinions were given on the basis of magazine photographs; he cites the fact that linen sheets in his morgue had never developed an imprint like the Shroud's, which was termed "too good to be true." This is not to say that Baden may not have something useful to contribute to Shroud studies, but the fact that skeptics quote him at this stage demonstrates their desperation in the medical arena. In the same vein (apologies!), Nickell's claim that the pathologists I cited have all been "religious devotees of the relic" is not merely incorrect, but preposterous, as is Schafersman's unverifiable notion that skeptical medical authorities have just not bothered to make their opinions known. The fact is that a number of investigators (Delage, Barbet, Modder, Cameron) approached the Shroud with an initial skepticism. It remains true that all informed and published medical opinion concurs in interpreting the Shroud image as the imprint of a crucified body. This evaluation comes from Protestants, Jews, and agnostics as well as Catholics, but even for the latter it is totally unjustified to pronounce them all religiously biased, with scientific judgement impaired. In sum, I stand by my statement that the only reasonable conclusion to be drawn from this body of evidence is that cited from the respected archaeological scientist Stuart Fleming – that the Shroud image is neither medieval nor artistic in origin.

McCrone and others contend that I have ignored strong arguments for human artifice, but suggestions that the image might be a painting, rubbing, or print have been thoroughly disproved by the recent analyses. It is established that the visible body image does not reside in a pigment, ink, or other coloring agent and that it has distinctly different characteristics from the bloodstains. My dismissal of McCrone's claims is more than amply justified by the battery of Commission and STURP tests. Even Mueller, Nickell, and Schafersman now accept the STURP interpretation of the image as a cellulose degradation product, but McCrone still insists that it is a water-color painting with a layer of pigment. Not only are the iron oxide and other possible pigment particles present only in trace levels far below the visible range, but their identification, origin, and distribution pattern are disputed. Heller and Adler (1981:93) identify three types of iron compounds on the Shroud – cellulosic and heme-bound iron and Fe_2O_3, the latter concentrated in the water stain margins and possibly derived from either of the former, from airborne dust, or from contact with jewellers' rouge on glass. Further, Riggi (cited in Heller and Adler 1981:97) found no evidence under electron microprobe of the mineralogical contaminants (Mn, Co, Ni, Al) invariably associated with iron-earth pigments of medieval artists, nor did Heller and Adler find such impurities in microchemical testing. The few isolated examples of undisputed paint particles, e.g. cinnabar, are completely consistent with dust deposition. Indeed, among the millions of particles on the Shroud surface, it would be surprising not to find traces of pigment, as the Shroud has been copied at least 60 times.

Even if one ignored the very compelling evidence to the contrary and granted McCrone's interpretation of the iron particles and protein, all one could conclude would be that minute traces of a solution or ointment containing pure haematite are present in the body imprint. This is of course a far cry from proving the image to be a painting. As STURP responded to McCrone's first pronouncements, "microscopic observations do not exist in a vacuum" (quoted in Sox 1981:61). McCrone is somewhat like Mearns's little man who "wasn't there again today." He declined at least two invitations to discuss his findings in the multidisciplinary framework of STURP; he has declined invitations to present his work at scientific congresses. He did not follow the STURP "covenant," which he signed, to publish in peer-reviewed scientific literature. And, as he admits, he has not responded in print to the arguments of Heller and Adler, Pellicori, Riggi, and Schwalbe and Rogers on the physics and chemistry of the image. He has abandoned his earlier claims of a synthetic iron oxide (post-1800) in the image and of a pigment enhancement of the genuine image.

I should interject at this point that the established facts as reviewed above are more than sufficient to refute the medieval-clever-artistry hypothesis. A forger **could have** obtained a Middle Eastern cloth, **could have** used some primate blood (and serum), and **could have** depicted the body in flawless anatomical detail, and the pigment **could have** disappeared, leaving a faint dehydration image – but that all of these unprecedented circumstances should have coalesced in the production of a single relic is virtually impossible to imagine. And yet, there are much greater problems in the "viable hypothesis of image formation" trumpeted by Mueller and Nickell.

Apart from McCrone, the skeptics have moved on to a more refined position not dependent on the identification of any pigment in the cloth, i.e., that the cellulose degradation was produced by a paint or coloring material **formerly** present. It should be noted that the earlier vaporgraphic theory could be resurrected with the same logic: that a reaction of bodily vapors occurred with a sensitizing material on the superficial fibers of the linen only or was provoked by sunlight, all evidence of the initial reaction now having "evaporated, been washed away, or otherwise disappeared." Because the Shroud is unique, every hypothesis of image formation must involve a set of unique conditions, and none can be rejected on this basis alone. Body imprints are invariably distorted, as Mueller remarks, just as paintings and rubbings invariably contain pigment layers (and distortion in three-dimensional projection). The new hypothesis of a "post-pigment image" has a certain built-in immunity, like postulation of an ancient occupation in regions where artifacts would not have survived. Clearly, to be testable and viable, the hypothesis must derive from or at least not conflict with the known elements of 14th century art.

This it manifestly fails to do. In addition to the four unprecedented features described above, there is no rubbing from the entire medieval period that is even remotely comparable to the Shroud, nor is there any

CRITIQUE AND REPLY

negative painting. Nickell's wet-mold-dry-daub technique was not known in medieval times, according to art historian Husband (cited in Sox 1981:88), and even that technique fails to reproduce the contour precision and three-dimensional effect, the lack of saturation points, and the resolution of the Shroud image. The bas-relief used would have been far more accurate than any example of 14th century wood carving or sculpture known; even later carvings by 15th /16th century masters of bas-relief do not have the fine detail of wounds and postures which would translate into the undistorted three-dimensional projections of Tamburelli, confirmed as accurate anatomically by the forensic pathologist Zugibe (1982:169-76). Similarly, even the blood flows painted in the greatest 14th century works of art are not at all comparable to those on the Shroud.

There are many more flaws in the "powerful case" for medieval artifice, and I must beg the reader's forbearance for what must begin to seem like the whipping of a very dead horse. There is no medieval depiction of scourge marks of such realism (radiation and fine detail) or correspondence to the Roman scourge. The nude figure of Christ is extremely rare, unheard of in an object for public veneration, and Shroud copyists generally saw fit to correct it. The wrist-nailing is unique, according to art historian McNair (1978:35): "I have studied hundreds of paintings, sculptures and carvings of Christ's crucifixion and deposition, from the 13th to the 16th centuries, and not one of them shows a nail wound anywhere but in the palm of the hand." Depiction of a non-circlet crown of thorns covering the head is extremely rare. The Shroud is unlike any 14th century or earlier artist's conception of the deposition and wrapping in linen. The portrayal of the face is extremely close to the Byzantine style, as Whanger has shown. It is clear, therefore, that clever artistry simply cannot be stretched to cover such a wide range of extraordinary circumstance, Innovation, even at genius level, is bounded by the cultural context and cannot diverge therefrom to the extent that the Shroud contradicts the 14th century milieu. From this massive conflict between the Shroud and medieval art 1 believe there can be only one conclusion – that the Shroud image belongs to the 1st millennium, with the corollary that it is the imprint of a body. These conclusions should now be considered well-documented archaeological judgements, approaching the level of certainty if normal standards are applied, especially since they agree exactly with the evidence from medical studies.

I have not invented this historical knowledge (dating and assessment) or failed to present it, as Schafersman and Pellicori maintain. The identification and dating of artifacts by their cultural affinities is part and parcel of archaeology. A web of intricate, interlocking, field-tested evidence is usually taken as proof, though not exactly comparable to proof in the natural sciences, as Maloney and Otterbein point out. With the medical, pollen, blood, pigment, and art historical evidence all pointing away from medieval forgery and collectively indicating the Shroud's origin in the ancient Middle East, the issue of Stage 1 authentication should have been settled after the archaeological confirmation of three cultural traits first hypothesized from Shroud studies – the Roman wrist-nailing, the 1st century Jewish placing of coins over the eyes and the supine, hands-over-pelvis burial posture. The skeptics, however, posit such miraculous qualities in the "clever artist" that, by the same criteria, no artifact, manuscript, or work of art could ever be dated or authenticated. And contrary to Alcock, science and history do proceed by decisions of validity and authenticity.

The possibility that the Shroud is ancient but not the burial cloth of Christ is only mentioned by Cole, who merely states a series of propositions without substantiation. It is **difficult** to build a case on this possibility, but it is not the hopeless case of medieval artistry. I do not believe it a "ritual" to examine all the Stage 2 alternatives, but there is of course a very compelling argument for the representation of Christ in the Shroud figure, virtually ruling out accident. The only real, though highly unlikely, alternatives to the full authenticity of the Shroud are therefore the early-forgery and imitation scenarios. The skeptics would do well to redirect their energies into these possibilities, if they are quite determined to remain skeptics.

Establishing the authenticity of the Shroud does not, of course, hinge on convincing every investigator, still less on resolving all difficulties and unknowns. Rather, authentication results from a process in which a minimum set of unique conditions and imposing probabilities has been established. Among these prerequisites is **not**, contrary to Jackson, a satisfactory explanation of the Shroud's early history and the image formation. Being confronted with genuinely ancient objects of unknown provenance is a common experience for the museum curator, and ancient technology cannot always be reconstructed by the archaeologist. The "lost" 1,300 years and the image origin may always remain unexplained – indeed, this prospect is beginning to appear likely – but data sufficient for authentication have been obtained from other aspects of the Shroud. The dating, geographical origin, and association with Christ are indicated not by an isolated feature or datum, but by a web of intricate, corroborating detail as specific as that used in the authentication of a manuscript or painting and certainly as reliable as many other archaeological/historical identifications which are generally accepted. This consistent mesh of detail, with layer upon layer of data from various disciplines, is more than circumstantial, but it is less than irrefutable. Perhaps the reason Pellicori and STURP support only Stage 1 is that they are not accustomed to the methodologies involved, a problem often encountered when, to paraphrase Pellicori, nonarchaeologists attempt to make archaeological judgements. The proper scrutiny of the evidence requires more of a legal than a laboratory method, and qualification by elimination rather than quantification is the determining factor.

As noted in the conclusion to my article, there can be no irrefutable proof of the past, since it cannot be repeated, and conspiracies on a massive scale, forgery of documents, bungling of excavations, etc., are always possible. In each of the examples of historical "fact" which I have compared with the Shroud – Tutankhamen's tomb, the dating of the Parthenon, Shakespeare's authorship, Hitler's death, the Lascaux paintings, the Shang dynasty – there is an element of the circumstantial, and nothing irrefutable, but careful investigation of the pattern of interlocking data, unique features, and the extraordinary circumstance required by alternative explanations leaves no reasonable doubt, and no substantial reason to doubt, unless one has a particular axe to grind. So it is with the Shroud.

The epistemological element in the question of authenticity of the Shroud is of equal fascination with the relic itself. Cole's espousal of extraordinary standards for emotional issues is a splendid example of the manner in which our preconceptions filter empirical data, especially in the degree of proof we require. And, as Burridge points out, so many of our supposed certainties, even in the natural sciences, are actually possibilities or probabilities that we need to be continuously reminded of the frailty and lack of absolute certainty inherent in our knowledge. But in an epistemological framework no stricter than that normally operative for judgements of history and science, the image on the Shroud of Turin can, I submit, be confidently ascribed to the body of Christ.

Later comments

John H. Heller and Alan D. Adler, Connecticut, USA – "The Shroud is classically an interdisciplinary subject. Meacham has approached this very complex problem in this light, and his paper is, therefore, wide-ranging. Though we disagree with some of the interpretation of data and some conclusions, the author must be complimented on a courageous synthesis.

"What is odd about the commentary on it is its impassioned attacks, not so much on the author as on the scientific work he quotes. The ad hominem aspects of these assaults are, at best, unfortunate. Readers can evaluate the bona fides of both the men and their work, as well as those of their detractors, by consulting *American Men and Women of Science, Scientific Citations*, and similar sources.

"The detractors predicate their arguments primarily on reports in the press and in private or parochial journals. There is a large body of material in these types of publications representing the views of credulous enthusiasts who want to believe in the authenticity of the Shroud. A smaller amount of similar material exists representing the views of those who are passionately opposed to authenticity. Neither of these strongly held viewpoints has any relevance to the scientific questions on the nature of the images and the stains. It is astonishing that critics of Meacham's article have attacked the credibility of the scientific research he cites without reading the scientific literature itself and addressing the scientific questions they raise with academic rigor.

"In contrast to the above popular, private, and parochial material, the scientific publications of the Shroud team (Accetta and Baumgart 1980; Avis et al. 1982; Bucklin 1981; Devan and Miller 1982; Ercoline, Downs, and Jackson 1982; Gilbert and Gilbert 1980; Heller and Adler 1980, 1981; Jackson, Jumper, and Ercoline 1982; Jumper 1982; Jumper et al. 1983; Jumper and Mottern 1980; Miller and Lynn 1981; Miller and Pellicori 1981; Morris, Schwalbe, and London 1980; Mottern, London, and Morris 1979; Pellicori 1980; Pellicori and Chandos 1981; Pellicori and Evans 1981; Schwalbe and Rogers 1982; Schwortz 1982) appear in established journals available in scientific libraries. In none of these publications is the "authenticity" of the Shroud addressed. These papers treat the scientific aspects the problem, and all opinions on the nature of the image, blood, water stains, etc., are examined in great detail. The multidisciplinary nature of these publications, ranging from mathematics, physics, and chemistry through biology and medicine, is part of the complex Shroud problem and must be considered in its entirety for an evaluation of the evidence.

"While authenticity cannot be established by any techniques now known to science, forgery can be, and the topic has been examined exhaustively. Possible eye-brain-hand techniques have been painstakingly analysed. Adventitious and accidental circumstances have been examined both theoretically and experimentally. All these data, involving dozens of investigators and tens of thousands of scientific man-hours, are set forth in the references just cited. A little less heat and a lot more light are what this problem requires."

CRITIQUE AND REPLY

Peter M. Rinaldi, Turin, Italy – "I find Meacham's paper complete, lucid, cogent, one of the finest presentations I have ever read on the subject."

Reply

I wish to thank Heller, Adler, and Rinaldi for their comments. It is most useful to have a complete listing of the work published to date by STURP members. Several recently published papers have data relevant to points raised in the comments on my paper. The question of image distortion due to projection or imprinting of a body form on a two-dimensional flat surface has been examined by Ercoline, Downs, and Jackson (1982:579). They conclude that the Shroud image does contain significant distortions which cannot be explained by anatomical variation or cloth stretching but appear consistent with a cloth drape over a three-dimensional body form.

The use of pigment in any eye/brain/hand coordinated artistic effort or in a rubbing from a bas-relief carving would seem to be definitively ruled out by the data marshaled by Jackson, Jumper, and Ercoline (1982) on the three-dimensional characteristics of the Shroud image, i.e. its precise contour shading. The virtual absence of pigment particles reported by microchemists Heller and Adler and microscopist Ercoline has been confirmed by microanalyst Riggi (1982:212), especially with regard to the traces of cinnabar or Vermillion (containing mercuric sulfide) claimed by McCrone to be present on the cloth. Riggi noted a total absence of mercury compounds among the mass of particulate matter aspirated from the Shroud by vacuum during the 1978 testing, yielding a quantity of material "enormously greater than that examined by either McCrone or Ercoline" on the sticky tape samples.

While the presence of blood traces on the cloth has been established beyond doubt by the chemical and physical testing, corroboration is seen in Bucklin's (1982:5) report that color photographs enhanced by image analysis systems reveal characteristic internal structures within the blood areas, with "physical separation of red blood cells from serum and localization of the cells toward the periphery of the blood deposits."

Finally, the biophysicist DeSalvo (1983:12-13) has described similarities between Volckringer patterns and the Shroud image in their visible reflectance and ultraviolet fluorescence characteristics, image detail, negativity, and three-dimensional reconstruction. DeSalvo proposes that lactic acid, one of the plant acids involved in the formation of Volckringer patterns and also present in human perspiration, may be responsible for the cellulose degradation image on the Shroud.

PART II – THE FALL

3. The Ultimate Test?

From 1978 To 1988 The Shroud Was at the pinnacle of the esteem in which it was held, both in the academic and popular mind. But a force was gathering momentum in the mid-1980s that would by misadventure and incompetent planning overturn utterly and completely this position of interest and awe in the eyes of the world. This force was of course the drive to carbon-date the cloth, in and of itself a quite logical step in the scientific study of the object.

Radiocarbon dating was invented in 1952. It is based on a very simple principle, namely that all living things absorb carbon through the food chain, and after death the radioactive isotope Carbon14 begins to decay. It has a half-life of 5730 years, so by measuring the amount present in ancient wood, bone, shell, etc. one can obtain a "date" (in years before the present) when the organism died. Beyond about 36,000 years the amount of C-14 remaining becomes too small to measure. There are a number of complications, and the measurement technology is very complex, since the proportion of C-14 atoms to other carbon atoms (C-13 and C-12) is extremely small.

Up to the late 1970s, the sample size required for conventional C-14 methods was too large to allow the test to be done on the Shroud. Two new methods for dating small samples became operational around 1980. One involved the use of an accelerator (called AMS dating) that could measure samples smaller than a postage stamp, down to about half a square centimeter of linen; the other was a system of gas proportional counting that required more sample than AMS but less than conventional dating. It seemed only a matter of time until the so-called "ultimate test" would be performed on the Shroud. There would however be a long period of increasingly strident altercation over how the test would be carried out.

THE ULTIMATE TEST? 53

This period is covered in the next few chapters, reviewing the issues as they were hammered out in the heat of the battle.

On October 13, 1988, the results of the radiocarbon dating of the Shroud were finally announced at press conferences in London and Turin. The age of the cloth was determined to be in the region of 1260-1390 A.D., thus seeming to prove beyond doubt that this object could not be the burial cloth of Jesus. With that announcement the Shroud of Turin morphed in the eyes of most people from being possibly the most important and fascinating archaeological object in the world to a forged medieval relic of little significance. That day back in 1988 is still very fresh in my memory, for it was the culmination of several years of effort, by me and many others, to have the Shroud dated. It was also the sad climax of several years of frustration over the faulty procedures, arrogance, Byzantine intrigues, machiavellian scheming and influence peddling that accompanied the planning of the test. The result was a disaster for the Shroud, and it truly marked the demise of the Shroud in the minds of millions of people who knew something of the fascinating image it held and the puzzle that it posed. The image and its puzzle are still there of course, but only a tiny percentage of those who formerly looked upon the Shroud with a sense of wonder do so today. For the vast majority, the C-14 result was the crowning and defining event in the encounter between the venerable relic and 20th century science. It was found to be medieval, a fake, maybe at best an icon of inexplicable realism, an oddity. But it was medieval, and thus could not possibly be the burial cloth of Christ.

The tragedy was that these views were not warranted by the evidence. The dating was a fiasco; the result may well be incorrect. It has not been corroborated by any follow-up testing, which for some inexplicable reason has not been allowed by the Church. Research done in the last ten years has cast grave doubts on the validity of the date as an age for the cloth as a whole. It is quite possible that contamination and/or repair works are responsible for the aberrant age of the single sample selected. The decision to take only one sample, and the location chosen, may well go down in the history of the Shroud as one of the worst single events, behind only the fire of 1532 and the "restoration" of 2002. There is firm evidence available now that the sample taken was not representative of the cloth as a whole, and that it provided what archaeologists and geologists call a "rogue" or "fictitious" date, i.e. one that does not provide a true age of the object or context it purports to date.

As an archaeologist, I had used C-14 dating many dozens of times on excavated samples, and found that it does generally **but not always** give accurate results. Most other archaeologists and geologists that I know have the same view; a few are more skeptical of its reliability. The debate within the professions has been largely about its accuracy in settling fine-grained chronological questions, for example the question of whether a city was sacked in 703 B.C. rather than 751 B.C. Rogue results were normally discarded without any follow-up research, when it was abundantly clear that something was amiss, whether it was due to contamination or "old wood" or residual material from an earlier phase or intrusive from a later one. Such rogue dates are common in archaeology and geology and they are usually not subjected to any further detailed study. Instead, the normal practice would be to seek more and better samples, obtain new C-14 dates and review the overall clustering pattern indicated by the dates. Such has been my experience as an archaeologist: I have excavated, submitted and interpreted around one hundred fifty C-14 samples from Neolithic, Bronze Age and Early Historical sites. Of these dates obtained, about 110 were considered credible, 30 were rejected as unreliable and 10 were problematic. I mention this merely to inform the non-specialist that rogue dates are quite common in the general application of C-14 in archaeology. As fate would have it, I had dealt with more rogue samples than most other archaeologists, and furthermore had been involved with several C-14 labs in investigating why some of these samples yielded results which simply could not be correct in terms of their real calendar date.

After the publication of my article on the Shroud in *Current Anthropology* in 1983, I was vaulted into the inner circle of Shroud researchers, by simple virtue of the fact that I had been able to publish such a comprehensive and favorable treatment of the subject in the most prestigious journal of anthropology in the world (see Scavone 1983). Of course it was an honor for me personally, but I had already published a lengthy article in the same journal a few years previously on South China prehistory. What was exhilarating and humbling at the same time was to be lifted from relative obscurity in the ranks of Shroud aficionados and suddenly to be ranked with the experts – people who had spent years in research or who had been involved in the 1978 STURP testing. Again as fate or luck would have it, the issue that was most pressing for the future of the Shroud and being most intensely debated in 1983, was one that I knew very well from first-hand experience.

In both the *Current Anthropology* comments and in Shroud writing generally at the time, I noted a lack of awareness of the pitfalls and uncertainties inherent in the C-14 method. To quote from the comments, Alcock said it was "sheer whimsy" to raise the question of contamination; McCrone claimed that "the impurities can be readily removed before dating, hence this argument has no validity"; Maloney thought that "the margins of error supplied with each date [give] a measure of accuracy" in the elimination of contaminants; Schafersman claimed that the idea of contamination was "absurd." In the Shroud literature, a similar absolute belief in the method is found among most writers. Wilson, for example, states (1978:264) that a dating accurate to a plus-minus of 100 years is possible thus "enabling the settling, once and for all, of the question of whether or not the Shroud is a 14th century forgery." Sox (1981:132) follows Wilson in thinking that C-14 dating the Shroud could "remove it once and for all from the Middle Ages, or place it squarely there for all time." Some STURP scientists unfortunately display similar misconceptions. Jumper et al (1983:176) claimed that the test "if 'negative', i.e. not first century, can **prove** lack of authenticity" (emphasis added). Dinegar, who heads the STURP C-14 group which claimed to have made a detailed study of the application of C-14 to the Shroud, stated that "sample preparation procedures can insure no error in date due to foreign contamination accreted over the centuries" (1982:6; emphasis added).

All of these statements reveal an unwarranted trust in radiocarbon measurement to produce an exact calendar date for any sample submitted. However, I doubt that anyone with significant experience in the dating of excavated samples would dismiss for one moment the potential danger of contamination and other sources of error. No responsible field archaeologist would trust a single date, or a series of dates on a single feature, to settle a major historical issue, establish a site or cultural chronology, etc. No responsible radiocarbon scientist would claim that it was certain that all contaminants had been removed and that the dating range produced for a sample was without doubt its actual calendar age. The public and many non-specialist academics do seem to share the misconception that C-14 dates are absolute.

Even the most elementary textbooks of archaeology and geology give a very different picture. "Contamination of samples may cause error in determination of reliable dates" (Heizer and Graham 1967: 165); "contamination of the sample may take place ... and removal of the contaminant from the pores spaces and fissures is almost impossible" (Goude 1977:10). "Carbon from other sources may easily be trapped in porous materials ... The archaeologist is the only person who is in a position to know of these contaminating potentials" (Stuckenrath 1965:279). Excavated samples are "liable to absorb humic matter from the solutions that pass through them (resulting in) contamination by carbon compounds of an age younger than its own ... there is also the possibility of exchange of carbon isotopes under such conditions ... That there are other risks of contamination and other pitfalls involved in this method is obvious enough" (Zeuner 1970:341-6). Stuckenrath noted that contamination could not always be detected or eliminated, even with specialized pretreatments. He cited discrepancies in "dates" of wood house posts in Alaska at 1800-1600 B.C. and of charcoal from hearths within the houses at 1000-800 B.C. Summarizing the attempts to date early man in North America, Wormington (1983:191) stated what must be a nearly universal view among archaeologists: "Over the years, we have learned that radiocarbon dating is not quite the alchemist's stone we once hoped it might be." The possibility of contamination is not of course in any way reflected in the margin of error given with each result. And every radiocarbon laboratory stresses the proper handling of excavated samples to avoid contamination additional to what may already have been deposited. The sample should be dried out immediately upon excavation to avoid mold growth, it should not be handled in a cloud of cigarette smoke or taken back from the field in a lunch box, it should not be placed in contact with a paper label, etc. These handling considerations are not simply for the sake of white-coated tidiness – contamination is a real danger for any C-14 material and it is realized as such by archaeologists and geologists in the field.

Unfortunately, this perspective had not been understood by those proposing to date the Shroud. In 1979, the much vaunted "Gove/ Harbottle Proposal on Carbon Dating the Shroud" (Sox 1981:161:167) outlined only standard pretreatment of the samples for carbonates and humic acids. It did not propose scanning electron microscope screening or other types of direct examination to check the state of the samples prior to testing – an omission which might have been rectified if the vicissitudes of the cloth over the centuries had been stressed, as an archaeologist would have done. Much worse, the 1979 proposal involved a small sample of cloth removed from the Shroud in 1973 for study by Prof. Raes of Belgium. McCrone and Sox had inspected the sample (apparently unstitched by Raes into two pieces) during a visit with Raes in 1976, and found that "the samples were kept in what looked like an old scrapbook for postage stamps" (Sox: 1978:48). Certainly most archaeologists would have rejected the use of samples subjected to a long separation from the object to be dated and held under unknown conditions of storage and handling.

Further, McCrone (1978:440) made his contribution by proposing to rely on "the person authenticating the Shroud samples as the same ones studied by Raes." The original sample was apparently not even taken from the Shroud in the presence of Raes. An art historian would certainly not have been satisfied that such a procedure could establish conclusively that the pieces were indeed from that sample removed from the Shroud in 1973, and that it had not been tampered with in the intervening years. Finally, the original Raes sample was taken at the junction of the side strip (believed by some scholars to be a later addition) and the (selvage?) border (possibly treated to prevent unraveling, and certainly more subject to contamination than the main body of the cloth). It could not be considered as a typical or representative sample of the relic. In sum, the proposal to use the Raes piece for C-14 dating was not an academically sound proposition; it was based on expediency (as the pieces had already been removed from the relic and were "available"). There is consensus now that, had the testing been allowed, it would have been the cause of great controversy regardless of the results. Yet Gove, in urging the release of the Raes samples, wrote that "at long last, the Shroud of Turin's true age will be established in the near future."

When STURP planned the 1978 testing, Carbon-14 was on their list. But it had not been approved, the official reason being that it was destructive. All of the other tests they proposed were non-destructive, i.e. doing no damage and leaving no mark on the Shroud. They were however allowed to lift loose fibers off the Shroud by means of sticky tape, and to perform physical and chemical testing of these fibers. This could be described as micro-destructive, in the sense that no mark would be left where the sticky tape had been pressed to the cloth and the fibers removed, but the individual fibers themselves would be destroyed in the course of the laboratory work. Conventional C-14 measurement at that time would on the other hand have required a rather large piece of the cloth, roughly 6 x 6 inches, and this was considered too much material from the precious relic to sacrifice. A number of other factors were involved: new methods of dating very small samples had been developed and were already yielding results, but were not yet in general practice; there was resistance in some quarters to this particular test due to the Shroud's long history of exposure to possible contaminants; some people in Turin and Rome believed that the Shroud had already been proved authentic and therefore did not need to be subjected to further testing. It was unclear how widespread these viewpoints were. There was also an undercurrent of anti-American feeling among some Italian researchers that had been fed by STURP's international recognition. Finally, it was rumored that the Pontifical Academy of Sciences was to be consulted on the matter. As I would soon discover, things were frightfully complex, and scientific considerations were only small part of the picture.

In 1984 I visited Turin and made friends with some of the leading Shroud authorities there. Notable amongst them were two Italian priests of very different temperament and outlook. One was Fr. Peter Rinaldi, leading light in the Holy Shroud Guild and the grand old man of sindonology, who had helped guide the STURP enterprise through the labyrinth of local Turinese church politics. He was a warm and charming person, and we kept in touch until he went on to meet his maker. The other was Don Piero Coero Borga, who represented the old guard conservative wing. Borga was director of the Turin Centro, an organization devoted to the study and cult of the Shroud. Both he and Rinaldi were engaged to the hilt in maneuvering to get the C-14 testing blocked or authorized, respectively. Another key figure that I met was Luigi Gonella, an animated pipe-smoking professor of metrology (measurement) at Turin Polytechnic. His greatest accomplishment in life had been that he cleared the way for the STURP tests of 1978, and for this he will always have a place in the Shroud pantheon. Unfortunately, he would later take on the dominant role in the dating of the Shroud, and he bears a large share of the responsibility for what went wrong.

Later that year I met two of STURP's leading figures, the chemists John Heller and Alan Adler, and spent several hours in discussion with them in a gazebo at John Heller's house in Wilton, Connecticut. Heller took me back to the train station that evening, and as we sat waiting for my train back to New York City, he told me in strictest confidence about a secret C-14 run that had already been made on a thread from the Shroud. He said it was done by the Livermore Laboratory in California, and the thread was cut into two segments. One end dated ca. 200 A.D., the other ca. 1000 A.D. He also said that starch had been identified on the thread. He did not know what margin of error there was on the dates, and thought it would be quite wide, as the test was only intended to give a rough idea of what an eventual C-14 date would look like. As it turned out, it gave conflicting indications. (This test in California was later confirmed to me by Adler, who said that he was in fact the one who had arranged it, despite C-14 dating being specifically forbidden in STURP's agreement with the Turin Archdiocese.)

At that time, it was believed that C-14 would eventually be done by STURP officially as part of the second round of more sophisticated testing they proposed. As I began to learn more of the personalities, issues and ambitions involved, it became clear that C-14 was rapidly taking on a huge and unwarranted importance, as I had already warned in the *Current Anthropology* article. There was a risk that it would overshadow all the other research that was being proposed. Unfortunately, this is exactly what happened, but in a massive and overwhelming manner that could not be imagined at the time.

In late 1985 I wrote a paper examining the entire question of carbon-dating the Shroud. There were many aspects that I felt were being overlooked or not sufficiently emphasized, by STURP and also by the carbon daters who were getting involved. A first draft was sent to some of the main players, and a few comments were received. A particularly curt reply came back from Heller, who said that STURP had lined up some of

THE ULTIMATE TEST?

the best C-14 labs in the world, and just who was I to be questioning their project? It appeared that no one was interested in discussing the issue in detail, since positions were already fairly well solidified and turf well established. STURP and another US organization ASSIST seemed to want input only from scientists, and the carbon-daters only wanted to deal with each other. Gonella seemed to have surprisingly firm views on the matter even though he had no experience whatever in it.

My C-14 paper was published the next year (Meacham 1986), and can be seen online at www.shroud.com/meacham.htm. It provides an overview of the issue as it had congealed at that time, and highlights some of the problems that would soon rise to the fore in a most dramatic fashion. The point that I hoped to drive home is that there are many things that can go wrong with C-14 dating; for some the cause is known, while the others are grouped under the term "rogue dates." It is important for anyone wishing to understand the normal archaeological use of C-14 to know that a single date or even a series of dates on a single object or feature is seldom if ever cited to answer important questions about the age of a culture or a site. To put a single radiocarbon date in the position of being the ultimate arbiter of the age of the Turin Shroud is a blatant departure from the way C-14 is normally used. There are simply too many pitfalls. This was not a position that went down well with the hotshots from the radiocarbon labs.

4. Maneuvering and the Grand Council

After My Trip To Turin In 1984, I begin to "dig" in earnest to find out exactly what STURP was proposing for the C-14 measurement. My first letter to John Heller, as mentioned above, brought a rather frosty response along the lines of "We've got some of the world's best C-14 experts lined up ... What do you think you have that they might have missed? ... It was hard to get this far so don't rock the boat now." I wrote back setting out in some detail the problems as I saw them, especially regarding contamination and the use of the charred material, and his reply exhibited a complete *volte-face*:

> Re the thrust of your letter on sources of contamination in C-14 sampling, your observations are well taken. I was completely unaware of them and appreciate your pointing them out. Clearly, you are perfectly correct and I will support you to the hilt. I will also urge your inclusion in STURP. Adler agrees with me and is as pleased as I am to have been made aware of possible sampling glitches.

This made a deep impression on me, as he had an entrenched position but moved immediately to square it in the face of new data. In later years I heard much disparaging talk about Heller, notably that Adler did most of the work and Heller was only in it to write a book, but his quick recognition of the problems I was describing was certainly admirable.

Unfortunately the same cannot be said for STURP as a whole. Despite having the support of Heller and Adler, and a good rapport with Rinaldi and Gonella (STURP's "patrons" in Turin), I never got any response from the leadership, namely John Jackson and Tom d'Muhala. I then wrote to the STURP Board of Directors in July 1985, suggesting that STURP needed to expand its C-14 committee to include archaeologists and others who made regular use of the dating method in their professional life. I pointed out as gently as I could some of the flaws that I perceived in STURP's approach and attitude, citing several statements made in print by STURP members that were inaccurate and would not have been made by a practicing archaeologist. I wrote:

> These statements are a compelling demonstration of the need for STURP to include archaeologists and historians in its ranks; the scientific study of an historical object does not take place in a vacuum, and data from the laboratory must be integrated into the interpretation of the object in acceptable social science modes. To my mind, this is a major weakness in the STURP organization and it has resulted in poor testing procedures and inaccurate statements in the past. In 1981, I wrote to STURP in a similar vein, but this letter was not answered nor apparently were its contents deemed relevant.

There was no answer to this letter either.

In October 1985, after learning of the disastrous reception of Dinegar at a major international C-14 conference (see below), I wrote to John Jackson, who was the leading light in STURP, enclosing a copy of a letter I had just received from an old friend and radiocarbon man (Henry Polach) whose vehemence regarding Dinegar's speech had surprised me. I wrote:

> While the situation is certainly not as bad as he [Polach] paints it, the fact that he and some of his colleagues have this impression is serious, and indicates to me that STURP has failed to win wide international support for its C-14 proposal among professional daters. I am also convinced, having researched the issue in some detail, that use of the charred cloth as the principal C-14 sample material from the main body of the relic is faulty, and dangerous in terms of its possible consequences for the study of the Shroud.

Again, I offered to cooperate with STURP to draw up a rigorous C-14 plan that would have the full support of the academic community. Again, there was no reply. STURP was on course for disaster, and it was largely of their own making.

I did manage to obtain, from Heller, a copy of STURP's super-secret C-14 "work package" proposal of 1984. As I expected, it planned to sample only the charred areas of the Shroud, with additional control samples from patches and backing cloth. Under principal investigator Robert Dinegar of STURP and coinvestigator Garmon Harbottle of Brookhaven National Laboratory, there were eight carbon dating specialists listed, one of whom, Robert Otlet of Harwell in England, I had submitted samples to and corresponded with previously, but never met. The *enfant terrible* among the others, as I would soon discover, was Harry Gove of Rochester, one of the inventors of the AMS method of C-14 dating. I had heard from Frs. Rinaldi and Otterbein that he was "trouble" but beyond that knew nothing of him. I would soon experience first hand his abrasive and supercilious nature. In 1996, he wrote a book about the dating of the Shroud; it is an incredible and offensive *mèlange* of fact, fiction, rant and self-trumpeting, liberally peppered with arrogance and ad hominem attacks on just about everyone involved who did not agree with him. I believe it will be clear from what follows how wrong he and most of the other C-14 experts were in their approach to this milestone test for the Shroud.

Alarmed at the direction that things were taking, in May of 1985 I also sent a proposal to Cardinal Ballestrero concerning the planning and implementation of a C-14 project for the Shroud. After pointing out the many possible pitfalls of an improperly designed radiocarbon dating, I suggested that the good cardinal appoint a panel composed of relevant experts "to study all aspects of the procedures, to make consensus decisions, to collect and submit samples for the C-14 tests, to examine all aspects of possible contamination or other distortions of the laboratory measurements, and to interpret the results." I went over again the C-14 proposal submitted by STURP in 1979, then the variant "Gove/Harbottle proposal" of 1981, and finally STURP's latest C-14 proposal of 1984. Having demonstrated that all of these proposals were flawed, I pointed out that they had been drawn up without the benefit of experience of actual archaeological applications of C-14 dating. It seemed to be treated as a matter solely for physicists and chemists, in spite of the professed ideal in archaeological dating of a close collaboration between field and lab. I concluded this letter to Ballestrero:

> Because of the Shroud's status as a religious relic and the esteem in which it is held by millions, it is necessary to proceed cautiously in the undertaking of what has been called 'the ultimate test of the Turin Shroud.' And it is essential to proceed under the principle of close collaboration between experts from relevant fields if the tests are to be successful in the broadest sense – that is, to obtain a valid, internationally recognized, scientific estimation of the age of the cloth. And, as people from all walks of life all over the world await this crucial test, it is essential to proceed. In my view, further postponement of the C-14 dating will damage the cause of the Shroud. In conclusion, I would urge the Church to take all steps to

guarantee that this most important of tests is conducted according to the most rigorous scholarly procedure that can be devised. The appointment of a panel as suggested would represent an effort to exclude, as far as is humanly possible, the effects of personality conflicts, cliques, national rivalries, and simple human error from the pursuit of the truth of the Holy Shroud.

Alas, much of this was prophetic in a negative sense: the panel was not appointed, and all of the mentioned detriments did rise to the fore. Unbeknownst to me at the time, a serious rift had already developed between Gove and STURP. Rather, to be more precise, Gove, though having formally agreed to participate in STURP's project as one of the eight collaborating C-14 experts, had taken an axe to the relationship. In June of 1985, at the 12th International Radiocarbon Conference held in Trondheim, Norway, there had been a contretemps between Gove and Bob Dinegar of STURP over the future direction of the move to date the Shroud. After the presentation of a laboratory intercomparison project on dating ancient textiles, which was conducted as a precursor to dating the Shroud, a question was asked from the floor about what the next step would be. Gove, in his inimitable style, relates what occurred:

> Dinegar rose and said he represented the organization STURP. He claimed that STURP was responsible for the intercomparison test. He noted that STURP had very close connections with the archbishop of Turin. STURP would take care of all the political arrangements connected with dating the shroud as well as that of announcing the result. He essentially advised the rest of us to wait until we got a sample and then just go ahead, like good technicians, and date it – then pass the results on to him. It struck me as a most extraordinarily arrogant statement.

This would have been a classic pot-kettle-black, except for the curious fact that Dinegar was totally correct. STURP was the body that was conducting the study of the Shroud, and like any archaeologist or geologist, they should have been the "submitter" of the sample and the labs should have dealt directly with them. Unfortunately, Dinegar was not an expert in C-14 dating and may have had no practical experience dealing with labs either. He made a bad impression on the C-14 people at Trondheim, and not only Gove. A few months later I wrote my old friend Henry Polach of the Australian National University Radiocarbon Laboratory for his opinion on the use of the charred material. What I got back stunned me. Polach said he had been at the Trondheim meeting, which was he said:

> ... quite good except for a some blemishes, such as the politico/religious representative of STURP who was not seen by me or any of my friends talking to any of the radiocarbon daters. His speech from the audience to the plenary can be summarized as: 'You worry about dating and we worry about getting the Shroud sample to some of you.' There were no comments in reply, which is indicative of saying 'who cares.' The sad thing is that a number of very serious people do care.

This incident was an important turning point, and Gove had gained the upper hand. "It was suggested" at the Trondheim meeting that Gove take on the task of writing a protocol for dating the Shroud. The enterprise seemed to be slipping even further towards a totally physicist-dominated one. Ironically, as it turned out, when faced with the thorny issue of variable chemistry over the cloth, or the question of possible contamination that might escape pretreatment, or of possible isotope exchange due to the 1532 fire, the response of Gove and the other C-14 "technicians" was precisely that all they needed was a little snippet of the cloth, no matter where from on the cloth, and they would merrily take it back to their lab, run it through their machines and produce a date for it.

In addition to gaining the advantage on the scientific side, Gove through his side-kick Vittorio Canuto (a scientist working for NASA) had begun courting the president of the Pontifical Academy of Sciences, a Brazilian biochemist named Carlos Chagas. (I would later meet Chagas at the Turin C-14 conference; he was a genteel and distinguished man in his seventies.) The purpose of this courtship was to bring the Academy into the issue, as a counterfoil to the complete control theretofore wielded by Gonella on behalf of Cardinal Ballestrero, so that ultimately the C-14 dating could be done free and clear of STURP. From Gove's slanted and self-idolizing book, it is also clear that he developed other more sinister plots and objectives, which he pursued with the tenacity of a bulldog in a china shop. Whilst remaining part of STURP's C-14 team he worked to undermine and replace it with his own plan. Later, he began to press for all other STURP testing to be blocked while the dating went ahead.

The fact that Gove's side-kick had a close relationship with Chagas proved most useful in advancing these goals, as did Gove's knack for wringing advantage out of every situation. For example, at the conclusion of the Trondheim session, when "it was suggested" that Gove draft the protocol, it was also agreed that the protocol, after being reviewed by the six laboratories to be involved, "would be presented to the authorities in Turin or the Vatican." When Gove sent round his draft for comment by the six laboratories, he indicated that he would send it to the Pontifical Academy of Sciences. Later, Gove relates that Chagas "seemed to be particularly pleased that the Trondheim group had emphasized [sic!] the importance of the involvement of the Pontifical Academy." This was a far stretch from what actually happened at Trondheim, but Chagas fell for it.

It is not easy to understand why Gove became so obsessed with dating the Shroud. From the account in his book it is clear that he made hundreds of phone calls, many to Brazil or Rome, sent hundreds of letters, faxes and cables, and spent thousands of hours plotting strategy with his sidekick. He made frantic efforts to contact ambassadors, senators, highly placed cardinals, and anyone else who he thought might be of use. The simplest explanation, that there was funding to be had, does not seem to fit, and Gove specifically rejects that as a motivation – not, of course, that his rejection of it would mean very much! He would say that, wouldn't he? But it does seem rather that it was all about glory, no matter which way the dating went. It was literally a win-win game for the C-14 folk: if the Shroud date came out 1st century, they were the ones who revealed this to the world; if it turned out to be medieval, they were the ones who proved it could not be Christ's.

For Gove, there may have also been two other factors: the AMS dating method was his baby (or so he ardently believed anyway); and after he began to lock horns with Gonella it became personal. Gove's published comments on Gonella, and some directed at me also, are defamatory; he quotes his sidekick as remarking: "How is the Pope to know that Gonella is a second-rate scientist and that the rest of us are super scientists?" According to Gove, Gonella was "unprofessional," "an obscure polytechnic lecturer nobody had ever heard of," "a trouble-maker of the first order," "malicious," "small-minded" etc. ad nauseam. All through the book Gove spares no effort to portray Gonella in the worst possible light. Ironically, in almost all of the issues described with such scorn by Gove, Gonella was right and Gove was dead wrong. But on the one that mattered the most, and which would lead to a flawed dating of the Shroud, Gove essentially ignored it and Gonella made a huge error.

The intense media interest in the subject must also have attracted Gove and some of the other C-14 daters. Teddy Hall of Oxford supposedly offered the BBC exclusive coverage of his dating of the Shroud sample, for a hefty fee. After the results were announced, Hall obtained a very handsome endowment for his lab from a group of businessmen. Garman Harbottle of Brookhaven may have also coveted the attention and glory. In one of his letters to Dinegar, Harbottle pointed out (as cited by Gove) that "STURP had done all the experiments, written all the scientific articles, been on all the talk shows and starred in all the films on the Turin Shroud."

Sounds as though he wanted in on the action! Gove professed a disdain for the press, but then seemed to relish each interview or reporter's query. He stated that all the media attention was "heady stuff." Overall, one gets the impression that Gove considered the Shroud dating enterprise to be his, and anyone who got in the way should be crushed. Unlike the others, for him it probably was not about the money, and maybe in the final analysis it was not even about the public attention or the glory, but rather his absolute fixation on and monolithic drive towards his objective, positively reeking of arrogance and dogmatism, bulldozing everything and everyone aside. In a military man or politician, this might be an admirable quality. In a scientist, it was pathetic. And he has the audacity to denigrate, over and over again, those he suspected of being "true believers." He said that he had dealt with STURP for ten years and "regard them as a pack of religious zealots." This is of course totally absurd, and merely serves to indicate how blinkered Gove's perception of reality was. This is all with the benefit of hindsight, as I had not yet met Gove or any of the other C-14 daters in person.

In his book *The Resurrection of the Shroud*, Mark Antonacci (2001) devotes most of a chapter to Gove's shenanigans. He concluded:

> Gove's attitude toward STURP was nothing less than blatant hypocrisy. Gove's obsession with STURP manifested itself in his deceitfulness, resentment, hypocrisy and unscientific behavior. Throughout his book, Gove seems to brag and gloat about his conduct and attitudes ... which never had any scientific or other valid basis.

Clearly Gove's involvement was most unfortunate for STURP and for the Shroud, but he would later be reduced to a mere carping nuisance when his lab was excluded from the project.

In my continuing correspondence with Gonella, he mentioned, in reply to my proposal of a panel to study the dating problem, that something was brewing, perhaps a meeting to discuss the issue. Although I did not know it at the time, this was spurred by Gove's approach to Chagas to involve the Pontifical Academy in hosting a meeting of representatives of the labs. Gonella said that Ballestrero was in favor of such a meeting but he (Gonella) would lobby for inclusion of other experts besides the radiocarbon boys. In November 1985, Chagas obtained approval from the Vatican for the meeting, after Ballestrero had agreed to it. It was to be held in Turin or Rome in June 1986. Perhaps my proposal of a radiocarbon panel to study the problem contributed in some small way to softening up Gonella and Ballestrero to the idea of a consultative meeting.

As luck would have it once again, I was organizing a small conference in Hong Kong for March 1986, centered around an exhibition of STURP photographs. Among those that I invited was Gonella; others were Rex Morgan (who arranged the exhibit), Heller, Adler, Rinaldi and Ian Wilson. The timing could not have been better, as there was a lot of activity at this time, and lots of gossip in the air. And of course, it did not do any harm for me to invite Gonella and provide his airfare and expenses, while he was in the midst of deciding whom to invite to the forthcoming C-14 conference! In addition to a meeting with the C-14 labs' representatives, STURP was pressing ahead with plans to conduct another session of direct testing of the relic in 1986, the British Society was concurrently planning its own tests, and another American organization (ASSIST) was putting together a wide array of proposals. There was strong opposition from the Turin Centro. Arriving in Hong Kong, Rinaldi and Gonella were brimming with news and gossip, particularly about the Gove-Chagas intrigues and the xenophobic attitude of the Centro. On the latter they reported that there was a deep bitterness and/or jealousy towards STURP, and one of the Centro's leading figures had made crude anti-American remarks. Gonella said that the Centro people did not support any further testing, since they believed that the scientific data had already proved the authenticity of the Shroud. Hardly anyone outside of a narrow band of supporters in Italy bought this. On the other hand, if there was to be another round of testing the Centro wanted to play a prominent role.

There was a major high level tug-of-war going on at this time between Chagas and Ballestrero, over issues related to the planned C-14 meeting: where it would be held, under whose auspices, who would chair it, who would be invited, etc. Gonella told me that Ballestrero wanted him to be in charge, with Chagas as a sort of ceremonial presence. The Gove axis did not see things that way, and at the continual prompting of Gove via Canuto, Chagas pressed the Vatican for control. I did not know it at the time, but one of the sticking points was over people nominated by Ballestrero to be invited, including Adler, Dinegar, Jacques Evin (a C-14 dater from France, another person that I had submitted samples to and corresponded with previously, but never met.) and me. Gove wanted STURP people to be excluded, and the meeting restricted to C-14 professionals and church representatives, a totally ludicrous position (as usual). Fr. Rinaldi wrote to me that he (Rinaldi) and Gonella were pressing to have me included but everything was up in the air, and a decision was awaited from Rome. Fortunately Ballestrero prevailed, and things seemed to have been sorted out when in April I received a letter from Chagas inviting me to the meeting, which was to be held in Turin on June 9-11. Later, I learned from various people that there had been an enormous struggle over where in Turin the meeting would be held, with Gonella arguing for the Turin Polytechnic as a neutral academic venue, and Gove/Chagas insisting it be in a Church institution such as the Archbishop's palace to negate the influence of Gonella and STURP. Reminiscent of the interminable squabble in Paris over the shape of the table for negotiations to end the Vietnam conflict!

For reasons that were never made entirely clear, the meeting was postponed just one month before it was due to start, and eventually took place at the end of September 1986. Rumor had it that the delay was due to a final appeal to highly placed Vatican officials from certain members of the Turin Centro who did not want C-14 or any further testing (by Americans) to be done. Meanwhile, STURP was gearing up on Gonella's advice for the 25 other tests it had planned, aiming at a week-long session to be conducted in the summer of 1986, and this would supposedly include the taking of samples for the C-14 dating. Needless to say, when Gove got wind of this plan, dozens of phone calls and faxes ensued. He was not the only one opposed to STURP's rush to start testing; the British Society also argued for a delay, as did ASSIST. But apparently STURP was not entirely ready to proceed, due to financial and personnel problems, and that fact could have been one of the reasons for the postponement of the C-14 meeting. As it turned out, because of the later furor over the C-14 results and the way Gonella and Ballestrero handled the situation, STURP never did get to conduct all the other tests that it had planned, and this was a great loss to the study of the Shroud.

During 1985 and early 1986 I had a lengthy correspondence with Gonella over the possible pitfalls of C-14 dating, amplifying on the concerns in my earlier paper on the subject. Of particular importance was the proposed use of the charred material as **the only** sample from the main body of the cloth. This seemed insane to me, and I argued the case back and forth with Gonella. At times he seemed close to agreeing, at other times he would fall back to the position that there should not be any problem using this material. I believe he genuinely wanted to limit the amount of material removed from the Shroud and any visible alteration to it, which is of course a legitimate concern, but he took it to extremes. The charred, he said, was "the obvious choice ... being hidden under the patches ... and the sample anyways has to be charred for the C-14 test." He did not seem to understand some of the issues, but then he was in unfamiliar territory; to my knowledge he had never studied the subject of C-14 dating and had no experience in it. He was however a physicist with a pure science approach, like STURP's.

In this correspondence with Gonella, I continued to hammer the issue of sampling strategy and possible contamination. I pointed out that "the edges are anomalous in my view because they were much more subject to handling, in more intimate contact with wooden boards when the Shroud was mounted, and may have been treated to prevent or repair unraveling." But I thought a sample from the edge could still be used, as long as it was not the only one: "The sampling strategy that I would hope for would aim at four distinct areas – the charred cloth, the adjacent uncharred cloth, an edge sample (the size of Raes', for CO_2 proportional counting), and a thread sample (the size of Baima's, for AMS)." In comparing to these other samples previously removed, I hoped to soften his opposition to "punching holes all over the cloth" as he put it once. But I sensed that the correspondence was not actually sinking in. In one of his replies he asked me what part of the Shroud I thought would not be affected by the forms of contamination I had enumerated; in another he stated that such concerns needed to be quantified, otherwise they would be merely speculative. He failed to understand that these concerns are normally dealt with by archaeologists and geologists **after** rogue dates have occurred. What was needed for the Shroud was an approach that minimized the likelihood of getting an aberrant date. He wondered "why should the Shroud be considered any more likely to be contaminated than any other sample routinely dated by C-14?" I responded that the principal and very important difference is that the Shroud is unprovenanced, has been in so many different handling situations, in contact with so many diverse substances, subject to such extremes in temperature and humidity, unlike an object that has been buried in a stable matrix for several thousand years. And of course, another huge difference was that, unlike ordinary samples from an excavation, with the Shroud it would be very difficult to go back and collect more samples to study the problem once it had arisen. Ultimately, these same questions were discussed at the Turin meeting, and not entirely satisfactorily resolved. The pity is that Gonella involved himself so deeply in this matter and took charge at the final stage, committing a huge error in the choice of sampling site and the number of samples. At the higher level of responsibility is Ballestrero, who delegated too much power to Gonella and failed to see the dangers in this.

The ASSIST organization was also attempting to get involved in the C-14 dating, and its General Secretary Paul Maloney had formed a sub-committee with three carbon daters. I had a lengthy correspondence with him on the question of using the charred material, and as an archaeologist he was more readily moved by my arguments than Gonella. He put together a 3-page discussion summary and circulated it to his subcommittee and all eight of the STURP consultants as well. It was entitled "Shall charred remains be used to date the Shroud?" but other issues were described as well, such as the use of small counters and their requirement of a much larger sample than AMS, an issue that Maloney placed undue importance on. Harbottle was motivated by this paper to seek out the views of several dozen fellow C-14 daters on my reservations about the use of only charred material, and one of them, Austin Long of Arizona, ran an experiment to confirm that charring would not result in any increase in the C-14 content of a sample. Harbottle brought to the Turin meeting a summary of the comments from colleagues and the results of Long's experiment.

I heard from Fr. Rinaldi that there had been some discussion about the possibility of an inspection of the Shroud during the conference, but he doubted that it would happen because of all the "red tape" required to open the reliquary. When I learned about the postponement of the conference, I decided to write to Chagas and Ballestrero on the definite value of such an inspection, plus of course I wanted to see the object myself. I said that we would no doubt be discussing such things as the condition of the cloth, its charring and other discolorations, the presence of a selvage border, etc. and most of the participants would not have seen it. Although the photographic record is good, there are invariably many details that only the eye can perceive, especially the eyes of so many experts. And since the charred material under the patches had not been seen since 1534, it was surely prudent to examine some of those areas if it was proposed to take samples from there. I concluded that in order to make the best empirical decision about the details of the C-14 protocol, it was highly advisable that a first-hand inspection be arranged.

The Turin conference

I arrived in Turin exhausted, early in the morning of the 28th of September 1986, and proceeded to the hotel where accommodation had been booked. It was a very nice, small hotel in the heart of the city. On arriving in my room, the first thing I did was to order a large "American" breakfast through room service, and draw a hot bath. Breakfast in bed does not compare with breakfast in the bath, especially after a journey of 20 hours by air! Luxuriously relaxed, I contemplated what would unfold over the next few days, and wondered if ultimately the Shroud would be well served by this gathering of C-14 hotshots and others who were interested. Dinner that evening was a thoroughly European affair, with copious bottles of red and white wine, mineral water, wonderful Italian food, and conversation at full throttle. I felt good as an American who on this occasion linguistically outdid all the Europeans present, alternating in conversation on my right in Italian, and on my left in French, and eavesdropping on Tite's valiant efforts in French. It just so happened that I had studied in France for one year, and in Italy for another, so (again as the fates would have it) was well prepared for this group. Seated next to me was Giovanni Riggi, one of Gonella's colleagues at the Turin Polytechnic. He surprised me with the information "to be kept strictly confidential" that it had been decided already that only three labs would get samples of the Shroud, and none of the small counter labs would be used because this method required too much material. It turned out he was right on both counts. But there would be strong resistance, as Gove was expected to provide trouble on several counts. Adler cautioned me as we parted for the night: "Prepare to get crushed tomorrow."

The venue that had finally been decided upon was the Archdiocese Seminary Building, a stone's throw away from the cathedral where the Shroud was kept. The agenda did not include any mention of a visit to see the Shroud, and one of the first things I intended to do was to raise a question about this.

Those attending the meeting were: Canuto; Paul Damon and Doug Donahue from the Arizona AMS lab; Jean-Claude DuPlessy from Gif-sur-Yvette and Jacques Evin from Lyon (both C-14 daters); Gonella and Riggi; Gove and his female friend Shirley Brignall (why she should have been invited escaped me) from Rochester; Hall and Robert Hedges from Oxford; Harbottle from Brookhaven; Michael Tite from the British Museum; Mechthild Flury-Lemberg (a textile expert who would have an enormous and terrible role later); Otlet from Harwell; Fr Rinaldi; Adler, Dinegar and Steve Lukasik from STURP; Enrico di Rovasenda and Chagas of the Pontifical Academy; and Willy Woelfli of the Zurich AMS lab.

It is worth noting at this juncture how Flury-Lemberg came to be involved. According to Gove's account, her name was first suggested by Hall to Michael Tite, who then wrote to her about taking a sample from the Shroud for C-14 dating. Gove and Chagas had been casting about to find a textile expert for the sample site selection and lifting, so that the remaining sliver of STURP's involvement in the dating exercise could be eliminated. Even though it was decided that no sampling would take place during the meeting, she was still invited to attend. Her remark in the opening round of discussion was that she did not see why C-14 needed to be done, but was willing to lend her expertise nonetheless. I recall feeling at the time that this was unthinkable – someone who knew nothing about radiocarbon dating and little about the Shroud, and who apparently had not seen the cloth or read the reports on its study, would be nominated to pick a spot and take a sample. Ultimately the responsibility for bringing Flury-

Lemberg into the Shroud arena lies with Hall. If one applies the principle of *de mortibus nihil nisi bonum* (speak no ill of the dead), there would be nothing more to say. But for the record let it be said that he was an arrogant and frightfully shallow person with no interest whatsoever in the Shroud, except for getting AMS dating and himself/his lab into the news. This is based solely (some might say unfairly) on the three days that I saw him at this conference, which included one lunch at the same table of four. But as the famous joke goes: the writer protests to the publisher that he didn't read all his rejected manuscript, as pages 98 and 99 were glued together. The publisher replies "I don't need to eat all of a bad egg to determine that it is bad."

Of the conference participants I knew Adler, Gonella and Rinaldi quite well. I had dealt with Otlet and Evin in correspondence over archaeological samples, and also had some pleasant exchanges with various people in the Oxford lab, but had not met them personally. Ironically, with the exception of Donahue, the other C-14 people struck me over the three days in Turin as moderately to unbearably arrogant. I began to wonder if my generally good experiences in dealing with C-14 personnel had been somewhat unrepresentative of what their ilk is really like. Or perhaps it was the framework of the meeting that brought out their worst side. Or perhaps the fact that these were the top dogs (so to speak) in the field. At this meeting, they may have felt that since they were the experts, no one else's opinion mattered, except the church officials', since of course the latter had the ultimate say over whether samples were released or not. They frequently attempted to pull rank, or browbeat, but anyone who knew Al Adler would know that this kind of thing would not work with him. And I had enough experience on the practical side of C-14 to challenge a lot of their assertions. Gove may have thought the conference would be a cake walk for the C-14 daters. It was not, although it must be said that STURP performed miserably: Lukasik and Dinegar were simply not up to the task, although they tried hard. Lukasik was fairly verbose, sometimes articulate, but would veer off into abstractions or irrelevancies. Dinegar was by contrast a man of few words and was more direct, but usually did not have an answer for the onslaughts from Gove or Canuto. Adler chose his comments carefully, usually sticking to chemistry, and seemed content to leave issues involving STURP to Lukasik and Dinegar.

The first day of the conference began with opening speeches and formalities. Cardinal Ballestrero gave a welcoming speech, and said he would leave so that the conference could get down to work. He then went around the room personally greeting each participant. He was a heavy set man in his seventies, and seemed to have a great weight on his shoulders. I spoke a few words to him in Italian, and he asked if I had studied the language. But there was little time for small talk.

The focus of the first day was on the need for C-14 dating, how many labs and samples should be involved, the use of control samples, whether the testing should be done "blind" (without the labs knowing which sample was from the Shroud), and the minimum amount of sample material required. One sticking point that arose early on was whether each of the now seven participating labs (with the addition of DuPlessy's AMS lab) would get a Shroud sample, or whether some would get dummies. There was considerable agitation over this, and also over the question of blind testing, neither of which seemed particularly important to me. The choice of sampling sites was crucial, but it was not addressed until the second day. There was an assortment of ideas on this issue; my suggestion was for two different areas on the main body of the Shroud, plus a sample from the backing cloth. Gonella opposed removing an "inordinate amount of material," stating that the sampling had to be kept to the minimum, about 50 mg or 2 square centimeters of cloth, and again affirming that all seven labs did not need to receive a Shroud sample. I thought back to Riggi's remark at dinner and worried that Gonella was going to bring about disaster if he insisted on this minimalist approach – 50 mg was a ridiculously small amount that would hardly allow for rigorous pretreatment. Hedges agreed with me that a much more sophisticated pretreatment, including fractions, could be done with more sample, but claimed that it would be difficult in this case because of the value of the relic. I thought: it is fourteen feet long, for Chrissake, and we are worrying over an additional few square centimeters! I was also concerned that not enough attention was being paid to the all-important question of where the samples would come from.

This concern was soon erased as discussion turned to the use of the charred material. Gonella said it was ideal because it was hidden under the patches. I argued forcefully that it should not be used because it was anomalous, and had been through a firing event possibly 1500 years after the linen was made. At this point, Harbottle produced the results of his questionnaire to colleague daters, and surprisingly quite a few of the comments he read out were in favor of avoiding the charred: "it could present a serious problem" ... "better to take undamaged material" ... "a possibility of exchange with gaseous combustion products" ... "why take a chance?" This was a pleasant surprise to me, and I felt vindicated that so many professional C-14 daters agreed that it was best to avoid the anomalous charred material. Then Harbottle outlined the experiment done by Long in which textile samples were charred in different conditions and then dated. No influence on the level of C-14 was found; Gove chimed in by saying that it was extremely unlikely there would be any exchange, especially across the gas-solid interface. Gotcha! I responded that my original concern was **not** with a possible exchange between the cloth and CO_2 in the air or in gases, but with contaminants that might have been on the cloth at the time. I cited my paper circulated the year before which had a chemical formula showing an exchange of carbon atoms between a substance that could possibly be present on the cloth with one of the components of linen. The argument went on for a couple more rounds, when Bob Otlet, who had hardly said anything thus far, injected this mysterious remark: "Yes, there is the burnt toast problem." At this, Gove and Harbottle squirmed, some of the others nodded, but most of us must have had a quizzical look. He went on: "If you want to remove the butter, you have to do it before you toast the bread. If it is all carbonized, you can't separate the butter from the bread." There was general nodding, and the tide had turned. The charred would not be used. But this would turn out in the end to be a pyrrhic victory.

The discussion moved on to statistical issues, and the sites to be sampled were never identified. I raised the question of a visit to inspect the Shroud, and Riggi seemed to have been prepared with an answer. It was terribly complicated, he said, as permission had to be obtained from the Italian State as well as the Pope, seals broken, the cloth taken out of the casket and carefully unrolled, then rolled back up and new seals attached; blah blah blah, I thought, recalling that I had written three months previously urging that this be arranged. Clearly what was arranged instead was an excuse to be trotted out. Gove was also annoyed at this, and said he had hoped not only to inspect the cloth but also that we might take a sample right then and there. He claimed that one did not need a million dollars worth of equipment, but a simple pair of scissors and a small camera, which he happened to have in his briefcase, would be quite sufficient. I hoped Dinegar or Lukasik would respond but they said nothing, so I countered that since it was a one-time event, a certain amount of preparation should be invested, and yes, the expensive equipment did have a role to play in the selection and review of the sampling site. Flury-Lemberg maintained that it did not matter where one took the sample from, since the Shroud was all a homogeneous cloth. Adler begged to disagree, citing the very different chemistries apparent in the scorched areas, the water stain margins, the image areas and the edges. I argued, as I had in correspondence with Gonella, that the edges were anomalous and might have been treated in some way. After more in this vein, Chagas put an end to the discussion by proclaiming that the Shroud was not an archaeological site, sampling should be straightforward and a single sample divided into six or seven pieces would be sufficient. Adler and I shook our heads in dismay. Although we did not know it, the seeds of the imminent disaster that was to befall the Shroud had been planted.

Day Three saw more discussion on the issue of possible dummy samples, and Gove threatened to withdraw from the project if he could not be assured that his lab would be receiving a real Shroud sample. Chagas gently chided him, reminding that he came from a democratic country and surely he would abide by the consensus reached. Gove somewhat sheepishly withdrew his threat. For a moment Gonella had a look of barely suppressed joy, but it was not to last. Gove tossed out the snide comment that "STURP seems to be on some sort of crusade to prove the Shroud authentic." A few minutes later, Gonella opened with the comment "Apparently Gove does not like the STURP people." Chagas weighed in at this point and said that we should keep the discussion to the issues at hand, and not let it degenerate into personal or emotional attacks. I was tempted to point out that the time for such an intervention by the chairman would have been after Gove's offensive remark, but held my tongue. This incident would come up later in correspondence with Chagas.

The discussion turned to the question of statistical analysis again, and I began to realize that what the labs were most concerned about was obtaining matching results from each lab, or if not, then at least the one outlier could be quite easily identified and rejected before calculating the radiocarbon age. This concern seemed to me misplaced; what was **much** more important was insuring that a rogue sample was not chosen. It would be a tragedy if every lab got the same result but it was wrong because there was something inherently wrong with the particular sample chosen. Adler agreed that this was the biggest worry. We raised the subject again of sampling sites, and now a consensus was forming that only one sample needed to be taken, cut into seven pieces, and distributed to the seven labs. I pleaded for a minimum of two sampling sites, even if one of them was the charred material under the patches. At this there was much chortling from Gove and Canuto, and Chagas dryly remarked that I had spent so much energy arguing against the charred that he was mystified to see me "reverse" my position. Adler tried to argue the point further, but Gonella would not support us. At this late stage the chairman's control of the meeting was the deciding factor, and he stated that a single sample was the consensus and moved on. I felt a *frisson* of anxiety, that the future reputation of the Shroud could be in jeopardy.

The conference ended "in a spirit of amity" as the official statement said. The time had come for carbon-dating the Shroud. The minimum amount of cloth would be removed to ensure that a result that is scientifically rigorous. Seven samples containing a total of 50mg carbon would be taken and distributed by the British Museum to the five participating AMS labs and two small counter labs. Charred material would not be used. The British Museum would provide two control samples for each lab. The samples would be taken by Flury-Lemberg immediately prior to other experiments planned by other groups. Three institutions would analyze the results statistically and a final report would be given to Cardinal Ballestrero and released to the public. Samples would be taken in May 1987, before commencement of the other testing.

Although much less than ideal, this "protocol" held out the prospect that at last the Shroud would be dated, and that the sophisticated tests planned by STURP and other groups would also be done soon. There was a cautious optimism in the air, but it was not shared by me. I was very concerned about the choice of sampling site and the fact that Flury-Lemberg was given this task. Some of the world's best C-14 experts had decided that any ol' piece of the Shroud would do, they just wanted to be sure that there was no substitution of samples. Once they had their little fragment in their pocket, they would whisk it back to the lab where the technicians would produce a date. I consoled myself with the thought that STURP would put the sample site under intense scrutiny, and surely would discover if there was anything suspicious about it. Unfortunately this last line of defence was removed, and the person mainly responsible for that is none other than Harry Gove, assisted as ever by Canuto and incredibly, by Chagas too.

I left Turin with a tinge of sadness for another reason, thinking it might well be the last time I would ever see my good friend Fr. Rinaldi, who was in poor health and getting on in years. So it was, though we continued to correspond. He passed away in 1993. A wonderful, charming man, the kind of priest that does the Church proud.

Moving toward the carbon dating

A few weeks after the Turin conference, things began to unravel. According to Gove's own account, in October 1986 "Chagas was having second thoughts about the tests STURP planned to carry out after the removal of the Shroud material [for C-14]. He was concerned about the floodlights and the X-rays and the ultraviolet radiation ... Chagas would like advice from the laboratories on the possible danger that these tests might pose to the shroud." If accurate, this account puts Chagas in an extremely bad light. He was asking radiocarbon labs for advice about the conservation impact of tests that STURP was planning on a textile? These were the very same labs whose directors mostly could not see the relevance of these tests for the carbon dating; needless to say, they would not have a clue about such a conservation matter. And yet, amazingly, they jumped in where angels fear to tread, and Gove, Harbottle, Hall and Donahue wrote to Chagas expressing objections to the STURP tests. This was probably also a political move, to finish the job of shoving STURP aside completely. The whole enterprise was shameful.

Gonella would write later about this move on the part of Gove and his cohorts:

> At the beginning ... they [the radiocarbon labs] had guaranteed us the utmost seriousness and completeness in the analysis, as well as promising to collaborate with the custodian of the Shroud, the Archbishop of Turin and with his scientific advisor, the undersigned. Seized however by a feverish desire for celebrity, they began to renege on their promises: no further interdisciplinary investigations; just the carbon 14 test. They even badgered Rome, bringing pressure to bear so that Turin would have to accept their conditions. ... Scientifically, I would have been happier and have my mind at ease if the dating operation had been carried out in the context of comprehensive, wide-ranging and thorough chemical and physical investigation of the Shroud as originally planned. The carbon-14 laboratories preferred to work independently and they did not wish to collaborate with other scientists, something that, from the point of view of scientific methodology, left me greatly puzzled and certainly not satisfied.

In December 1986 I got wind of this from Gonella, and was angry enough write to Chagas in fairly strong terms. According again to Gove, Chagas described it as an insulting letter. When I read this, I wondered if Chagas had ever actually received a real insult, as he was a pleasant and charming fellow. I reproduce the correspondence here as it sheds light on how the process was corrupted, and how the Academy took the official line that this was quite alright. I wrote:

> Dear Prof. Chagas,
> I was most distressed to learn recently that certain participants in the Turin C-14 Workshop had taken it upon themselves to raise anew the question of other planned testing of the Shroud and its supposed 'impact' on the relic. Aside from the fact that this question is totally outside their area of expertise, this action reflects an attitude hostile to the proper scientific study of the relic, as indicated in the provocative and improper remark made at the meeting

(regrettably allowed to pass without reprimand by the chair) that 'STURP is on some kind of crusade in their zeal to study the Shroud, in the full glare of publicity.'

The consensus arrived at in the Turin Workshop ('Conclusions and Procedural Steps') represents, in my view, a program with several major weaknesses, constructed by committee and motivated not only by scientific considerations but also by 'politics', the desire to cater to the various personalities involved, and the ultimate appearance of the project in the eyes of the general public.

In spite of its shortcomings, however, the 'Turin protocol' was a consensus elaborated through negotiation. The conclusions were agreed upon in gentlemanly fashion 'in a spirit of amity' and, more importantly, in an effort to give due consideration and weight to the various interests and perspectives represented.

The timing and relevance of the other testing programs were discussed in Turin at length, and the agreement on this point (on which I have serious reservations) is expressed in item 4 (first sentence) of the Conclusions paper. An attempt now to alter this agreement through backroom dealings appears to me to be subversive and under-handed, and I would not hesitate to withdraw my support of the 'Turin protocol' if this very weak provision for the securing of contextual information relevant to the C-14 samples is not respected.

I sincerely hope that you and the Academy, as chairman and co-organizer of the Turin Workshop and in the spirit of our accord laboriously hammered out, will endeavor to insure that the consensus, as expressed in the Conclusions paper will be strictly adhered to.

No faction should be allowed to maneuver, through whatever connections they may have, their priorities to the fore or erect obstacles to the procedural steps recommended after having failed to obtain majority support for their position at the Workshop. Either we have a basic agreement and protocol or we have none, in which latter case the Workshop will have been little more than an academic debate, and the authorities responsible for the Shroud would be justified in re-considering the entire program for radiocarbon dating.

With every hope that the C-14 and other testing of the Shroud will proceed smoothly,

A reply was swift in coming. According to Gove, Chagas did not deign to reply and asked the director of the Academy's office to reply for him, and this reply was drafted by Canuto. Regardless of who its author was, it was weak and illogical, but it did confirm one very important piece of information – the backroom dealings that I heard about were indeed going on.

Dear Prof. Meacham,
This is in reply to your letter of January 5, 1987, to Professor Carlos Chagas, who has asked me to answer on his behalf.

Notwithstanding our dismay at noticing that the central motivation of your letter are topics and arguments that were part of a private correspondence (between the President, the Cardinal of Turin and the Vatican Authorities) that was intended to remain private, I must point out that the choice of words like 'backroom dealing', 'subversive' and 'under-handed', can only reflect your lack of appreciation of some basic facts:

1) Your 'reprimand' of Prof. Chagas in the discharge of his duties as Chairman of the meeting is at the same time disrespectful and naive: disrespectful to the President of the Pontifical Academy of Sciences, who has accumulated an unprecedented forty years of experience in chairing international meetings, and naïve for it misses entirely the main point. In fact, giving the floor to a speaker is not tantamount to agreeing with what is going to be said.

2) The duty of Prof. Chagas regarding the Shroud (as requested of him by the Authorities of the Vatican) entails his presenting the whole spectrum of potential pitfalls, doubts and shortcomings of all intended experiments, no matter when and by whom the former are brought to light, so long as they are scientifically sound.

3) Prof. Chagas himself brought up the very same points during his final remarks in Turin, as our review of the Records of the Meeting has confirmed.

4) Prof. Chagas is a biophysicist with a time-honored experience regarding damage induced by radiation, the Shroud being just one such example.

Your further allegation of 'factions maneuvering to bring their priorities to the fore after they have failed in their attempt in Turin', is particularly unpleasant for it implicitly puts into question the ability of Professor Chagas to arrive at a balanced decision once he has given equal opportunity to all the parts involved to express their points of view.

Much as the Carbon-14 dating process was scrutinized by a panel of experts, so should future experiments of any kind concerning the Shroud. This is, and will remain, the firm position of the Pontifical Academy of Sciences in discharging its duties as an unbiased, non-partisan advisory body to the Pontiff on scientific matters.

As for your possible withdrawal from the Turin protocol, you may feel free to take whatever action you deem necessary.

Sincerely yours,

Renato Dardozzi

It was not difficult to deal with this mush. Gove claimed that I wrote back and apologized to Chagas; as usual, he got it wrong. I replied in February 1987:

Dear Ing. Dardozzi,

I have your letter of Jan. 27, and clearly we have very different attitudes, perspectives and concepts of protocol. Nevertheless, one should always aim at being constructive; this was the original intent of my letter of Jan. 5, in spite of the strong language employed.

Let me assure you and Prof. Chagas that no disrespect to him was intended. My criticisms were directed at those who I believed to be attempting to subvert the consensus hammered out at Turin. I had no knowledge of the 'topics and arguments' in the private correspondence you mentioned, and it is disappointing to glean from your letter that the Academy is not pressing for strict adherence to the conclusions and procedural steps drawn up in the Turin Workshop. As stated in the fifth paragraph of my Jan. 5 letter, I hoped that Prof. Chagas and the Academy would work to uphold the provisions of the Turin protocol.

If my criticisms apply to Prof. Chagas as well as to certain individuals involved in the C-14 controversy, let me stress again that I certainly do not intend any disrespect, unless it is considered that criticism itself constitutes a disrespect, as your letter seems to imply. In fact, I have great respect for Prof. Chagas, deriving from the fine and dedicated manner in which he chaired the Turin meeting. You will recall that I stated this in rather lavish terms at the end of that meeting. This was not an attempt to flatter or curry favor, but a sincere expression of praise. By the same token, criticism should be taken as an equally sincere communication of views. I trust that you would agree that every one of us is on occasion capable of error or of having subjective bias influence our decision-making. Yet you find it 'disrespectful' that I point out what I perceived to be a minor error in the chairing of the meeting, and 'particularly unpleasant' that I implicitly put into question the ability of Prof. Chagas to **always** arrive at a properly balanced decision. Allow me to elaborate further on these aspects:

1. I believe that most independent observers would agree that the proper intervention of the chair should have occurred after Prof. Gove's inflammatory and gratuitous remarks casting aspersions on the motivations of STURP members, rather than after Prof. Gonella's simple observation that 'Prof. Gove apparently does not like the STURP people.' My comment was certainly not naive; that an inflammatory remark like Gove's did not draw any rebuke from the chair was a simple error, compounded by subsequent events seen in retrospect.

2. I believe however that Prof Chagas did an excellent job overall in chairing the meeting, insuring that all participants had equal opportunity to express their points of view. The Turin protocol represents a balanced consensus obtained at the meeting. What I objected to was a private tampering with the consensus at a later stage, initiated by a certain faction, during which time other participants in the workshop had no opportunity to comment further on the issue raised. Nor did the scientists whose proposed experiments were in question have the opportunity to respond. Nor were views sought from other, dedicated scientists who have devoted considerable time and energy to the proper study of the Shroud. It can only appear to the outsider that the Academy has taken a position on the promptings of a few influential individuals, without input from other scientific circles, and thus not in the manner of an unbiased, non-partisan advisory body.

Again, I wish to emphasize that these critical views are offered in good faith, in the belief that subjectivity and bias affect us all, and that procedures need constantly to be reviewed in order for an organization to be as unbiased as humanly possible.

I must confess to being completely unaware of the basic fact in item 2 of your letter, and I feel certain that other scientists interested in the study of the Shroud were also unaware of it. Would it not have been a more non-partisan approach to have raised the question of possible pitfalls or doubts of the intended experiments directly with the scientists concerned, so as to allow them to respond to or clarify any problems or critique? Such an inter-play between proponents and critics of a proposed project is the normal procedure for an outside body to determine whether the project is designed on a scientifically sound basis.

I do not recall any mention during the Turin meeting of the Academy's intention to review and approve all intended experiments on the Shroud. The date of May 1987 for C-14 sampling and other testing was fixed primarily as the earliest date possible for the organization of the other testing. My own position and that expressed by several other participants is that the C-14-test must take place in the context of the other testing. This sentiment was incorporated in a compromise form in item 4 of the procedural steps, and it constitutes part of the scrutiny of the C-14 dating process by the panel of experts. Rather than altering one of the crucial points of consensus arising from the Workshop, would it not be better to consider amending item 11 instead, if necessary?

I trust that the Academy will give due consideration to this suggestion, and strive to promote harmony among those who have a genuine interest in the scientific study of the Turin Shroud.

It is interesting to note that the Vatican did finally decide that the role of the Pontifical Academy of Sciences ended with the Turin conference, and all future decisions regarding research and testing of the Shroud would be made by the Archbishop of Turin. Chagas had wrongly interpreted his brief, and had made a mess of it as regards the perceived "threat" posed by STURP's proposed testing. He was removed from the fray by the Vatican.

"The Lord works in strange ways," and so it was to be with the unwarranted and improper attempt by Gove, Chagas and cohorts to remove STURP from the picture. In January I sent Gonella a copy of my letter to Chagas, and remembering the private statement from Riggi on the eve of the Turin Conference, I suggested that since Gove, Harbottle et al were working to change the terms of the protocol, why not kick them out and select two or three AMS labs to do the dating? I wrote:

> I believe that as a scientific program it could be greatly improved ... an absolute minimum of sampling sites should be two (better three) ... the charred material could be one of the samples ... fractional dating should be performed. ... An enormous responsibility has been laid on someone [Flury-Lemberg] who knows little about either the Shroud or C-14 – only a committee could cook up something like this! ... Gove/Harbottle/Chagas maneuvered STURP completely out of the C-14 program (and it was surprising to me how little STURP fought), and tried to block their other testing programs as well, so it would be superb irony and justice to see them (Gove and co.) put out of the picture as well. It is pleasing to imagine that such things might be possible, if the Cardinal really has been delegated full authority for the Shroud [as I had heard from Fr. Rinaldi].

It would be nice to believe that my suggestion had anything to do with the final decision to use only three labs, but more likely it was in Gonella's mind all along, as Riggi had told me on the eve of the Turin meeting. I heard from several sources that the number of labs was going to be cut to three, and that STURP and other groups would not be allowed to run any of its planned testing until after the C-14 dates were announced. This was a sad state of affairs, as STURP was the main group studying the relic. Clearly Michael Tite of the British Museum was only in the picture as a referee of sorts; he would not be directly involved in the sample-taking or in the interpretation of the results. Sensing an opportunity for a small group to play a role in the project, I contacted two Italian archaeologists I knew – Roberto Ciarla and Maurizio Tosi – both of whom had worked in the Middle East. Together we formulated a proposal to be involved in the sampling and in the final interpretation of the results. Unfortunately Gonella did not take up this offer, and in the end chose his colleague Riggi, plus two textile experts who knew nothing about the Shroud, to assist in selecting the sampling site. This was a terrible decision on the part of Gonella, matched only by his equally appalling handling of the announcement of the results.

In April 1987 things certainly hotted up! The Turin newspaper *La Stampa* ran a story about the forthcoming carbon dating of the Shroud and cited Gonella to the effect that "two or three laboratories would make the measurements" once approval had been granted. This story plus the subsequent leaking of a letter from the Vatican to Ballestrero set off another maelstrom of activity on the part of Gove and Canuto. Once more, dozens of phone calls, faxes and cables went flying around, as Gove attempted to circle the wagons and obtain commitments from the other six lab directors that they would stand firm and not accept such a serious alteration in the protocol to be engineered by Gonella. The wording of Gove's telegram to the British Museum, and the other lab directors was incredible: "In my view, Gonella and STURP are being deliberately mischievous concerning carbon dating. If the Turin Workshop agreement is not followed to the letter, I am no longer willing to be involved." This from someone who had been actively campaigning over the previous few months, using every connection he could find, to change precisely that agreement, concerning the other tests planned by STURP and other groups. It is hard to understand how such blatant hypocrisy could be maintained. He drew up a letter to Chagas declaring that "the undersigned wished to reaffirm their strong and continuing support for the conclusions and procedural steps agreed to by the delegates to the Turin workshop ..." Among the signatories to the letter were Hall, Damon,

Donahue, DuPlessy, and Woelfli. Eventually a similarly worded letter to the Secretary of State of the Vatican and to Ballestrero was signed by representatives of all seven labs, many of whom had been involved along with Gove in the blatant attempt to alter part of the very procedures agreed at Turin that they were now urging strict adherence to.

An official letter from Ballestrero was sent to all participants of the Turin conference in October 1987, to announce that three labs had been selected for dating the Shroud: Arizona, Oxford and Zurich. It would be AMS only; Harwell and Brookhaven were dropped "because of sample size considerations." Gove was out, and for many of us this was entirely appropriate comeuppance. The Cardinal even described specifically the obstructionist maneuvers:

> ... some participants in the Workshop ... stepped out of the radiocarbon field to oppose research in other fields, with implications for the freedom of research of other scientists and on our own programs for the Shroud conservation that asked for thorough deliberation. Besides, when the competent Authorities advised me they deemed we ought to proceed with three samples, a concerted initiative was taken to counter the decision, with the outcome of a telegram send to H.E. the Cardinal Secretary of State and myself by some participants in the Workshop, a telegram where the meaning of my introductory words at the Workshop was heavily misinterpreted.

One would have thought that such a clear and sharp condemnation would have put an end to the lobbying efforts of Gove and Canuto. But *au contraire* it set off yet another and final round of frenzied activity. After more dozens of phone calls, they believed that they had lined up all seven labs and the British Museum to insist on adherence to the Turin workshop agreement (the part that they agreed with, anyway). Gove, Harbottle and Canuto began to draft a letter to the Pope informing him that Ballestrero was being badly advised by his scientific adviser Gonella. Harbottle wanted to contact National Public Radio and the *Skeptical Inquirer*. Gove and Harbottle held a press conference in New York to warn of the dire consequences of proceeding with only two or three labs. Gove and Canuto made frantic efforts to involve the Papal Nuncio, the US ambassador to the Vatican, the senator from New York and many others. Gove wrote a letter to the director of the British Museum in which he stated that the effort to carbon-date the Shroud had become "a somewhat shoddy enterprise" and that the Museum might come to regret their involvement in it. (After the C-14 dating was announced, I mentioned this letter in a press release and it was cited several times in the media. Gove was furious, and for someone who had obtained so many items of private correspondence or memoranda by hook or crook, he could still have the pompous audacity to write: "How Meacham obtained it is a mystery to me, and his misuse of it confirmed that he, like Gonella, was willing to toss principles aside when it was convenient. ... He had no right to have a copy of the letter or to refer to it out of context." Highly amusing stuff!)

Reading reports in the media of the press conference given by Gove and Harbottle in early 1988 prompted me to send a statement to the press myself, to counter some of the nonsense they were spreading. I sent this statement to the *New York Times* and *Chicago Tribune*:

> On Jan.17 you reported the rather strong comments of two New York physicists 'outraged' at being dropped from the project to date the Turin Shroud by carbon-14. It is ironic, however, that these two scientists are now calling so stridently for adherence to the 'protocol' agreed at the Turin conference in September, 1986.
>
> I attended the Turin meeting along with representatives of the C-14 labs and experts from other fields. In January, 1987, the Director of the Pontifical Academy of Sciences in Rome revealed, in correspondence with me, that these same scientists now so outraged were working behind the scenes to change certain provisions of the protocol not to their liking. I wrote to several laboratories then involved to point out the dangers inherent in such maneuvering, but none reacted until they were dropped from the program.
>
> The 'protocol' agreed in Turin was in fact only a recommendation from the assembled experts to the church authorities. There can be no claim that the Vatican or Turin have broken the agreement. If anyone violated the Turin protocol it is those who attempted to use their influence in the Pontifical Academy to have it amended.
>
> The dating of only three samples instead of the recommended seven will still yield a scientifically valid result, within the limitations of the C-14 method. It is alarmist (and possibly self-serving) to claim that seven laboratories must be involved to produce a reliable C-14 date on a piece of cloth.
>
> Much more important than the number of samples is the provenance of each sample. The NY scientists had originally, in 1978, proposed to date a piece removed from the Shroud in 1973, even though this sample had been passed around and held in less than rigorous scientific conditions (in an old photo album at one stage). They then proposed to date the charred material from one of

the burn marks, but this plan was roundly rejected at the Turin conference as unreliable.

Finally, they wished to take a single piece and divide it into seven samples. To me, as an archaeologist with 17 years' experience in the application of C-14 dating to field contexts, this proposal seemed absurd. One should seize the opportunity to date samples from different parts of the cloth, avoiding a possibly anomalous (e.g. starched) area. This is the major scientific question now relevant. The dating of the Shroud is not, after all, a laboratory inter-comparison experiment. Three dates from reputable labs, hopefully on samples from three different sites on the relic, should give a good indication of the radiocarbon age of the cloth, and whether or not random contamination or other problems exist which require sophisticated testing techniques.

Gove continued on with his campaign, trying to persuade the representatives of all seven labs to form a united front, against what he called the dictatorial behavior of Gonella. Finally, after contacting Victor Weisskopf, one of the most senior physicists in the world and being gently rebuffed, Gove realized that "it was another case of my clutching at any straw" and the game, this time, was over.

5. The Dating

Cardinal Ballestrero's Letter Of October 1987 at last set the ball rolling towards a radiocarbon dating of the Shroud, despite the continuing and sometimes frantic machinations of the Gove-Canuto-Harbottle axis, now without Chagas, particularly in a last ditch but futile campaign to forge a united front amongst the original seven labs to insist on no reduction in their number. The appeal of dating the most famous relic in the world with all the attendant favorable publicity was too strong for the chosen ones to resist. Representatives of the three labs met with Michael Tite of the British Museum and Gonella in London in January 1988, supposedly to find out if their "stringent requirements" would be met, but in fact to accept the conditions which Gonella was setting. The basic parameters of the new protocol were spelled out: each laboratory would send a representative to Turin to witness the sample taking which would be "under the supervision of a qualified expert"; control samples of known age would be provided by the British Museum; the whole procedure would be recorded by video; the labs would submit their results to the British Museum and a statistical institute in Turin. A date for the sample-taking was not announced, but rumored to be in the spring. It was hoped that results could be announced by the end of 1988.

One certainly felt that an historic occasion was approaching; I doubted that a bulls eye date of first century would be obtained, but was cautiously optimistic that a result would indicate some antiquity for the Shroud, perhaps back to the 4th or 5th centuries, owing to some intractable contamination. This could be taken as a good indication that the Shroud was the genuine article. I made one last effort to persuade Gonella of the need for the small team of advisory archaeologists that I had suggested, particularly for the selection of sampling sites. Again, I put it to him in the strongest terms that a minimum of two sites was needed. By this stage, he was not listening, and I did not receive a response. Fr. Rinaldi kept me informed of what he learned of the developments, and it was clear that Gonella was proudly running the show. No one knew just how much he was going to ruin it, but there was a shadow in my mind of continuing nagging worry that he would take the sole sample from a bad location, and the Shroud could be assigned an incorrect age.

STURP was not out of the picture entirely, as Gonella responded to one of Gove's last ditch initiatives with the remark that if the results from the three labs were contradictory or not statistically conformable, a further sample could be taken when STURP carried out its testing program in June. For a brief interlude, in the early months of 1988, it appeared that the STURP tests were on track. It is unclear what finally diverted them, whether it was continuing pressure from Chagas and the Pontifical Academy, slighted over the manner in which they were taken out of the picture, or whether it was the failure of STURP to raise the funds and personnel on time. Perhaps a major factor was Gonella's total involvement in the C-14 planning, with little time to devote to arrangements for a complicated series of tests. At some point it was decided by someone that STURP's testing would have to wait until the carbon dating results were obtained. This would prove fatal.

STURP's testing strategy had veered sharply off course in any event. Lukasik sent me a copy of their draft protocol for examination of the Shroud, and it was an extremely one-sided document with a strange and undue emphasis on conservation. Perhaps they had felt the sting of the Gove/Chagas allegations that their tests were too intrusive. Their general approach was summed up thus: "advances in conservation constitute the only justification for any test proposed at this time ... [so that] future scholars can extract more definitive information." They even argued against C-14, since "verification of the age of the cloth is not needed for its conservation." Other tests were rejected if their objective was merely "to satisfy the curiosity of the investigator." It was a sharp turn away from what had been STURP's great strength – its drive for knowledge and understanding of the relic.

I wrote a long letter arguing against the new stance and strategy, copied with a covering letter to Gonella. I used a *reductio ad absurdum* that is familiar to archaeologists: if future scientists will have much more sophisticated methods, then no research at all using any limited resources (such as archaeological sites) should be done now. The most important part of the letter was a suggestion that I made regarding "radiocarbon coordination," in view of what seemed then to be the imminent lifting of samples for dating. I assumed that STURP was going to conduct their direct testing shortly after the C-14 samples were taken. I suggested:

1) That a micro-sample (say 3 to 5%) be removed from each lifted sample before they are dispatched to the C-14 labs, and these tiny pieces be either sent to STURP, or held in Turin, for detailed testing by STURP for contaminants -- something which the C-14 labs will probably **not** do. They will more likely conduct the standard pretreatment, and even this might need to be severely limited because of the critical sample size involved. Such testing on the micro-samples would also provide corroboration, or otherwise, of the pretreatment performance re contamination.

2) That STURP run a specific set of examinations at the points where C-14 samples were lifted. I am thinking particularly of micro-Raman spectroscopy and/or an analytical spectrometer ... for any alien organic or inorganic compounds; uv florescence for scorch damage not visible to the naked eye; and other types of testing which might reveal any other anomalies in the area sampled.

There was no response from either Lukasik or Gonella. Looking back and knowing what we know now, it was a huge pity that these two suggestions were not taken up. The fault lies squarely with Gonella, since, as his power consolidated, he ran (and seemingly reveled in) a one-man show for the decision-making on all aspects of the carbon dating enterprise save the laboratory's own internal procedures. STURP was clearly in disarray, and Gonella probably had to leave them on the sidelines. The organization was near the end of its corporate existence.

Even though Gove now realized that his was also a lost cause, he did not quit the field. He wrote a letter to *Nature* comparing the new procedures for dating the Shroud with those agreed at the Turin conference in 1986. He stated: "All these unnecessary and unexplained changes unilaterally dictated by the Archbishop of Turin will produce an age for the Turin Shroud which will be vastly less credible than that which would have been obtained if the original Turin Workshop Protocol had been followed." He still worried single-mindedly about the possibility of an outlier due to a laboratory error, failing to see, as he had ever since the question of dating the Shroud arose, where the more important and more likely problems might lie – contamination and anomalous sample. He positively scoffed at the notion that any ancillary testing might be relevant to the C-14 enterprise; he quotes Ian Wilson's reaction to the news in March 1988 that STURP would not be allowed to do their testing until after the Shroud had been dated: "Wilson thought this was a very bad move since he believed that a carbon-14 date must be bolstered by other scientific data ... this was absolute nonsense. Other tests should take place only after its age was known." Elsewhere Gove commented on

STURP's desire to "characterize the sample" before it was dated by saying "whatever that means." **This** was the absolute nonsense! Clearly he had no concept of or interest in investigating the chemistry of a sample prior to running it through the standard pretreatment. The three selected labs were equally blinkered, they would conduct no research on where the sample should come from, and they planned to treat their prized Shroud fragment largely as they would any other archaeological specimen.

By March of 1988, a shroud of secrecy (so to speak) was drawn over all arrangements for dating. There were rumors, but hard information was lacking until late April when press reports confirmed that samples had been taken. The senior representatives of the three labs been summoned to Turin and were present as observers at the sample taking. They were called to the Cathedral at 4:30am and the operation began. A lively discussion ensued between Gonella and Riggi on the one hand and the two textile experts, Vial and Testore, on the other concerning where the sample should be taken. One of the textile men is said to have asked, on noting the dark stain on the chest [blood stain from the wound in the side], "what's this?" Gonella and Riggi finally decided to cut a single strip approximately 1 cm wide by 8 cm long, weighing 300 mg., right next to the small cut that had been made in 1963 at the corner of the cloth to provide the textile expert Raes with a sample. The reason, as Gonella told Al Adler, was that "the Shroud was already cut there." Adler called this the worst possible reason. The sample was adjacent to a seam that joins the main body of the Shroud with the side strip, which seems to be of the same cloth but was attached by a stitched seam at some unknown time. This seam had to be trimmed away by Riggi before dividing the sample into equal segments to give each lab.

What is remarkable is how poor the planning and execution of this project was, despite all the brouhaha and the months of secretive preparations, in addition to the disastrous choice of sampling site and the disastrous decision to take only one sample. It is hard to imagine that, in all the months that had passed since the Turin conference, Gonella had not given due consideration to the location where material was to be removed, and that it was decided only after discussion on the very day of sampling. Riggi was brought in to do the cutting, although he had no expertise in textiles. Riggi was also given the responsibility of video-tapping the proceedings, a conflict of interest one could argue. He would later treat this video as his personal property, and charge the BBC a hefty sum for use of several segments in a documentary. What is even more amazing is that, after all the exhortations by Gonella that the amount of material removed from the relic had to be minimal, Riggi cut **double** what was actually going to be given to the three labs. He then cut the 300 mg strip in

THE DATING

half and divided one half into three segments, the other half being retained as a "reserve piece." Presumably, if there were any discrepancies in the results obtained by the three labs, this reserve piece was going to be used for another run. Gove's constant harping on the possibility of lab error or statistical outlier must have registered with Gonella, so he came up with this precaution. My constant harping on the need for a minimum of two sample sites obviously did **not** sink in, nor did the distinct possibility, as plain as the nose on your face to anyone who has done archaeological dating, that if the first run gave discordant results a second run on the same sample would very probably produce similar results.

Unfortunately, Riggi failed to cut the half into three equal segments. The Arizona sample was only 40 mg, whereas the other two were approximately 50 mg. He then shaved about 10 mg from the reserve. Later, there were significant discrepancies between the weights of sample material made on the spot and by the labs. Even more mind-boggling is that Riggi was allowed to keep the seam trimmings, **and** to take sticky tape samples from another part of the Shroud with blood stain, **and** to run his vacuum over the Shroud in a zigzag pattern that he appears not to have planned in advance or plotted at the time. Riggi would later distribute the trimmings and the tape with blood-stained fibers to researchers in Texas, earning a stern rebuke from Ballestrero's successor. His involvement in this operation was a huge mistake on the part of Gonella.

In addition to Riggi's shenanigans, the labs were told the age of the historical known-age control pieces, a fact that rather diminished their value as controls. Paradoxically, the pretense of "blind testing" was maintained for the whole dating exercise, despite the fact that everyone knew that the Shroud weave was easily recognizable. Even if the samples were shredded the Shroud fiber could probably be identified by the labs, since there was so much technical data published by STURP. What happened next simply beggars belief: to maintain the pretense, Ballestrero and Tite took the samples into a private area, out of view of all the people in attendance and of the camera, and put them into vials labeled with numbers. These vials were then brought out and presented to the representatives of the three labs. This secrecy gave rise to the allegation, quite absurd on the face of it, that Tite had conducted some sleight of hand and switched the real Shroud samples with others of medieval age. There are still quite a few Europeans who believe to this day that the samples were substituted and the C-14 date that was later obtained is not from a piece of the Shroud. Loading the vials in private was a totally unnecessary and ridiculous procedure, another major error on Gonella's part.

Standing on the sidelines through the eventful proceedings of that morning were the lab directors: Hall, Hedges, Damon, Donahue and Woelfli. Their only apparent role was that of couriers – to await the delivery of the vials into their hands. No microscopic, physical or chemical examination was done on site, since these could of course be done back in the labs. What is surprising to learn is that, once they had brought the vials back to their respective labs, very little scrutiny of the sample was carried out. Not one lab photographed the samples they received properly, i.e. both sides and with a scale. The samples were examined under a microscope, and a few alien fibers picked out, but no lab reported anything suspicious, even though later a STURP chemist found that threads from the adjacent Raes sample had high levels of aluminum, a high occurrence of cotton fiber intermingled with the linen, some kind of coating or encrustation, a high degree of oxidation, and FTIR spectra markedly different from threads elsewhere on the Shroud. Certainly the labs were not in a position to know all the results of all previous investigations of the Shroud, but they could have consulted with STURP personnel, or they could have requested comparison fibers from other parts of the Shroud. The fact that they did neither indicates an over-confidence in their ability to date the samples through standard procedures. It seems very likely that this was a huge mistake, and as Ray Rogers of STURP chemist remarked: "there will be hell to pay when the truth comes out!"

The samples were prepared by a standard pretreatment procedure that consists of alternating acid and alkali washes. In the case of Arizona, Gove reports that the lab also consulted Proctor and Gamble about an agent to clean textiles, and actually used an industrial detergent they recommended. Woelfli wrote to me later about the pretreatment methods used on the Shroud sample at his Zurich lab, basically the same acid-alkali baths. He reported that the Shroud sample was subdivided into five pieces, with one being run without any chemical pretreatment, the others with varying degrees of wash. This led him to state quite confidently that they found "no detectable contamination." Of course, all that this result really shows is that any contamination present was equally soluble or resistant in the acid and alkali washes as the cellulose of the linen, or that such contamination was shielded by the cellulose substrate. This situation has been noted to occur with archaeological specimens, as I had remarked already in my paper on carbon dating the Shroud. It does not prove by any stretch that there was no contamination present. The only way to do this is to look and to test!

Arizona was the first lab to run Shroud samples, on May 6, 1988. Donahue and Damon invited Gove to witness the event, "out of respect for his efforts" and probably feeling a little guilty at having let the side down by accepting Turin's conditions eliminating the other labs. In perhaps the most revealing incident in his entire book, Gove recounts that, arriving at the lab, he was asked to sign the following statement:

> We the undersigned understand that the radiocarbon age results for the Shroud of Turin obtained from the University of Arizona AMS facility are confidential. We agree not to communicate the results to anyone – spouse, children, friends, press, etc. until that time that results are generally available to the public.

This prohibition is normal in C-14 labs in any event, as the client owns the date and the lab does not have the right to release it except with the client's permission. Everyone connected with the Arizona facility signed. Gove signed. He goes on to recount: "... despite the agreement I had signed, I told Shirley [Brignall, his companion] the result that had been obtained that day." In sum, he gave his word to his colleagues, as a scientist and a gentleman, and he broke it the very same day. As we say in the South: "Nuff said!"

In July a newspaper in England reported that the Shroud's C-14 date was medieval, proving it to be a fake. This was roundly denied by all parties, but it was clear with so many people involved, even though they were sworn to secrecy, some whether at the top or the bottom could not be trusted to keep their word, and the results were going to leak out. By September it was confirmed that all three labs had completed their C-14 measurements and had sent the results to the British Museum. By this stage there was a constant stream of "leaks" all pointing towards a date in the 13th to 15th centuries. I called Fr. Rinaldi to ask him if he knew anything, but he had only seen the same reports in the press as I had. He said that Gonella and Ballestrero were convinced that one of the labs had let the results be known, and that Turin would issue a statement in the next few days. Fr. Rinaldi shared my concern that these rumors might very well be true, and we spoke about the possible impact on the Shroud and on believers. I asked him how he would feel if the date came back 14th century. He said he had always had a nagging suspicion that the Shroud was too good to be true. I replied that it was too good to be a forgery! Fr. Otterbein of the Holy Shroud Guild wrote me most prophetically that "if the rumored C-14 date turns out to be true, all the other evidence for authenticity would be tossed aside." This was of course precisely what I had been warning for several years already. The next looming problem was how the matter would be handled by Turin. And it was here that, once again, Gonella made another great mistake.

Fearing that the Shroud's reputation was about to be totally ruined by a very poorly planned and quite possibly incorrect carbon dating, I composed a letter to the British Museum which I copied to Gonella and STURP, hoping that any one of them would realize that more testing needed to be done before any definitive conclusion could be reached. I also sent it to several news agencies, along with a copy of Gove's previous letter to the Museum (my use of which caused him to be so riled). My statement read:

Comments On The British Museum's Involvement In Carbon Dating The Turin Shroud

The attached letter by Prof. H. E. Gove raised serious questions about the involvement of the British Museum in this project. I would agree with the statements of Gove in his penultimate paragraph, but for entirely different reasons. The Museum's role was restricted throughout the exercise to one of certification of the samples and of the results – merely the function of a notary.

However, through the use of its name and immense prestige, it would appear to the public that the Museum was involved in a more substantive, archaeological role. Sadly, this was not the case, at least as far as anyone has been able to pierce the shroud that has been drawn over the whole proceedings. Since being invited by the Pontifical Academy of Sciences to participate in the planning of the carbon dating, I have raised numerous questions that went unanswered, and lodged numerous objections that went unheeded.

The major and very serious flaw in the dating project is that only one sampling site was chosen. I understand that the Museum had no part in this decision, and did not even have an input as to which site on the cloth would be sampled.

No testing or physical measurements were conducted on the site in question, to ascertain if it had been damaged or altered in any way by the fire in 1532. This criterion for the C-14 samples to be tested was recommended unanimously by the Turin Commission on Carbon Dating. This condition was ignored, and the samples were taken from a scorched area.

The site to be sampled was apparently pre-decided by Gonella and his associate Riggi – both of the Turin Polytechnic – in conjunction with an Italian textile 'expert' of their acquaintance. Presumably this 'expert' did visually examine whether any repair or restoration work might have been done in the sample area. However, I am informed by Dr. Stuart Fleming, formerly of the

Oxford Laboratory for Archaeology and now with the University of Pennsylvania, that a skilled medieval restorer 'could certainly have re-woven a damaged edge to a standard not visible to the naked eye.'

The carbon-dated samples were taken from a single strip cut from the Shroud only 2-3 cm away from the selvage edge, in which a different kind of fiber with traces of cotton appears. This selvedge stitching was apparently done to attach a side panel to the Shroud at some point in its history. During the Intercomparison Experiment involving known age linens, conducted by the British Museum as a precursor to the dating of the Shroud, the samples were specifically taken "away from selvages". But samples from the Shroud were taken very close to the selvage. There would seem to be no valid reason for this choice; it was, apparently decided by the Turin participants and not by the British Museum.

The entire affair does appear to have been 'a somewhat shoddy enterprise' in Gove's words, not under properly stringent scientific controls. The sampling methodology was poorly planned and ad hoc; it seems to have been determined by individuals who have no experience in collecting samples for C-14 dating or in applying the results of such dating to actual field situations.

In sum, the British Museum has much to answer for in its involvement:

1. Why did it acquiesce in the reduction of samples to be taken from seven to three, against the recommendation of the Turin Commission?

2. Why did it agree to the elimination of the small counter laboratories, which employ a more reliable counting system?

3. Why did it agree to only one sampling site, thereby raising the possibility of an anomalous zone being dated?

4. Why did it agree to the sampling of a scorched area of the cloth, again in conflict with the recommendation of the Turin Commission?

5. Did it approve the choice of the textile 'expert'? And is it satisfied that his visual inspection of the sampled area is sufficient to rule out any possibility of a restoration/re-weaving of that area?

6. Why did it not follow its own guidelines in the inter-comparison experiment and insist that samples be taken well away from selvedges? Or is 2-3 cm. considered to be 'well away'?

> Clearly the full weight of the Museum's expertise was not brought to bear on the project and its involvement does not add any credibility whatever to the results.

This was carried in a few newspapers, just days before the official announcement of the results. But it did not have the intended effect of causing Tite or Gonella to moderate their interpretation and statements to the media. Gove reacted angrily, writing that I knew perfectly well that the sample did not come from a scorched area. Needless to say, he was wrong as usual; at the time I had reason to strongly suspect that the area had been mildly scorched. Some time before sending out the letter to the British Museum I had written to Barrie Schwortz and Vern Miller, STURP photographers, asking about a discoloration of the C-14 sample area:

> Now it appears to me, studying the published color or black-and-white photographs I have from 1931, 1973 and 1978, that the C-14 sample came from a mildly scorched area. It certainly appears, from the photo published by Pellicori and Evans in *Archaeology*, to be of the same medium brown tone as some of the scorches around the patches. The enhanced B&W photo in *National Geographic* shows this in dramatic fashion.

The area appeared to be anomalous, much darker than the rest of the cloth. Ironically, the color photograph of the area taken by Miller and published in Gove's book shows very clearly that this area is quite a bit darker than the adjacent cloth. Miller responded to my inquiry with the following:

> The area of the C-14 sample does not seem to have the uv characteristics of a scorch, but it is heavily stained. I would really suspect that there was a lot of pyrolysis [product] and water stain ... We know when the water went on and this agrees with the C-14 results ... There would have been a lot of debris and contaminant in the water, especially at the margin. The sample is right in a water boundary which is highly contaminated ... All the contaminants which were in the water and on the cloth would have been concentrated there ... This area is as highly stained as any area on the cloth. It is striking. I don't see how they could have chosen a worse location.

It should never have been sampled for dating, and under no circumstances should it have been the only sample taken. It took me a few hours of investigation to reach that basic conclusion, yet people like Gonella and

THE DATING

Gove who had spent countless thousands of hours involved in this carbon dating fiasco never did this very basic piece of homework. Reviewing the uv fluorescence photographs later confirmed that it did not fluoresce as a scorch would, but based on the chemistry Adler wrote (1996) in the journal *Archaeological Chemistry*: "In fact, the radiocarbon fibers appear to be an exaggerated composite of the water stain and scorch fibers thus confirming the physical location of the suspect radio sample site and demonstrating that it is not typical of the non-image sections of the main cloth." In 2002, the remarkable unrepresentativeness of this area was fully and dramatically explained by Ray Rogers (discussed in more detail below).

The results were announced simultaneously in London and Turin on October 13, 1988 – a day that is burned forever into the memories of all who had researched or been intrigued by the Shroud. The averaged results of the three labs indicated a date of between 1260 and 1390 A.D. for the cloth. All three labs had produced very similar dates, the main reason being that they used splits of the same sample and followed essentially the same procedures in measuring them. It was presented to the public as a 95% probability that the flax used to make the linen was harvested within the quoted time frame. This was of course only a statistical probability of measurement scatter, and had no bearing at all on whether there was contamination, isotope exchange, re-weaving, or any of the various other possibilities that might put the date in question. Scientists and statisticians were quoted in the media to the effect that the chances of the Shroud actually originating in the first century but giving this C-14 result was one in ten million, or some other meaningless figure. Many newspapers carried a photograph of Hall and Tite in front of a blackboard with the date written on it, followed by an exclamation point. Hall seemed to have a slight smirk, since things had clearly gone as he thought they would. This single picture became for many people the defining moment in the Shroud's twentieth century investigation.

The Shroud writer Ian Wilson attended the announcement of the results in London. He describes his reaction:

> [it was] nothing less than a real body blow ... This statement [of the Shroud's age] rendered worthless all my historical researches on the Shroud, on which I had been then been working for more than twenty years. It also negated much of the medical and other evidence that had equally impressed me. The Shroud simply could not possibly be any true shroud of the historical Jesus. For as those

on the platform collectively insisted, the odds against this were now 'astronomical.'

The probability statements obviously influenced affected many people, but they were little more than scientific fraud perpetrated on an unknowing public. Hall showed his ugly, ignorant side with this remark: "There was a multi-million pound [sic] business in making forgeries during the fourteenth century. Someone just got a bit of linen, faked it up and flogged it." Yes, this incomparable object, arguably the most intriguing object in existence, was merely "faked up" by someone and then sold off. Brilliant Oxford scholarship! Tite was more diplomatic, pointing out that the evidence only related to the age of the linen and told us nothing about how the image was made or the intentions of the persons who presumably made it.

In Italy, Ballestrero and Gonella were in a more delicate position than the British scientists. What they said represented the Church's official position on the outcome of the dating. For Shroud believers, their words were literally the shot heard round the world: the Shroud has been dated to the 13th - 14th centuries, and there is no reason to doubt the result. The Church would accept the radiocarbon laboratories findings but still held the Shroud to be a priceless and beautiful icon whose image remains a mystery. It was even claimed that the "icon" had in the past produced some miracles, with the implication that it should still be considered holy. Headlines around the world the next day screamed the contrary: "Church accepts that Shroud is medieval/fake/not authentic." Fr. Rinaldi described this to me as a public relations catastrophe for the Church, not to mention for the Shroud. It was presumably Gonella who decided on this line for Ballestrero to take, and it was without doubt the worst possible way to handle the results. Sadly for Gonella, who had done so much for the Shroud in fighting for STURP's study in 1978, it would be his swansong and his lasting legacy; he was totally out of his depth and stubbornly refused to listen to those with experience in the field, despite urging and pleading from all quarters. It was the tragic outcome to a disastrous project.

6. Grappling with the Result

The Shock Of The Shroud's C-14 Dating had an immediate effect: millions of people came to a snap judgement that it was a fake. The enormity of the situation surprised even someone like me who had been warning that too much emphasis was being placed on this single test. People who had previously asked me about the Shroud were now announcing to me that it was "proven" a medieval forgery. What struck me was how little all the evidence against this interpretation seemed to matter; C-14 was to most people like a magic litmus, and the result was in. Cardinal Ballestrero's and Gonella's handling of the announcement of the results undoubtedly played a part amongst Christians in this widespread acceptance of the date as the true age of the Shroud.

The reaction in Italy was somewhat different from the rest of the world. Fr. Rinaldi wrote to me that:

> The Cardinal has been crucified in Italy for his stand, for swallowing hook, line and sinker, and almost gleefully proclaiming: 'We now know the truth! The Shroud is not what we thought it was, but at the very least it remains a beautiful icon.' Of course Gonella shares the blame and I must tell you he is very unhappy ... he has since been in the USA where he met some of the STURP people who took him apart and blamed him for everything that has happened.

And rightly so, as he failed in the most crucial aspect of any scientific project – to involve people who have experience and expertise. While furious debates raged in Italy over the reliability of the C-14 date and whether the Shroud could really be a medieval forgery, elsewhere there seemed to be an overwhelming acceptance of the date and hence the presumption of forgery. It took me a few days to decide to try to introduce some doubt into the mass media reporting on the date. I prepared a press release with what I believed were the strongest points, and faxed it out to news agencies and major newspapers. It read:

SHROUD C-14 DATE UNRELIABLE, ARCHAEOLOGIST CLAIMS

The carbon-dating of the Turin Shroud has not established the true age of the relic or proved it to be a forgery, an archaeologist involved in the project has claimed. The dating results recently reported have indicated an age of only 500 to 900 years, prompting claims that the Shroud was now shown to be a medieval fake. But the samples came from an unrepresentative section of the cloth, according to William Meacham, an archaeologist at the University of Hong Kong who participated in the early planning of the tests. He maintains that the dates may relate more to an incident in the history of the Shroud than to its origin.

The sampling procedure was seriously flawed, and this round of testing has proven nothing about the Shroud as a whole. The samples were taken from a repaired corner that had also been scorched in a fire in 1532.

He pointed out that a medieval restorer could have woven new fibers into the cloth as part of the repair, and that isotope exchange during the fire could have introduced new C-14 atoms into some parts of the cloth. The C-14 date may reflect the influence of the 1532 fire rather than the actual age of the linen.

All three samples taken from the Shroud and dated at laboratories in Arizona, Oxford and Zurich, were lifted from a single spot on the cloth – a fact that Meacham said severely weakened the credibility of the results. He cited two factors that led to the faulty procedure: pressure from the labs for identical samples, and pressure from the Vatican to limit the number of samples taken.

Technical Note: One of the major compounds present in the Shroud linen, carboxyl, is known to exchange C-14 atoms with compounds in other substances at temperatures above 300 degrees C. In the 1532 fire, the Shroud was burned by drops of molten silver from its casket at approximately 850 C; the scorched areas around the burns were almost certainly heated to 400-500 C when the molten silver dropped onto the cloth. No precedent has been found in C-14 dating comparable to this situation, i.e. an ancient object involved in a fire long after its manufacture, in spite of a request sent to over 40 labs by the director of one of the labs in the Shroud project.

Only a committee of scientists and priests could have come up with a C-14 procedure like this, said Meacham, who attended a conference in Turin organized by the Vatican in 1986 to advise on the program for dating the Shroud.

The British Museum's participation was limited to a purely certifying role, while the group of American scientists (STURP) which originally developed the proposal for C-14 dating of the Shroud was excluded altogether.

Meacham called for another round of testing, with samples from at least two other sites on the cloth, before any firm conclusions could be drawn about its age. However, he said that C-14 dates should not be regarded as infallible.

Carbon dating often produces results that vary from the true age by hundreds or thousands of years, usually for reasons that remain unknown. Such 'rogue samples' are quite common in archaeology, and their aberrant dates are generally ignored. In the Aegean, where there were tight historical controls, a number of prominent archaeologists had recently disdained the use of single dates altogether. Prof. P. Betancourt and his colleagues remarked on the fact that 'so many dates have proven to be useless because of contamination and other causes.'

And Prof. W. Woelfli, director of the Zurich lab where one of the Shroud samples was dated, remarked in a recent paper 'no method is immune from giving grossly incorrect datings when there are non-apparent problems with the samples ... this situation occurs frequently [in carbon dating].'

Meacham had circulated a paper at the Turin conference warning that the results would mean little if scorched or charred cloth was used and if only one sampling spot was chosen.

Prior to the release of the C-14 results, most of the scientific analyses of the Shroud had pointed to authenticity. The Shroud was extensively tested by scientists in 1978, who concluded that the image on the Shroud was the genuine body imprint of a male crucifixion victim.

Because of the accuracy of details in the image and the absence of paint, pigment or dye, one of the STURP scientists involved in the testing concluded that 'it would be a miracle if it was a forgery.'

In the pre-internet age, it was difficult to gauge the news coverage of a press release like this. I received a few clippings later in the mail, but there were no telephone calls or faxes from reporters, a fact that suggested to me that this side of the story was not getting much coverage in the media. After a few days, I decided to send out another statement, and this one **did** evoke some response:

SHROUD DATED 200-1000 A.D. IN SECRET TESTING; RESULTS INCONSISTENT WITH RECENT DATES

A closely-guarded secret testing of the Shroud of Turin in 1982 by an American C-14 laboratory yielded conflicting dates of 200 A. D. and 1000 A.D., an American archaeologist involved in Shroud research claimed today.

Mr. William Meacham of the University of Hong Kong said that members of the US scientific team which examined the Shroud in 1978 informed him that a single thread was later tested at the University of California nuclear accelerator facility.

He said separate ends of the thread gave quite different results, and the presence of starch was also detected during pretreatment. These findings were never published because C-14 testing did not have the approval of the Turin authorities at that time. Prof. L. Gonella, scientific advisor to the Archbishop of Turin, was only informed of the results in 1986, at a meeting that Meacham had attended.

Recently completed C-14 tests are reported to indicate a date of 1000-1500 A. D. for the relic, which bears the image of a male corpse with wounds of crucifixion. Extensive testing in 1973 and 1978 had indicated that the image was a genuine body imprint with stains of human blood.

Meacham said the recent C-14 tests proved nothing at all about the Shroud as a whole, since all three samples dated by Arizona, Oxford and Zurich had been taken from the same spot on the cloth – a corner that had been scorched in the church fire of 1532.

It is also possible that this area was re-woven by a medieval restorer, since it is just next to a selvage edge and side panel that were added to the Shroud at some time after its original manufacture.

The Shroud may not be one homogeneous cloth as far as its chemistry is concerned. We already know of significant variations from one point to another, and the radiocarbon content likewise may vary significantly.

The recent testing was very poorly planned. It is astonishing that samples from at least two or three different points on the cloth were not taken for dating. Archaeologists who make frequent use of C-14 results are accustomed to samples occasionally giving aberrant results, and would normally not attach much importance to a single date, or in this case, three dates on a single spot.

Meacham said he had repeatedly urged Gonella not to rely on one single site for dating the Shroud, especially in view of the previous test results from the California lab. Criticism of Gonella surfaced earlier this year when 4 of the 7 labs originally planned to do the testing were dropped from the program. Meacham cited a letter he had just obtained that was written by one of the labs' directors to the British Museum in January of this year, in which the current C-14 project was described as 'a rather shoddy enterprise ... which the British Museum may live to regret.'

Meacham felt the matter could be easily clarified by another round of testing under proper controls, especially in view of the small amount of material needed to obtain a C-14 date. There should be at least 5 or 6 dates on various points on the cloth before we can say anything definitive about its radiocarbon age.

After two weeks the subject of the Shroud had run its course in the press. I realized that it was going to be difficult to move the mass media or the mass mentality until there were new developments. It seemed to me very likely that Ballestrero and Gonella would favor a new round of testing, including all the tests that STURP was planning, plus another C-14 run on samples from different sites on the cloth. And why not? There was everything to gain and nothing to lose. This was eminently logical, but as often happens in Church or any other politics, logic does not always prevail.

Amongst Shroud researchers, there was a wide variety of views on what should be done: some thought efforts should now be focused on the image question; others agreed with me that another round of C-14 dating, properly organized, was certainly called for; still others thought that the Shroud should be left alone, as it was a mystery beyond the ability of science to explain. Most did not accept the C-14 date as the true age of the cloth. The only two that were rumored to have done so, and dropped out of Shroud research as a consequence, are Eric Jumper and Bob Dinegar, but neither ever made any statement to that effect. David Sox of the British Society had already experienced doubts about the Shroud following McCrone's claims; after the C-14 dating he rushed a book into press titled *The Shroud Unmasked*; its subtitle was perhaps the one of the rashest statements ever made about the Shroud – "Uncovering the Greatest Forgery of All Time."

Several people in the Shroud community wondered how Fr. Rinaldi would cope with what must have been a terrible blow. He had spent most of his life promoting the Shroud. The answer was not long in coming. He sent out a "pastoral letter" a few days after the results were announced. It showed a remarkably calm and composed attitude, preserving respect for the object even though it now seemed that it was not what many people had believed for so long. A handwritten note at the top of the page said: "This message I sent to my Shroud friends to console them, and to console myself while consoling them!!!" The letter read:

Dear Friends,
It has been a long time since you heard from me. Bear with me, please. They have been busy months for me. Difficult, too, I doubt if the cause of the Shroud ever went through more trying times than it did during the past year. Surely you must know by now that scientists, using the ultimate test, the carbon-14 analysis, have dated the origin of the Shroud to the 14th century A.D. This would mean, of course, that the Shroud is not the burial cloth of Christ.

Let me say, first of all, that not all the experts accept the results of the test. Some of them are actually calling for a new test on good scientific grounds. I was intrigued by what one of them told me: 'Valid or not, the results of the carbon-14 test in no way solve the mystery of Christ's image on that cloth. The test has not said the last word on the Shroud.'

The position of the Church

The Church, which for centuries has venerated the Turin Shroud much as it did other sacred icons, never officially stated that the Shroud is actually the burial cloth of Jesus. It could hardly have done so without the support of historical and scientific proofs. It was exactly in order to determine the true origin of the Shroud that Church authorities agreed it should be examined by a group of scientists. Now that the verdict of the carbon-14 test is in, the Church will not question the results. Any disagreement among the experts on their validity will have to be settled by them.

Whatever the scientists' decision, the Shroud will continue to be a highly revered object. It is unquestionably the most impressive visual representation of Christ's sufferings, the only one of its kind in fact known to exist. Renowned art experts and pathologists refuse to believe it could be the work of a medieval forger. As one of them said: 'I find it much easier to believe it is the actual burial cloth of Christ than to believe it is a 14th century artifact.'

There is no question in my mind that the Shroud image will come again under the most intensive scrutiny by the experts. A Turin Shroud official told me: 'No stones will be left unturned to solve the mystery of that incredible portrait.'

The Church has nothing to fear from the truth

Shortly after the results of the carbon-14 test were announced, a friend met me in front of the Turin Cathedral. Placing his hand on my shoulder, he said mournfully: 'I feel terribly sorry for the Church and for you.'

'You can't be serious,' I told him. 'Do you really think the Church will fall apart because the Shroud may not be what many of us supposed it to be? The Church has nothing to fear from the truth, provided, of course, it is backed by solid facts. For one thing, in the case of the Shroud, it was the Church that took the initiative to find out the truth. Besides, my friend, what makes you think the carbon-14 test marks the end for the Shroud? I might be persuaded to accept the results of the test only when someone will demonstrate beyond all question, how a medieval artist produced so extraordinary an image as that of the Shroud.'

A silent witness to Christ's death and resurrection

People constantly ask me how I reacted to the news that the Shroud could be a medieval forgery. Had the carbon-14 test placed the origin of the Shroud in the 1st century A.D., I probably would have burst in a joyous 'Alleluia!' But the fact is that, aside from what the experts have said or may yet say about the Shroud, it will continue to be, in the words of Pope John Paul II, 'a unique and mysterious object, its image a silent witness to the passion, death and resurrection of Christ.'

Doubtless, that incomparable portrait, which no artist could have produced, will outlive all the scientists' tests, and will continue to touch the minds and hearts of countless people for ages to come. As for me, as often as I glance at the image of the Man of the Shroud, my heart still says: 'It is the Lord!'

A sign of our faith and hope in Christ

One thing does trouble me: the thought that the simple faith of many good people may be somewhat shaken by this turn of events. This could be due to an exaggerated notion they have of the importance of the Shroud in the scheme of our Christian faith. When lecturing on the Shroud, I often reminded my listeners that for us Christians, it is the Lord that matters, not the Shroud. If the Shroud does have a meaning, it is because it speaks to us of His sufferings as no other image does. But, at best, the Shroud is only a sign of our faith and hope in Christ. He and He alone is our greatest and dearest possession, the supreme gift of the love of the Father to us.

If I am grateful the Shroud came into my life, it is because it has brought me closer to Him, and, too, because millions of people, through the Shroud, were given a new and deeper awareness of Him who said: 'Crucified, I will draw all men to me.'

With my best regards, a promise to-keep in touch with you on all future Shroud development. Pray for me.

Cordially in Christ,

Peter M. Rinaldi, SDB

Reflecting on the fact that the Church had been quoted all over the world as accepting the radiocarbon results as being the true age of the Shroud, it occurred to me to write a "letter to the editor" of the official Vatican newspaper *Osservatore Romano* to try to provoke a response clarifying the Church's position, and to set the stage for a new request for C-14. In this letter I used many of the points made in the two press releases cited above, but tried to put the issue in terms the Church might find acceptable. It began:

The Turin Shroud – a Medieval Fake?

On October 13 the news came on the BBC, in their lead story at 11 hours GMT: 'the Roman Catholic Church has stated that scientific tests have shown the Holy Shroud to be a medieval forgery.' I listened in utter disbelief. Although rumors had been circulating that the results of the carbon-dating tests were far short of 2000 years, it seemed almost unthinkable that the Church would officially declare the Shroud to be a fake on the basis of this single test. The next day's newspapers confirmed the BBC account; the Reuters dispatch was headed 'Vatican Concedes Shroud is a Fake'.

As an archaeologist who has been closely involved in the study of the Shroud and in the planning of its C-14 testing, I consider this conclusion to be highly premature, if indeed it is the actual position of the Vatican.

The truth is, the carbon-dating of the Turin Shroud has not established the true age of the relic or proved it to be a forgery. We now have an indication that the Shroud might date from the Middle Ages, but there are problems with taking the present carbon-dating results at their face value. ...

One of America's foremost archaeological scientists, Dr. Stuart Fleming of the University of Pennsylvania, has pointed out that a medieval restorer could have woven new fibers into the cloth as part of the repair. It is also possible that isotope exchange during the fire could have introduced new C-14 atoms into some parts of the cloth. ...

It is clear that another round of testing should be conducted, with samples from several other sites on the cloth, before any firm conclusions could be drawn about its age.

At the Turin conference in 1986, organized by the Pontifical Academy of Sciences to advise on the proper procedures for dating the Shroud, I circulated a paper warning that the results would mean little if scorched or charred cloth was used and if only one sampling spot was chosen. Sadly neither of these caveats was taken up, and the Shroud is now branded a fake on the basis of an inadequate and flawed testing procedure. The solution is straightforward enough; another round of very sophisticated testing should be done, with samples from at least three points on the cloth.

And surely we must not forget all the other evidence from this fascinating object, which has baffled and intrigued scholars and the general public for centuries. Its mystery remains; its image and remarkable blood flows still contradict the forgery hypothesis.

On present evidence, its possible antiquity, and even its possible association with the body of Christ, cannot be ruled out.

I sent a copy of this letter to Fr. Rinaldi and asked if he knew anyone in Rome who could help to get it published. He wrote back:

I called a friend on the editor's staff and asked what the chances might be that they would publish. 'Not one in a million,' he told me. 'You must have noticed that, except for the official communiqué on the results, the *Osservatore* has been silent on the whole issue, while other newspapers both Catholic and secular have registered all sorts of protests and criticism of the way Cardinal Ballestrero handled the October 13 press conference. For the time being the *Osservatore* (i.e. the Vatican) wants to stay out of it.

Although the damage done to the Shroud's reputation was severe, several researchers supported my contention that we should now proceed and do it right. Samples needed to be taken from 3 or 4 points on the cloth; each of these sites thoroughly examined and tested; the samples themselves thoroughly screened; intensive pretreatment with the resultant fractions dated. And **if**, at the end of it all, we still have a medieval age, then we would have to acknowledge the very real possibility that, difficult as it is to conceive, the Shroud really could be a medieval cloth. But if different dates were obtained it would have a tremendous impact on the masses and the mass media. Actually it would only be a confirmation of what those of us who use C-14 regularly already know – that one can never trust a single date no matter how reliable the sample appears. Without corroboration from a suite of other measurements and other data the date from one sample means very little.

I wrote to STURP, ASSIST, the Holy Shroud Guild, the British Society, and several other Shroud organizations in Italy, France, Spain, Mexico, Australia, etc. outlining all the reasons why the C-14 date just announced might be incorrect, and proposing direct action:

> Now what occurs to me is that all those who have studied the Shroud need to come together in pressing for the ancillary testing and for another round of C-14 measurement, with specific attention focused on the sites where samples for C-14 are lifted. This is of course exactly what should have been done the first time round, but now it is crucial that it be done and without the usual Italian delays in getting things moving.
>
> What I have in mind specifically is some sort of petition addressed to Cardinal Ballestrero from all those who retain an interest in and respect for the Turin Shroud. This would also be good for media consumption, as it would show that scientific interest in the Shroud has not evaporated, that those who have studied the relic closely have not closed the book on its possible authenticity, and it would create a new sense of drama that something else is happening and will shortly produce new results that may or may not corroborate what has just been announced.
>
> A letter to Cardinal Ballestrero might go something like this:

'We the undersigned have followed with great interest the scientific studies of the Turin Shroud. As scholars, researchers and enthusiasts of this unique object, we are dismayed by the impact of the carbon-14 dating and the near-universal tendency now to dismiss the Shroud as a medieval fake. We believe that there are many questions which deserve further research, and urge Your Eminence and other responsible authorities to permit such investigations to proceed as soon as they can be organized, hopefully by the Spring of 1989.'

'In particular, we are most concerned that the true radiocarbon age of the Shroud may not have been established by the recent tests, owing to the exclusion of the small counter method and the sampling of only one point on the cloth. We urge that further sampling be permitted of at least two other areas of the Shroud, and that this second round of dating be under the direct supervision of archaeologists experienced in the use and field applications of C-14 dating. A wide array of sophisticated analyses should also be conducted at these sampling sites to insure that they are not in any way anomalous. Only with such comprehensive examinations can we obtain evidence on which to base conclusions regarding the possible authenticity of the Shroud of Turin – which remains one of the most fascinating objects in existence.'

'We pray that Your Eminence will give urgent consideration to this petition so that the physical reality of the Shroud may be clarified without undue delay.'

Let us make this an international outpouring of concern over the reputation of the Shroud – proven through extensive examinations to be the most extraordinary mystery which a single measurement cannot and should not settle.

The pressure to conduct the first C-14 test came mainly from the scientific community. If there is to be a second, the impetus will have to come from Shroud enthusiasts, who are unwilling to accept on the present totality of evidence that the Shroud has been **proven** to be a medieval fake.

The response was underwhelming. Some societies thought the Shroud should now be left alone; others thought the data needed to be studied in detail; still others could not make any decision. Some leading Shroud figures in Europe embraced the conspiracy notion that somehow the samples were switched. STURP was having huge administrative, financial and political problems trying to get its second round of testing organized. Ian Wilson of the British Society was favorable but doubted that Turin would allow a new round of carbon-dating anytime soon; he said his Society would focus on tests that would shed light on the image. Otterbein of the Holy Shroud Guild proposed to wait for the official publication of the C-14 data in a scientific journal.

I decided to go ahead and draw up a detailed C-14 proposal, which I did over several days. This was sent to Ballestrero, with a covering letter setting out all that was wrong with the first dating, and strongly urging him to authorize another round to find out if the results obtained already would be corroborated. I copied the proposal and letter to Gonella and STURP. There was no response, and I would soon learn that the effort was wasted. On everyone's mind was the question of the general tests that STURP and the British Society were planning, which Gonella had indicated were slated to take place after the carbon-dating results were announced. Unfortunately, circumstances conspired against them. The mass snap judgement on the Shroud as medieval fake made fund-raising much more difficult, but before that problem could even be addressed came word that Ballestrero would be retiring soon. Fr. Rinaldi wrote me in November 1988 that STURP's planned new phase of research was in doubt:

> I hear all kinds of noises from the Cardinal's residence. He is so fed up with the totally unexpected adverse reaction, that he is not likely to move on anything, all the more since he is resigning his mandate as archbishop any day now, having reached the age limit, 75 years old, as prescribed by the Canon Law.

It transpired that Ballestrero was well and truly stunned by the reaction, and the blame was put squarely on the shoulders of his adviser Gonella. With Ballestrero retiring, Gonella would certainly be out of the picture. An entirely new ballgame would begin with the appointment of a new archbishop, and the prospects for any early move towards testing, radiocarbon or other, were probably remote.

The scientific publication of the results occurred in the journal *Nature* in February 1989, in an article with twenty-one signatories – senior staff at the three labs where the dating was carried out, plus Tite. They asserted that the results provided "conclusive evidence that the linen of the Shroud of Turin is medieval." In March, Ballestrero announced his retirement. The curtain had closed on the drama, but the debate was just beginning.

On the counter-attack was Rev. Kim Dreisbach, an Anglican priest and long-time Shroud scholar in Atlanta, Georgia, who prepared a massive and impressive compilation of all the evidence in favor of authenticity, calling it the "overwhelming preponderance of evidence." He circulated it to dozens of people, and the press, but his efforts like mine met with little success in getting across to the mass media what a travesty had occurred. Foremost in people's minds would be the simple litmus test of carbon dating. It was becoming clear that it would be extremely difficult to change the mass snap judgment based on the dating. At the time I felt confident that, after Ballestrero's retirement and a suitable period of months rather than years, Turin would allow another C-14 run, and why would it not?

Quite unexpectedly, in August 1990, the Vatican made an announcement that held out a flicker of hope – it would consider proposals for new scientific tests on the Shroud. The statement called the C-14 results "strange" and pointed out that they conflicted with previous scientific findings. This made me feel that perhaps my letter to the official Vatican newspaper might not have been a wasted effort. I sent a copy of my proposal already submitted in 1989, but alas this apparent openness to new research was closed as suddenly as it had appeared, for reasons known only to the inner sanctum of the Curia. The new archbishop of Turin, Cardinal Saldarini, made it known that only proposals regarding the conservation and preservation of the Shroud would be considered.

Meanwhile, the skeptics were of course having a field day, with the full weight of the scientific establishment's "conclusive evidence" that the Shroud was medieval. Hall in particular proved to be something of a boor (which I already knew), with his smug remarks about "Shroud believers being onto a loser" and equating them with "flat-earthers." Several writers accused me and others of being true believers who would never alter their belief in the Shroud's authenticity. This was patent nonsense, and I responded to one of them:

> At a minimum we need another round of C-14 sampling, with at least 2 samples of main body cloth. I would share to a degree the view of *The Economist*, and probably the majority of people who have ever heard of the Shroud, that all that remains are relatively trivial questions of how and when the Shroud was faked, **if** it is really 13th century and therefore not a real gravecloth of a crucifixion victim. I doubt that much importance will attach to the confirmation that Heller and Adler were right all along and the image consists of nothing more than the degradation of the cellulose, and the bloodstains are human blood.
>
> The over-riding issue remains the C-14 date, in my view, and the Shroud's origins must be sought from further testing. If as I believe, and the preponderance of other evidence indicates, the Shroud is really from antiquity and the period of crucifixion, then I am moderately confident that a sophisticated C-14 dating procedure

such as the one I have suggested will turn up indications of anomalies in the radiocarbon content of the cloth and at least strong indications of an earlier age.

If on the other hand the cloth was shown to be consistently of a 13th/14th century radiocarbon age even after all the pretreatment fractions had been measured, then I think it would be very difficult indeed to argue that the cloth was any older than that. It would also remain very difficult to argue that it was faked in the middle ages, unless there is dramatic new evidence from the image analysis.

I am reminded of a metallurgist in Canada who spent the better part of her career investigating how bronze was ever invented, with all the unlikely conditions that have to be met. She finally came to the view that, with our present state of knowledge and the extremely unlikely possibility that all the necessary pre-conditions would ever have converged, the only tenable scientific conclusion was that bronze could not have ever been invented! She was only a short step away from von Daniken [popular writer attributing all advance in human civilization to visits from aliens].

As months went by, Cardinal Saldarini made it obvious that a second C-14 dating was not going to be allowed in the near future. Several writers raised the possibility that the reason for this was that the Church had already done it, secretly. This would be the only logical explanation for why it would refuse to allow a confirmation of a result so highly damaging to the Shroud, but as pointed out previously logic often does not play a part in ecclesiastical decisions.

Gove alleges in his book that not long after the Shroud dates were announced a sample was sent by a private customer in Italy to the IsoTrace AMS Laboratory in Toronto, for dating on a commercial basis. He said that "scientists at Toronto were readily able to identify it [as belonging to the Shroud] because of its unique weave. The measurement at IsoTrace agreed with the values at Arizona, Oxford and Zurich." In 2004 I spoke on the telephone with Ted Litherland, director of IsoTrace, and he confirmed that a sample thought to be from the Shroud had been received from a customer and dated by them. I asked him about its characteristics such as dimensions and weight, and any distinguishing characteristics; he said someone else in the lab had processed the sample and promised to get back to me with whatever information was in the file, except the actual date, as that information belonged to the client. He believed they had not taken a photograph of the sample. Despite repeated reminders from me, he never did respond as promised, but I got an email from Gove affirming what was in his book and stating that no one at IsoTrace was going to tell me anything more. He was right, and I suppose their loyalty to Gove meant more than a mere promise over the telephone.

While it remains possible that a sample was secretly dated by the Church, the IsoTrace story is surely incorrect, par for Gove. Firstly, Litherland told me he could not remember who had "identified" it as coming from the Shroud. It seems doubtful that any of the technical staff at the lab would be familiar with the Shroud's unusual weave. It turns out that an Italian Shroud researcher did send several linen samples to IsoTrace over a period of three years, but these were from the Sudario (facecloth) of Ovieto in Spain and also some first century textile fragments that he had experimented with. Further, the "reserve" piece held by Turin was examined by a textile expert in 1998, and found to weigh 136mg, exactly the amount that should be left after 164mg were cut from the 300mg strip for the three C-14 labs. It seems highly unlikely that the Turin authorities would have cut another sample from the relic for dating, especially after the departure of Ballestrero. The IsoTrace dating of a sample from the Shroud was just more Gove nonsense.

As the full impact of the carbon dating sank in, a number of Shroud writers and devotees opted for strange theories to "explain" the date, notions that ranged from the possible to the far-fetched and absurd. A commonly held view was that the Resurrection had impacted the cloth in some way such that its chemical composition had been changed and C-14 measurement was no longer valid to calculate its age. This possibility was given a degree of respectability by a physicist at Harvard, Dr. Thomas Phillips. In a letter to *Nature* published at the same time as the report on the dating, he wrote that if genuine the Shroud was present at a unique physical event – the resurrection of a dead body – and as such could not be studied scientifically. But he argued that one could speculate that a resurrection could have radiated heat, light and energy, possibly in the form of neutrons (after a loss of protons). This process would have resulted in the conversion of some carbon-12 in the burial cloth to carbon-14, and thus a radiocarbon age much younger for the cloth itself. In a letter to Gove, he said that as a high-energy physicist, he considered anything to be possible unless there was a measurement that contradicted the possibility.

Hedges of Oxford wrote a reply to Phillips, also published in *Nature*, stating that there was no plausible biological mechanism for a human body to produce such a surge of neutrons. Hedges further argued that if a miraculous event was proposed, it would be futile to conduct scientific investigations. Perhaps Hedges did not realize that in the Catholic Church there is a long tradition of exactly that, and only when natural explanations have been exhausted is the possibility of a miracle considered. In the case of the Shroud, the exact concurrence between the carbon date and the first reliable historical date is simply too overwhelming to invoke a supernatural coincidence. If the carbon date had been 1740 A.D., or 2240 A.D., then perhaps, but it is simply too far a stretch to have the miracle of the Resurrection produce by accident a radiocarbon date precisely corresponding to the first secure date for the Shroud in history. Was God toying with our science? Most people would scoff at such an explanation, and I never put any credence in it.

The first natural scenario to be developed to explain what might have skewed the carbon date was put forward by a textile specialist from Manchester, England. John Tyrer wrote that the 1532 fire must have produced intense heat inside the casket, and:

> In these circumstances, moisture in the Shroud would turn to steam, probably at superheat, trapped in the folds and layers of the Shroud. Any contaminants on the cloth would be dissolved by the steam and forced not only into the weave and yarn, but also inside the flax fibers' very lumen and molecular structure. The Shroud is known to contain all kinds of contaminants, including microscopical fungi and insect debris as well as pollens and dust of all kinds. ... Under the circumstances, contaminants would have become part of the chemistry of the flax fibres themselves and would be impossible to remove satisfactorily by surface actants and ultrasonic washing.

This scenario drew upon some of my previous observations about contamination that was present on the Shroud, and it had the merit of coming from a textile chemist who could speak authoritatively about how such normal contaminants might be driven into the cellular structure of the cellulose.

Dan Scavone, then professor of history at the University of Southern Indiana, was also investigating the possibility that contamination could have thrown the date off by a significant amount. One of the people he contacted was a mathematician with a rather abrasive character who was ridiculing the notion that the date could be wrong due to contamination. I wrote a lengthy reply outlining the case in some detail. The problem with contamination as an issue, as I had already pointed out to Gonella a couple of years before, is that it is difficult to quantify because it is usually an unknown. The arithmetic seems impressive, i.e. that something like 50% or more of the bulk mass of the sample would have to be contaminant in order for a first century linen to produce a C-14 date of 1300 A.D. And there is an appeal also to common sense: it would surely be obvious if a textile was so heavily contaminated. Even though it may seem unlikely, it is unjustified to leap to "highly unlikely" and then to "could not possibly be." And even if it seemed unlikely, it could happen. In the case of an ancient "charcoal" specimen from Hong Kong, it was found on specialist examination to be unfired old wood composed "mainly" of organic material which had over time seeped into the lumens (cellular structure) of the wood. And, when a sample of linen was specially prepared in a laboratory with 60% contamination from microbial residues, it was not obvious at all to the naked eye.

Speaking strictly of bulk contamination only, as opposed to other kinds, it is important to realize first of all that such contamination of samples, even from near ideal archaeological conditions does occur and sometimes the dates are off by considerable amounts. Often the type of contamination is not identified, and one cannot exclude the possibility without detailed investigations. My paper drafted in 1985 detailed a large number of such cases, such as the modern wood samples from Monte Amiata in Italy, the samples (of say 50 g) would have seemed at the time to need to contain 500g of old carbon to yield the dates that were obtained. Of course there is now a known mechanism that produces the backward contamination, and it is not bulk replacement of the carbon but rather depletion (due to volcanic gases) in the immediate environment where the sample lived.

But in many other cases there is still a possibility of bulk contamination or replacement of the cellulose by more recent substances, in spite of the rather large proportions that would have to be present. The proposition certainly has not been disproved, and some observations would support the notion that there has been substantial contamination of the sample area of the Shroud. The more important are, first, the remarks of Prof. Ettore Morano (1978) who examined Shroud threads under the scanning electron microscope and found "the surface of the fiber presents a 'filthy' aspect with abundant deposit of extraneous contaminating material intimately connected with the individual fibers." This was noted at magnifications of 8800 and 17,500. The other observation comes from Vern Miller, whose remark has already been cited above about the heavy discoloration and staining in the area of the C-14 sample. It should be obvious from his and Morano's comments (and recall that Morano examined threads from a relatively "clean" area of the Shroud) that contamination is a very real possibility, and when contaminants (such as starch) are in intimate contact with the sample for long periods of time they can and do work their way into the cellular structure of the sample.

The other possibility that has not been excluded, and that merely seems unlikely at the common sense level, is that the area sampled for C-14 was the subject of medieval repair. The more I thought about this question the more ridiculous it seemed to me that only one sample was lifted, especially from that very curious area near the sewn border where the side strip is missing and which is discolored as if scorched. It is not enough to say that there is no visible disturbance to the weave, just as it is now not sufficient to qualify a female athlete by simply verifying that s/he has female genitalia! We know from human biology and from modern surgery that there is more to this question than sometimes meets the eye! If a frayed edge was repaired by a good medieval restorer one cannot be certain that there would be visible traces of the work. It is noteworthy that the Oxford lab picked out a few obviously intrusive fibers (as seen under the light microscope) and these were identified as cotton, possibly from a medieval repair. The restorer may have also used linen and other fibers not now distinguishable from the Shroud's original fibers. The extremely simple point was this: another measurement on another sample would completely and easily dispel this notion, or give it real credence. What an impact there would be now if another sample gave a result of 200 A.D., as the California lab supposedly found on a thread that had starch at one end.

To be honest, I felt privately that these scenarios were unlikely, certainly not impossible and not excluded by the data, but still unlikely. To my mind, the most likely explanation of the medieval date was isotope exchange, whereby the carbon atoms, or even only a few C-14 atoms, are exchanged with contaminants that may have been on, in or in contact with the cloth at some point in its history. In my symposium paper I gave an example of the type of exchange reaction that could alter the C-14/C-12 ratio. Al Adler mentioned to me several others, which in the right conditions would also produce the same effect. There is no way to rule out such disturbance to the original C-14 content, and thus no way ultimately to prove that any C-14 date is accurate. We simply do not know all the instances in which carbon or just carbon-14 may be introduced into a sample. It is instructive to recall just how rare the C-14 atom is in ordinary carbon: if one imagines a path of sand three feet wide stretching all the way to the moon, and all the grains of sand as carbon atoms, there is only **one** that is C-14. That is the incredibly small ratio of carbon-14 atoms to all the other carbon-13 and carbon-12 atoms. So the addition of a very small number would have a dramatic effect on any date.

I had a brief correspondence with Woelfli of the Zurich lab, and he castigated me for trying to shake the "solid date" that had been obtained. He also wrote very curiously that the isotope exchange reaction that I had cited "is really the jottings of some armchair chemists, because such an effect had not been observed so far." Here, he was very wide of the mark, since I had already pointed out that virtually all archaeological specimens of charred material, notably charcoal, were burnt at or near the time of their origin, so any exchange reaction that might have been induced by heat would not make a noticeable difference in the C-14 date. I pointed out that Harbottle had asked some 30 radiocarbon colleagues for examples of samples fired much later than their origin, and no one provided any. I also made a simple example – let us say that a 100-year-old wooden beam in a Bronze Age temple had been painted with a substance containing significant amounts of one-year-old carbon. Let us say further that the structure burned some 300 years after being painted, and in the fire there was a carbon exchange between the wood and the paint. When a charred piece of this beam is found and dated 4000 years later, the exchange will not be noticed because at that remove the ages of the beam and the paint are indistinguishable. Thus it would be for 99.9% of all archaeological and geological charcoal. I have not yet been able to find in the literature a single example of a C-14 dated sample that was scorched/charred in a fire some 500 or more years after its origin. One would need a dozen such cases before asserting that "the effect has not been observed."

The debate over contamination and isotope exchange would soon be ratcheted up to a new level, with significant new propositions coming respectively from Texas and Russia! These are discussed in the next chapter.

Meanwhile, a weird "theory" was gaining currency in Europe: the Shroud had not been dated at all, but rather someone had substituted medieval samples in order to discredit the Shroud. A researcher I had considerable respect for wrote:

> I see no point in requesting new carbon tests. The reason is simply because the date given us raises suspicions. If the date announced had been, say, sixth century, there would have been room for discussion and for arguments about contamination, samples cut from beside the side-strip, etc. etc. But that the three laboratories came up with what has been announced as practically identical results, and that these results coincide with the accusation of Pierre d'Arcis – whose ghost we thought we had laid to rest – smells strongly of some procedural deviance prior to the actual tests. You know, and I know, and most people know, that the Shroud is not a medieval artifact. Most of us accept that the three laboratories did the cleaning of the threads and the testing correctly. What went 'wrong' happened somewhere else.

This struck me as totally illogical and unbelievable, on two counts. First, if there was some skullduggery involved, then all the more reason to ask for confirmation by another round of testing. Second, who would do such a thing, and why?

The mantle of leading conspiracy theorist was taken up by a French monk, Brother Bruno Bonnet-Eymard, a member of the ultra-right "Catholic Counter Reformation in the Twentieth Century." The idea was that the agnostic and leftist establishment was terrified of the Shroud and its powerful message, so a way was devised to bring it into disrepute. Bro. Bruno made the startling accusation that Michael Tite of the British Museum had switched samples just before they were put into the vials, a sleight of hand that went unnoticed (presumably) by Ballestrero. This conspiracy scenario was developed with bits and pieces of "evidence" that Brother Bruno picked up during visits to the three laboratories, interviews and correspondence with their staff. Discrepancies in the weights and sample sizes, odd occurrences such as the failure to videotape the samples being placed in the vials, flukes such as the suspected suicide of one staff member at Arizona – all was woven into a huge conspiracy theory of the "Hitler-is-alive" variety and printed in a glossy magazine-style publication that was sent to Shroud researchers. It was surprising that Tite did not sue, as the allegations were certainly libelous.

It has been a source of amazement to me that conspiracy theories about the C-14 dating of the Shroud continue even today to have such a following in Shroud circles, particularly in Europe. Another version was that the three lab directors conspired to date non-Shroud samples, and discard the genuine ones. It was also suggested by two German writers that a high-ranking official within the Church was a party to the subterfuge, in cahoots with Tite. According to this outrageous scenario, a medieval date for the Shroud served the Church, because it wanted to demote the Shroud in order to repress the secret that Jesus did not really die on the Cross. The Shroud, these writers asserted, proves this, therefore it needed to be brought down.

In my opinion, it is ludicrous to suggest that Michael Tite, or the three lab directors, or Cardinal Ballestrero, or some shadowy Vatican figure, would be involved in arranging the switching of samples, substituting some other material for genuine Shroud samples. Like most other outlandish conspiracy theories, it cannot be disproved, as it is impossible to prove a negative, but they do not deserve serious consideration, even though some prominent Shroud researchers have embraced the notion that somehow the samples that were dated were not really from the Shroud. This tendency arises from a deep and understandable consternation with the amateurish, shoddy and incompetent way the sampling was done, and from anguish over the result which seems to contradict everything that 20th century science and scholarship learned about the Shroud.

The conspiracy theorizing is fed by people who have no experience in fieldwork and who make evidentiary mountains out of accidental molehills. Everyone who has done fieldwork will know that errors occur in recording, especially when done by people not accustomed to performing the task at hand. Exactly how many C-14 operations had Riggi or Gonella been involved in prior to orchestrating perhaps the most important one of all? Absolutely nothing should be deduced from minor anomalies in the dimensions or weights of the samples as reported first by Riggi and then by the labs. Weird stuff happens, notes are written wrongly or misread, coincidence enters as well, for example that Riggi with a pair of ordinary scissors would cut ad hoc a piece that after trimming weighed exactly 300.0 mg. Having dealt also with about a dozen C-14 labs over the course of the last 30 years, and having seen firsthand the arrogant behavior of most of the C-14 luminaries at the Turin meeting in 1986, I am not surprised in the least that the labs did not properly record the samples on receiving them. But this does not lend the slightest credence to the allegation of subterfuge or dishonesty. Though some were arrogant and abrasive, the people involved in dating the Shroud were sincere and honest scientists, and there is no reason to doubt their integrity.

Another critical approach was adopted by Remi von Haelst and others, who pointed out that while the control textile samples of various ages yielded internally consistent results, the Shroud samples did not. Oxford's results were a little too far from Zurich's and Arizona's, which overlapped nicely. There are several technical statistical tests that the Shroud C-14 results failed. To me as an archaeologist who had used C-14 on dozens of occasions, it seemed like this argument led nowhere. Hedges answered this argument effectively, I thought, when he acknowledged the statistical discontinuity but noted that whatever factor was involved, it would not change the results by hundreds of years. This issue was revisited in 2000 by Bryan Walsh and Larry Schwalbe, who argued that the inconsistencies indicated that the laboratories actually measured different C-14 concentrations in their subsamples. Whether the differences arose from contaminants or an admixture of cloth material is yet to be determined, but they argued that until the carbon-daters account for the source of the systematic difference (a fact which they neglected to mention in their formal publication of the results), the dating had to be viewed as incomplete. And more importantly, the assumption of global homogeneity of C-14 over the entire Shroud cloth was unjustified. When seen in this light, there is something to be said for the argument. But to most people, even scientists, it would appear to be clutching at straws.

7. Three Scenarios

Garza-Valdes, Mattingly and ... Gove again (!)

In The Early 1990s, A Doctor from San Antonio by the name of Leoncio Garza-Valdes was investigating an unusual lustrous patina or varnish on several valuable Mayan jade artifacts in his personal collection. He believed that microorganisms form biogenic varnishes which coat the surfaces of desert rocks, forming a kind of patina or luster on the surface, the so-called "desert varnish." On his Mayan jades he found a similar coating of bio-varnish, or "bio-plastic coating" as he termed it. Garza thought this coating had built up over a considerable time, from some as yet unidentified microbial agent or agents, somewhat in the manner of a coral reef, forming a hard, transparent and protective coating. The thought occurred to him that an old textile like the Shroud might have a similar coating, which would not have been noticed by the C-14 labs, and further that such a bio-plastic deposit could account for the very late date for the Shroud.

Acting on a strong impulse, but little in the way of advance planning, Garza decided in 1993 that "the best way to test my hypothesis was to go to Turin and try to study samples of the Shroud." He faxed off a letter to the new Archbishop, Cardinal Saldarini, and though there was no reply he and a Spanish priest that he had contacted "boldly made our preparations to travel to Turin." Apparently he was under the impression that it was possible to simply go to Turin and persuade someone to let you study actual specimens of the Shroud. Yet amazingly, this is exactly what happened!

In his book *The DNA Of God?*, Garza (1999) describes meeting with Gonella for several hours, noting that it did not go well at first, but towards the end Gonella seemed to soften and said he would speak with Saldarini and inform them of the result. Meanwhile, Gonella told Riggi about Garza's ideas, and Riggi then went to meet with Garza at his hotel. After a conversation lasting half the night, Riggi invited Garza and his priest friend to lunch at his house the next day. When they arrived, Riggi had taken out the trimmings from the Shroud C-14 sample and allowed Garza to examine them. Garza relates:

> I knew the critical moment would be when I could examine a linen thread under the microscope to check for the presence of the bioplastic coating. So when Riggi removed a thread from the trimmed edge, I was nervous as I put it under the microscope. My nervousness did not last long; immediately, I saw a bioplastic coating on the fibers. I quickly took a picture with the microscope camera and called to Father Cervantes and to Riggi, 'It's there! There's bioplastic coating on the sample!' Even an untrained viewer could see the fibers of the thread completely covered with bioplastic coating, as well as some fungi, clear interference in the radiocarbon dating. Each of us took turns looking at the fibers, and it struck us all that somehow this coating was a thing of beauty in itself. It was an incredible moment for all of us. ... Riggi was convinced from the moment he saw the coating.

Garza then, in his characteristic go-for-it manner, asked Riggi if he could take a few small threads back to San Antonio for further study. Again, quite amazingly, Riggi agreed and gave him the samples then and there. Riggi retained the three pieces of cloth that constituted the main trimmings from the C-14 sample. Garza prepared a paper on his observations and his theory that a bio-plastic coating had thrown the carbon dating off by 1300 years. In parallel to this research, he was also developing a hypothesis regarding the Shroud image, namely that it was caused by the relative thickness of the coating. In June of 1993, he presented his views in a paper given at a congress of CIELT, the French Shroud organization, held in Rome. It was not well received, especially his hypothesis that the bacteria were responsible for the divine image. Somehow, this just did not seem right!

Undaunted, Garza continued his work on the thread samples he had obtained from Riggi. He enlisted the assistance of Stephen Mattingly, professor of microbiology at the San Antonio branch of the University of Texas, and they were able to obtain a small grant from the National Science Foundation. Their analysis would seem on the face of it to have been very thorough. Garza examined the threads under scanning electron microscope and found the fibers were "completely covered by the bioplastic coating" as well as fungi. He also sent samples to Dr. Paul Bierman of the University of Washington facility who according to Garza found that certain areas were high in manganese, others had a high iron content, and some high in calcium. Garza interpreted this to mean that the bacterial residues had both mineral and organic elements. Fibers were also studied under the infrared microscope for spectroscopy, and "the organic component of the bioplastic coating was immediately obvious."

Garza was now more convinced than ever that what was dated in 1988 by the three radiocarbon labs was a combination of cellulose from the linen and bioplastic coating. And he seemed to have the experimental evidence to support this claim. He checked his hypothesis by putting the threads through the same pretreatment procedure that the radiocarbon labs had used; at the end the bio-plastic coating was still there, undiminished by the acid-alkali-acid washes.

The reaction of the C-14 labs was predictable: massive skepticism. Timothy Jull, one of the senior staff members at Arizona, was quoted in *Time* magazine as saying that "the only people who have ever seen these bacteria are Drs. Mattingly and Garza-Valdes. In my opinion, our sample of the shroud was very clean, and there was no evidence of any coating." He added that even if the hypothetical varnish existed, the amount necessary to throw off the dating by 1300 years would have been visible to the naked eye. The key words to notice here are "in my opinion." It would be demonstrated quite conclusively later that the Shroud C-14 sample did indeed have a coating, and it was clear that the labs did not conduct the kind of testing that would detect it.

Garza organized three seminars to discuss the developing "bio-plastic hypothesis" with Shroud and radiocarbon experts. Among the people that participated in the seminars were McCrone, Adler, Scavone, Gove, Donahue, Dinegar, Fred Brinkman of the Holy Shroud Guild and Riggi. Adler agreed that something was present, but he was cagey about calling it "bioplastic." McCrone did not accept Garza's interpretation, still holding out for his painting hypothesis, whereby the Shroud was painted with iron oxide in a gelatin binder. The big surprise was Gove's reaction. It was reported by Scavone in a newsletter of the British Society:

> Dr. Harry Gove attended and was, albeit reluctantly, quite impressed with the work being done in Texas. After some lively debate during the informally designed Round Table and, later that evening, the observation of Shroud threads under the microscope, Gove said on Saturday, September 2, that he had observed what Garza had been asserting: that actual cellulose accounts for only 40% of a Shroud thread, the bioplastic coating accounting for 60%. What the laboratories dated, therefore, will have been the recent

accretions of micro-organic life, and the hard coating they form, more so than pure Shroud linen.

When this was published, Gove backtracked and said he doubted that it was more than 10%, but Garza claims that Gove told him at the time that it seemed to be more than half. Garza commented: "When the Newsletter appeared, Gove was upset because he did not yet want his views published. He was in a difficult position, because it looked as though he was throwing dirt at the rest of the radiocarbon profession." And, one might add, he (Gove) was almost ready at that time to publish a book in which he threw tons of dirt at people like me who argued that contamination could be a major factor that was not being given due consideration.

Garza then pulled off another astonishing coup – he convinced Riggi to provide two of the three pieces of trimmings for a secret carbon dating after chemically removing the bioplastic coating. Riggi required a written protocol, which Garza duly provided, and the samples were brought to San Antonio by Riggi personally in 1994. What happened next was an example of rank amateurism, and the waste of Shroud material, although it must be said that the trimmings Riggi had were an even more unrepresentative and less reliable sample material than the main C-14 samples had been. They were marginal to the marginal. In the chemical treatments Garza and Mattingly had devised for removing the bioplastic and rendering the cellulose pure, a buffer was mistakenly used that contained old carbon. When the samples were dated at Arizona (with the samples' identity withheld from the lab personnel), the results were in the region of 3000 to 1500 B.C. They had been contaminated backward by dead carbon from the buffer. When the reasons for this foul-up were discovered, there was great annoyance all round: Garza with Mattingly for selecting a carbonaceous buffer, Riggi with Garza for wasting the precious samples, and the Arizona lab with Garza for running a Shroud sample without informing them. Reflecting on the episode, Garza tells the tale, putting their errors in an interesting perspective:

> The problem with the radiocarbon scientists, was that they were overconfident; they were sure they had the final answer. But I believe that in this life, sooner or later, each of us receives a lesson in humility, and this [the dating of the Shroud] is their lesson. Mine was in not checking the chemical composition of the Tris-borate [buffer] ... The scientists did not realize that their sample was not clean. They must sooner or later acknowledge that they made a big mistake and had an unsuspected contaminant. The longer they take

to recognize that the date they obtained in 1988 was from a contaminated sample, the worse it is going to be.

However, Garza was not finished yet. He made contact with Dr Rosalie David of the Manchester Museum, who had been puzzling over the dating of Egyptian Mummy 1770. The radiocarbon date on its the linen wrappings were some 1000 years later than the historically established age of the mummy itself. She had concluded that re-wrapping was most unlikely, and that there was probably a contamination of the linen that produced the late date. Garza invited her to one of his round table meetings in San Antonio, and she was brought along a sample of the linen from Mummy 1770. Garza put it under the microscope and was quick to find the culprit: "There it was, a beautiful bio-plastic coating present on the bandages that had been used to wrap the mummy." Others at the round table concurred. Together with Gove and Mattingly, she and Garza hatched a scheme to run a test on another mummy to determine if the bio-plastic coating was indeed throwing off the C-14 dating of linen mummy wrappings. They chose a mummified ibis, a bird sacred to the ancient Egyptians that was often used in rituals and buried as a sacrifice. Garza had one handy, as he had purchased it at auction a few weeks before. It was christened Danny the Mummy in honor (?) of Dan Scavone. It had never been unwrapped, but presumably x-rayed, since clay ibis models were sometimes used instead of the real bird.

The plan was simple: to date linen, bone and tissue samples, and compare the results. Garza had already examined a sample of the linen under the microscope and confirmed that it had a similar bio-plastic coating to that on the Shroud, but that the coating was thinner on the ibis wrapping. He predicted a discrepancy of at least 500 years. The results turned out almost as Garza predicted: the bone and tissue samples had a radiocarbon age of about 2490-2730 years, whereas the linen's age was 2150-2310 years. This experiment was published as a scientific paper authored by Gove, Mattingly, David and Garza (1997).

The experiment met with little acceptance by the radiocarbon community. The main point raised against it was that the ibis might have a diet of marine fish, which could introduce a degree of lag due to the well-known world-wide oceanic reservoir effect. David pointed out in response that the ibis were bred in captivity far from the sea, and that its C-13/C-12 ratio did not suggest a marine element. She also considered it most unlikely that the ibis mummy once sacrificed would have been re-wrapped later. Unfortunately, these were not certainties, and there were still other possible factors, notably the possible influence of agents used in the mummification process. And the ibis could have been re-cycled a few centuries after it was buried. The problem with the experiment was that it was poorly designed, and for this our friend Gove must bear the lion's share of the responsibility, firstly because he was the C-14 expert among the participants, and secondly because he was the senior author. There were too many variables, and it involved comparing apples with watermelons anyway. What should have been done, as is crystal clear from reading Garza's account, was a dating run on two or three samples of the mummy linen with normal pretreatment, and dating of another few samples of the same linen from which the bio-plastic coating had been removed. By this time, early 1997, Garza and Mattingly believed they had perfected a technique of chemically removing the bioplastic from the cellulose, leaving the bioplastic as a hollow tube, and of course they had learned the hard way to avoid the use of a carbonaceous buffer. The cellulose and bio-plastic could have been dated separately. This would have been a superb experiment, and it might have proved something. As it was, nothing was established at all, and we were left with a batch of possible interpretations.

Garza did not think so, however. He was totally convinced that he had discovered the key to the Shroud's incorrect C-14 date:

> Where do we go from here? Do we keep testing and testing? Gove has suggested testing samples from a mummified bull in the Smithsonian Museum in Washington. We could run the test on as many animals as possible, but the results will always be the same. I don't know why we keep looking and looking. We have already tested the Shroud, Mummy 1770, the Maya Itzamna Tun, and Danny the Mummy. Every case has produced that abnormal result. ... I am convinced that at the present time, the radiocarbon dating of ancient textiles is not a reliable test.

Garza was also concurrently pursuing other lines of research: he believed that the Shroud image was due to the thickness and texture of the bio-plastic coating, as mentioned above. He also found microscopic fragments of oak in a sticky tape sample that Riggi had taken in 1988 from the occipital region, suggesting to him that the cross bar of the cross that Christ carried was made of oak rather than pine as traditionally believed. Riggi's tape sample was taken from an area with a bloodstain. He had also given Garza a portion of this tape for study, with fibers containing minute traces of blood. Garza invited Drs. Victor and Nancy Tryon, DNA specialists at his San Antonio campus, to examine the samples. They reported the presence of human DNA, and were able to clone and replicate a few segments – hence the sensational title of Garza's book *The DNA Of*

God? When this claim about Christ's DNA having been identified was broadcast, it was the straw that broke the camel's back as far as the Turin Church was concerned.

Even earlier, in 1995 Cardinal Saldarini had issued a press release stating that no new sample material had been taken from the Holy Shroud since 21 April 1988, and that no residual material from that sample was in the hands of any third party, but:

> if such material exists, the Custodian [of the Shroud, i.e. Saldarini] reminds everybody that the Holy See has not given permission to anybody to keep it and do what he wants with it. The Custodian requests those concerned to give the piece back to the Holy See. ... there is no degree of certainty about whether the material in question on which these aforesaid experiments have been carried out actually comes from the fabric of the Shroud ...

This seemed clearly aimed at Garza's work, and also at Riggi and Gonella for having retained the material and given it to others to study. They in turn felt that they had retained the material under the authorization of the previous archbishop, Ballestrero, for legitimate research. This was a major snafu, and one that need not have come about. But worse was to come, and it would be the end of Garza's Shroud adventure.

He prepared a paper on his findings of the wood microfragments to be presented at an international Shroud conference in Turin in June, 1998. On the day he was to present his paper, "The Oak of Golgotha," the chairman Baima Bollone unexpectedly skipped over three speakers and called Garza to the podium. After he made his presentation, Baima asked Ghiberti to read an unscheduled paper. In it, Cardinal Saldarini declared Garza's research to be officially invalid. Later, Garza tried a dozen times to speak with Ghiberti on the phone, but his calls were never returned. Garza concluded: "I did not realize that, at the end of the twentieth century, some people still hope to nullify scientific findings with political declarations. But I am glad, at least, that the Inquisition is no longer in power."

This was the unpleasant end of Garza's involvement in Shroud studies. It also marked the rise to prominence of Ghiberti, a Turinese priest who would later play a major role in the disastrous "restoration." Reviewing the rejection of Garza's work not quite two years later, in a paper also presented at a Shroud conference in Turin, I wrote:

> What is of particular concern is why the Church has done nothing to assist the investigation. The treatment meted out to Garza-Valdes is especially baffling. Whatever may be the personalities, the rivalries,

the improprieties, etc., it is nonetheless true that this man made a major discovery that has very important implications for the C-14 date. If there was any doubt about the Shroud fibers he obtained, or the manner in which he obtained them, why was he not given the opportunity to work on formally certified fibers from the Shroud? Two or three tiny 5mm fibers from different points on the cloth, similar to those removed previously for Frache, Filogamo, Zina and Baima, would have been sufficient. Instead, detractors of the Shroud were given the basis to claim that the fibers Garza examined may not even have come from the relic. One can only wonder, yet again, at why Church officials seem to make matters worse for the Shroud!

Ghiberti and the new archbishop, Monsignor Poletto, were sitting in the front row as I delivered these remarks. Ghiberti could be seen to be annoyed, perhaps even furious. Poletto however seemed to be puzzled by what I was saying, and even seemed to nod slightly in agreement as the last sentence came through in translation. Alas, what he would do to make matters worse for the Shroud would far surpass anything I could ever have imagined, or indeed anything ever done before in the relic's history.

It is clear that Garza-Valdes did much to stimulate research, but unfortunately most of his ideas and hypotheses did not pan out. The bioplastic hypothesis was finally put to rest when I located a copy of Garza's report, apparently to the National Science Foundation on the grant he obtained. This report contained quite a number of good color photomicrographs of what Garza claimed was the coating; none of them could be verified as anything other than the normal characteristics of flax. In one the "bio-plastic coating" as identified in the caption had the typical nodes and joints of flax structure.

Kouznetsov: promise, then scam

In marked contrast to the sincerity evident in Garza-Valdes, the saga of Dimitry Kouznetsov raises questions of the most basic sort. Unknown like Garza to the Shroud community, he also gave a paper at the same 1993 CIELT conference in Rome where Garza presented his first paper. The Russian Kouznetsov had previously made contact with Italian Shroud enthusiast Mario Moroni, and with John Jackson of STURP. Moroni and Jackson had both been investigating how the fire of 1532 might have influenced the C-14 date. He had also corresponded with Marie-Claire Van Oosterwyck-Gastuche (a French critic of C-14 dating) and had found his way to a foundation set up by the Frenchman Guy Berthault, which provided a grant for his research. His paper at the CIELT conference, and a subsequent one published in a prominent scientific journal, were powerfully argued, and he seemed to have even better experimental evidence that Garza and Mattingly concerning how the Shroud's C-14 date was wrong. For the next four years Kouznetsov was the toast of the Shroud world, especially in Italy and the USA, with numerous lecture tours and consultation visits. Then everything began to unravel, and he wound up disgraced and deported.

I never met Kouznetsov, but in 1993 he sent me a copy of his paper given at the conference, and a handwritten letter with lots of doodles and funny-looking characters drawn in the margins. He seemed to have a good command of the physics and chemistry behind radiocarbon dating, and identified potential problems in the dating. He concluded that, after corrections for a variant original delta C13 and for isotope exchange caused by the fire, "the age of the Shroud of Turin could be **not less** than 1,900 BP [before present], i.e. not less that approx. A.D. 100. This struck me as rather far-fetched and unjustified, even though with my limited knowledge of the technical details he discussed, I could not see anything particularly wrong with his arguments. It seemed to me that he could well have the key to what went wrong with the Shroud dating, and that would of course be a huge step forward, regardless of the reliability of his "corrections." It was would be interesting to see how the radiocarbon establishment responded.

Apparently, no one bothered to look into his background or his credentials. His affiliation, and that of his co-author Andrey Ivanov, was given in his 1993 paper as Laboratory of Physico-Chemical Research Methods, Moscow State Center for Sanitation and Ecology Studies. In a paper published in 1994 the affiliation of the two had changed to the S.A. Sedov Biopolymer Research Laboratories. A potential problem, not noticed by me at the time, was that both these "laboratories" had the same address. A greater problem, which either escaped the attention of everyone, or was quietly hushed up if noticed, was that he had previously published several treatises supporting creationism. This should have sent up warning flags, not because creationists are dishonest, but because this field is known to have attracted quite a few "scientists" of dubious repute. One thing that I did notice about their 1995 paper was that an entire paragraph was a verbatim text of what I had written in my 1985 paper, and strangely it was followed by no less than six references, making it appear to be a summation of the views of these various authors. My name was not among them. Another instance of this was in the use of the quotation that I had dug up from Woelfli et al ("The C-14 method is not immune to grossly inaccurate dating when non-apparent problems exist in samples from the field ...") This was attributed as "quoted in Stevenson and Habermas, 1990" who had taken it from my press release. But these were minor quibbles and not worth mentioning when such great issues were being fought out.

In brief, the Russians' argument against the C-14 dating of the Shroud was two-fold:

1) A ratio of carbon-13 to carbon-12 was wrongly assumed to be a mean value for plants of -25 per mil. When one takes into account the processing that occurs when flax fibers are processed, organic matter such as fatty substances driven out, and the resultant fibrous material made into textile, a lower value (-19 per mil) should be taken as the "normalization standard." This would result in a C-14 date for the Shroud of ca. 790-860 A.D. instead of the 1260-1390 as published by the three labs.

2) Experimental data from a simulation of the 1532 fire indicated that "there is a high probability of a very significant enrichment (up to 40%) of linen by 14C, both old and modern, during an isotope exchange reaction." For this experiment, they constructed a closed chamber and created an atmosphere that might be expected inside the casket, with gases and other combustion products from the fire. They used first a modern linen sample and an archaeological linen sample dated to 760-840, and both showed enrichment of the carbon-14 content. Later from Moroni they obtained a piece of archaeological textile from Israel that was C-14 dated to 386-107 B.C. After running this sample in their fire-simulation chamber its C-14 date was 1044-1272 A.D. – obviously a huge shift and a serious challenge to the dating of the Shroud.

Their results were published (Kouznetsov et al 1996) in a prestigious scientific journal, *The Journal of Archaeological Science*, after a peer review process. The three labs that dated the Shroud were informed about the paper during the review, and Arizona prepared a response on behalf of all three, which was published in the same issue of the journal. Damon, Donahue and their colleague Timothy Jull stated that they were unable to reproduce the Russians' results, and launched an attack on the methods and equipment, always a good backup argument. Kouznetsov and colleagues had not done the appropriate controls, their equipment was "untested" and their attention to "standards" had been lacking. The Arizonans concluded that "even if the carbon displacements proposed during the heat treatments were correct, no significant change in the measured radiocarbon age of the linen would occur." And they further stated that "other aspects of the [fire simulation] experiment are unverifiable and irreproducible." Gove's comment was that this was "about as strong language as reputable scientists generally permit themselves to use when disputing what they regard as a fraudulent claim." He was no doubt right about their intent, but wrong as usual overall. The Arizona lab found itself sued for libel, and finally settled out of court, for making a much more direct suggestion of fraud regarding another scholar.

Kouznetsov replied in the newsletter of the British Shroud Society, suggesting that the Arizona lab had not faithfully replicated all the steps of his fire simulation model, and cast doubt on some of the scientific calculations the Arizonans had used. According to Ian Wilson (1998), Kouznetsov used some very complex physics formulae that had actually been worked out by Jackson (in a draft response to the Arizona rebuttal), without any acknowledgement to that effect. Unfortunately, one of the formulae contained an error that Jackson only discovered later. This led Jackson to ask Kouznetsov about the unattributed use of his work, but "not a word of apology or explanation was forthcoming. All communication simply very abruptly ceased." Wilson further remarks that this was most unbecoming behavior especially since Jackson had generously hosted some six US visits by Kouznetsov.

It did not end there. Wilson himself became involved in a "venture" with Kouznetsov:

> Meanwhile, yet more questionable behavior on Kouznetsov's part was beginning to come to light, some of this involving myself. After he and I met for the first time in Rome he requested a copy of my original 1978 book on the Shroud, which I duly sent him. Shortly after his receiving this he said he hoped he might be able to get it published in Russian, news which I warmly welcomed ...
>
> In September 1995 Kouznetsov phoned me to say that he had already obtained thousands of advance orders for the book, and that a translation was well in hand for publication in May 1996. All that he needed from me, and urgently, was a formal letter authorizing him to handle everything pertaining to the Russian-language copyright, a nicety which a bureaucratic printer in St Petersburg had demanded. As Russia was a 'very poor country' he asked if I would accept just a two per cent royalty and include a note to this effect in the letter.
>
> Shortly after my compliantly writing and faxing the requested letter all communication ceased, which initially raised no alarm bells, as contact had never been more than spasmodic and I knew him to be often away from Moscow, for several months at a time. But then in the March of 1996, I learned to my astonishment that he had been hawking my letter among various Americans, asking them to finance my book's Russian-language edition in return for

guaranteed large profits. Sums running into tens of thousands of dollars had apparently changed hands. My suspicions duly roused, I immediately tried contacting him to ask him to explain himself only, like John Jackson, to meet a wall of silence. The American financiers, at first incredulous of my concerns for them, initially received bland reassurances from Kouznetsov. But when no Russian translation appeared on the due date they met with the same silence, along with a complete absence of any returns from their 'investments'.

There were rumors of dozens of Baptist churches in Texas having contributed tens of thousands of dollars for another project that Kouznetsov had touted. By now a huge black cloud had developed over his name, and it burst in December 1997; he was arrested in Danbury, Connecticut on charges of attempting to pass stolen checks. He spent six months in custody, but was released and deported before the case came to trial. It was a very sad situation. It seems that at the beginning Kouznetsov did some genuine research. His colleague Ivanov (now with "Natalija Nesterova University, Moscow"), whom I met in Turin in 2000, stands by the work they did and the claims made in the papers. It may well be that Kouznetsov was corrupted by the attention and availability of funding in the west; it is perhaps more likely that he was a something of a con man from the beginning, flopping about on the margins of the scientific world enjoying the limelight and looking for easy money.

Marino and Benford: invisible patching

At a Shroud conference held at Orvieto, Italy in August, 2000, two American researchers put forward a totally different explanation for the C-14 date. Joe Marino and Sue Benford proposed that "the Shroud has literally been patched with medieval material from the 16th century, in the C-14 sample itself, [a fact that] explains the medieval carbon dating results." They cite the report from the textile laboratory in Derbyshire that Oxford sent a few "rogue fibers" for examination: the fibers were determined to be cotton of "a fine, dark yellow strand ... [that] may have been used for repairs at some time in the past." Marino and Benford noted that the weave pattern and thread size in the C-14 samples had variations that suggested a heavier, blended material than in the rest of the Shroud. Adler is cited arguing that there were chemical differences and that "the radiocarbon samples are not representative of the ... bulk of the cloth." The statistician Bryan Walsh is quoted: "there is an apparent gradient of radiocarbon measured on the Shroud sample with the higher levels of C-14 measured at increasing distance from the edge of the Shroud linen" and, in addition, that the C-14 dating results did not pass the Chi Square test, meaning that "the samples cannot be considered identical, or rather, from the same representative sample." The authors match Walsh's statistical gradient with the shift in weave pattern and fiber density, and find a correlation between "the medieval material spliced into the original weave, and what Walsh has portrayed statistically."

As an experiment, the authors submitted unlabelled enlargements of photographs of both the Zurich and the original uncut C-14 samples, to a European-trained weaver in Ohio. He immediately recognized the disparate weave pattern and differences in thread size, stating "there is no question that there is different material on each side ... It is definitely a patch." He said that medieval weavers would try to repair an unraveling by matching the original cloth and by stitching a small amount of new material into the old, such that it was invisible to all but the trained eye. Another expert in weaving that they consulted believed that each side of the Zurich sample was woven independently.

Although they marshaled some good evidence, their thesis was open to criticism on several counts. First, neither of the authors was a textile specialist, or a scientist, so they were stepping into a subject way beyond their knowledge. Second, there were two textile experts present at the sample taking, and neither of them reported any anomaly or reason to suspect that the sample was not the same as the rest of the cloth. Third, ancient weaving techniques could have produced the kind of shift in weave and fiber that they pointed out as evidence of the "patch." Fourth, and most importantly, did textile repairers in medieval times have the skill to produce such an invisible patch or re-weaving, with work so fine that it would not be noticed by two 20th century textile experts? This is a possibility that I discussed with the archaeological scientist Stuart Fleming in the 1980s, and he believed that it was indeed within the realm of possibility that a skilled medieval repairer could re-weave a damaged area so that it would not appear to the naked eye. However, it struck us as an extremely unlikely scenario. And further, it is doubtful that any restorers could have done a re-weaving that would not be immediately obvious to a textile expert with a magnifying glass.

Shortly after their paper was presented, I put these questions to Marino and Benford, and urged them to find at least one textile historian who could answer these questions in support of their thesis. My own view was that it was most unlikely. A few weeks later, they wrote back informing me of new developments. They had succeeded in finding not only a textile historian but one of the best in the world, who felt that they had a good case. Dr. Thomas Campbell, Associate Curator, European Sculpture and Decorative Arts, The Metropolitan Museum of Art, described the sixteenth century French weavers as "magicians" and said "it was very difficult to identify their repairs." Their case was considerably strengthened, but even more dramatic corroboration was to come, from a most unexpected quarter.

A revised version of their Orvieto paper was posted on Barrie Schwortz's website www.shroud.com with particularly fortunate timing. Barrie had just persuaded Ray Rogers, the most prominent scientist member of STURP who had quit the Shroud field after an altercation with John Jackson in 1982, to come out of "retirement" and review a new book (Antonacci 2000) which made some spectacular claims about the image. Rogers' first impression of the Marino-Benford hypothesis was that it was plainly wrong and would be easy to refute. And he had physical evidence to draw on, in the form of several threads from the Raes sample that Gonella had sent him in 1979. The radiocarbon sample was cut from immediately below the site of the Raes sample. Photographs show the details of this location. At the very least, some warp yarns continued from the Raes sample into the radiocarbon sample. Some weft yarns may also have appeared in both samples. If the sampling area were indeed a patched or reworked location, the characteristics of the Raes sample should have been shared to a variable extent with the radiocarbon sample. The Raes sample had a common border of about 4cm with the C-14 sample, although this border was entirely with the "reserve" piece not cut into segments and distributed to the labs. Nevertheless, if there was any sort of repair or re-weaving of a frayed edge, it would certainly continue the last few centimeters to the end of the cloth, as indeed Marino and Benford had postulated.

Rogers set about with total confidence in his ability to shoot down the notion of a re-weaving, and while he was at it the claim for a bio-plastic coating as well. Both seemed to contradict everything he had learned from the intensive investigation conducted by STURP, and the proof would be in the Raes threads. What Rogers found bowled him over. There was indeed a coating of some sort on these fibers, one that he had not seen before on the thousands of Shroud fibers on the sticky tape samples that he had examined under the microscope. Furthermore, the number of cotton fibers present was vastly higher than in other areas of the Shroud, and they appeared not to be superficial but embedded in the threads. His curiosity well and truly piqued, Rogers went on to do an extensive series of tests on the Raes threads. In a summary that he and I sent to Cardinal Poletto (the latest of many futile attempts to persuade the Turin Church authorities of the need for new C-14 dating), we described why the area of the Raes and radiocarbon samples was anomalous, with the following chemical and physical characteristics:

1) The Raes/C-14 area did not fluoresce, and therefore its chemical composition was different from the main cloth. This is seen clearly and beyond doubt in the fluorescence photographs taken by STURP in 1978. There is absolutely no question about this fact.

2) The yarn in that area was coated with a gum that contained both dyes and mordants (common technology through millennia for dyeing linen). It had been colored for some purpose. Most of the added color appears on the outer surface of the yarn in that area. Photomicrographs document this fact. None of the main part of the cloth had any of this gum-dye-mordant coating.

3) The linen had been bleached by a different technique than the main part of the cloth: it shows very little lignin at growth nodes.

4) The lignin in the anomalous area gives the microchemical test for vanillin, a component of lignin that decreases with time. The lignin in the main part of the Shroud does not give the test (nor does lignin from Dead Sea Scroll wrappings). It is reasonable to conclude that the anomalous area has a different age than the Shroud, and that it is younger than the main cloth.

5) As Raes observed, there is cotton in the yarn of the sample taken for him. It is easy to find inside the segments of yarn. The only cotton that is found on the main part of the cloth is a superficial impurity.

6) SEM analyses by Adler proved that fibers from the anomalous area have twice the concentration of aluminum as other areas. Aluminum is used as a mordant for the ancient Madder root dye that exists in the anomalous area. Microscopic views, documented with photomicrographs, prove the presence of Madder dye on hydrous aluminum oxide mordant.

7) Madder root dye is largely alizarin and purpurin. These can easily be detected in the anomalous area. No other area of the Shroud is coated with Madder root dye. Alizarin has been used for over a century as an acid-base indicator in chemistry: its properties are known in detail, and its presence in the area has been documented with photomicrographs.

8) The hydrous-aluminum-oxide mordant is instantly soluble in hydrochloric acid. The color of fibers from the anomalous area changes instantly when treated with the acid, and the colors obtained depend on the pH of the solution (as expected from the dyes).

9) The gum coating on the outside of the yarn is soluble in water. It can be observed under a microscope, and the soluble gum is redeposited when the water is allowed to evaporate. The gum is not a biogenic polymer (as Garza Valdes and Mattingly believed), and it does not give any test for proteins. The gum quickly hydrolyzes in acid, and it hydrolyzes somewhat more slowly in sodium hydroxide solution. It gives the color test with iodine that is common to plant gums like gum Arabic (bright yellow). There is nothing like that on the rest of the cloth. Such gums were items of commerce for millennia, it was not a natural impurity on linen, and it was used to stain/dye the yarn. Photomicrographs are available to document these observations.

10) Careful microscopic viewing of yarn segments from the Raes sample showed a unique, end-to-end splice (photomicrograph available). The main part of the cloth was woven using overlaps of yarn when one batch of yarn ran out and another was added to continue weaving.

Hugely compelling stuff, one would have thought. But alas, the prelates in charge of the Turin Shroud still did not get it.

*   *   *

With these three major scenarios for an incorrect dating of the Shroud circulating in the period 1995-2002 and receiving wide attention, there was a continuing hope that the Turin Curia would finally "see the light" and give approval for another round of testing. It did not happen, largely because of the focus on conservation set by Cardinal Saldarini, and continued in the most disastrous manner by Cardinal Poletto. Radiocarbon scientists were also not convinced of the need for another dating, but their motives may not have been purely for the advancement of knowledge. One respected US carbon-dater told me he thought it would be a "setback for carbon dating" if it was discovered that the widely publicized date on the Shroud turned out to be wrong. I responded that surely this discovery would be more important than any concern about the public's impression of C-14 dating reliability. Ian Wilson reports a telephone conversation with Gove in 1997 in which Garza's bio-plastic hypothesis was discussed, and he quotes Gove as saying that the main obstacle to greater acceptance of Garza's findings was "the face-saving concerns" on the part of the three labs which did the Shroud dating. There were thus two entrenched groups resisting any re-dating: the Turin Curia and the radiocarbon labs, for their respective irrational reasons.

8. Where Do We Stand with "the Date"?

The Truth Is, And The Great Shame Is, as of 2005 some seventeen years (!) after the dating was announced, we simply do not know. The scenarios reviewed above are all supported by some experimental data or observations, and certainly cannot be ruled out completely. However, it would not require very sophisticated testing to determine which if any of the three is the true culprit. For each scenario there would be a crucial factor or indicator that would rule it in or out. The easiest to test would be the idea of re-weaving or patching; another sample from anywhere in the main body of the cloth would corroborate or demolish this hypothesis. Regarding Garza's bioplastic, with current knowledge and technology, it would be a straightforward matter to isolate, identify and effectively eliminate any coating or other encrustation that was found on any newly removed sample. The most difficult of the three scenarios to test would be that of isotope exchange, but it is highly unlikely that any such exchange would be uniform across such a large cloth. If several samples from different sites close to and quite removed from the scorches showed consistency in radiocarbon content and delta C13, this would be good prima facie evidence that isotope exchange was not a factor.

It is clear today, just as it was in October 1988, that the date of 1260-1390 is not the "conclusive evidence" that it was claimed to be. In his last word on the subject, in a manuscript written just before his death in June 2000, Adler (2002) addressed the issue in these terms:

> ... a radiocarbon dating examination was authorized and carried out in 1988. As this examination assigned a 14th century date to the Shroud, it only exacerbated the polemics. Unfortunately, the protocol recommended by a convened panel of experts for the taking of proper cloth samples for the radiocarbon analysis was not followed. Only a single sample was taken and that was from a most

unsuitable location, i.e., from the edge of a bounded water stained scorch area where evident repairs had been made. Therefore while this dating study can claim good precision for its reported date, it cannot assign any accuracy to the Shroud's historical date as it is not clearly established that the location sampled is typical of the rest of the cloth. In order to check this point, fibers from the radiocarbon samples show a distinctly different spectrum and therefore it can be inferred that their composition is not typical of the rest of the cloth. Why this is so is not entirely clear, but it does establish the fact that the accuracy of the radiocarbon date can be questioned on the basis of direct experimental evidence. Many theories and explanations have been advanced to attempt to resolve the dating inconsistencies but the matter can really only be resolved by further experimental investigation of cloth samples from the Shroud itself.

At present (November 2005) it certainly appears that re-weaving is the scenario best supported by the data. As summarized above, there are numerous anomalies between the Raes/C-14 area and the rest of the cloth that strongly suggest repair of some kind. There are also the continuities in the weave that would seem to argue against it, in addition of course to the fact that the area in question was inspected by two textile experts prior to the C-14 sample being taken.

It has also been said that there is no record of any repair to that area. This is not entirely correct. One of the people known to have made some repairs to the cloth was the Venerable Sebastiano Valfre (1650-1718). A 19th century book on the life of Valfre (Kerr 1896), gives this description:

> Sebastian had a great devotion to the Shroud of Turin and would visit it every Friday if at all possible. When the relic of Christ's Passion was moved to the Guarini Chapel in the Cathedral of Turin in 1694, Victor Amadeus asked Sebastian to sew on a backing cloth and to mend it in several places. This gave Sebastian many hours with the Shroud during which he gave free rein to his devotion. [It was said that] Blessed Sebastian knelt for hours as he did his work, speechless, and with the tears flowing down his cheeks.

During these "many hours," could he have effected a perfect repair to the corner where the C-14 sample came from? An Italian work on Valfre (Lanza 1898) gives this fascinating detail: "... near the edges of the cloth certain areas were unraveling ... Valfre repaired the unravellings between the border and the cloth of the Shroud." The Italian text (*fra l'orlo e la tela della ss. sindone*) has exactly the same meaning and is equally obscure as the English translation, but this phrase together with the use of "near the edges" is strongly suggestive of the seam that separates the side strip from the main cloth. Clearly, there could well have been some unraveling in the Raes/C-14 corner, and some repair involving gums or resins, but reweaving that could not be detected?

Despite the reputed skills of late medieval French reweavers, what I find very difficult to conceive is that any early restorer could have made a repair by weaving new fibers into the cloth with such perfection that it could not be detected by the eye of a trained 20th century textile expert assisted by a magnifying glass. Vial and Testore declared, "We carefully inspected the Shroud and we are sure that this sampling piece was representing the whole Shroud." Vial further noted as cited in Benford and Marino (2002) that he "examined carefully the cloth all along the warp and filling of the threads concerned, without noticing any splicing." Thus far a search for examples of other similarly undetectable repaired medieval textiles has not born fruit. Of course, if there really were invisible reweavings, then they would be, well, invisible.

Rogers did find what looks like a splice on one of the Raes threads, and it could have been missed by Vial and Testore, as it is not visible in enlarged photographs of the Raes sample. But if there were dozens of splices they surely would have been noticed, since all of them could not have been so perfectly executed. And this feature may not be a deliberate splice so much as an accidental mélange during spinning. Perhaps it is a mistake to put much confidence in the examination by Vial and Testore, with their eyepiece magnifiers, but I find it hard to reject their testimony outright. It may well be that on this point (and not much else) Flury-Lemberg is right: ancient spinning and weaving involved all kinds of irregularities, changes in pattern and thread characteristics. Rogers on the other hand is totally convinced that the Raes/C-14 area was made from a different linen than the main part of the Shroud, and that its date of manufacture does not correspond to the manufacture of the main Shroud cloth. It is not comfortable being opposite Ray Rogers on an issue that he knows so thoroughly. I certainly keep on open mind on the subject however, and would happily eat this page if I am wrong. As pointed out above, and literally hundreds of times to Gonella and the various Turin authorities, the reweave hypothesis is dead simple to confirm, or rebut. All that is needed in a tiny amount of cloth (less than the size of one's little finger nail) from somewhere else on the Shroud.

If new fiber material (and younger carbon) was not introduced by a reweave, then whatever gum, resin or other substance used to treat and protect a repair and/or to prevent further unraveling would then become a potential contaminant. This could be similar to Garza's bio-coating, but

Rogers found that the gum coating on the Raes threads dissolved in water, and thus would not have survived the C-14 pretreatment. Garza however reported that the coating on Riggi's threads resisted the acid-alkali-acid pretreatment. He also reported being able to completely dissolve all the cellulose of the linen leaving only the empty tube of the bio-plastic coating. Rogers positively blasts this claim to smithereens:

> Garza-Valdes ... claimed to have dissolved the linen fiber from inside the 'bioplastic-polymer' coating on a Shroud fiber with strong sodium hydroxide (NaOH). That was utter nonsense.
> In the first place only about 10% of cellulose is soluble in strong base (try it and see). He could not have dissolved the linen fiber without dissolving all of the less-stable biopolymers. The important fact is that any 'bioplastic polymers' would dissolve and/or hydrolyze much more rapidly than would the cellulose. They are largely made of pentose-sugar units (like the coating on the Raes/radiocarbon samples). This is a danger of failing to use controls in an experiment. He should have tried some authentic biopolymers and reported the results.
> I used the same concentration of NaOH to make my 'tube' as Garza-Valdes used. Cellulose swells in base: the fibers get larger. They also change crystal structure. The process is well known, and it is called 'mercerization.' The center of the linen fiber tends to have a hole down through it, the medulla. When the fiber swells, the hole gets large and the walls of the fiber appear to get thinner. You end up with a 'tube.' It is a simple, known process. Garza-Valdes has confused the public, making it ever harder to get Shroud science back to reality.

Rogers also makes a very convincing argument against the claim of a significant bio-plastic coating deriving from microbial agency. All organisms that fix atmospheric carbon dioxide in large amounts use some pigment (like chlorophyll), water, and light. The main carbon-fixing algae and bacteria are all colored, yet no pigments were found in/on the Shroud cellulose. His analysis of the coating found a chemical composition that does not correspond to what would be expected from bacteria. STURP testing of non-image non-bloodstain Shroud fibers by microchemistry, pyrolysis-mass-spectrometry, and laser-microprobe Raman spectroscopy did not reveal any components present other than those expected of flax, i.e. there were no amino acids, sulfoproteins, porphyrins or other substances that might be indicative of a biopolymer deposit. There were no anomalous indexes of refraction, and no amorphous materials cementing fibers (except for the recently discovered pentosan gum coating on the Raes/C-14 area threads). And recent Fourier Transform Infrared Spectroscopy done by DeBlase (2000) on fibers from the "reserve" piece cut for radiocarbon dating, also revealed no indication of substances that might be associated CO_2 with a significant microbial deposit. Finally, the coup de grace for the bio-plastic hypothesis is that the kind of bacteria that can bring in carbon from in the air do so by photosynthesis. In order for that to happen, they need light, and usually moisture. For most of its existence the storage conditions for the Shroud have been dark and dry.

In response to Rogers' critique, Mattingly has argued that the bioplastic deposit begins to break down as it ages, and its end products resemble cellulose. He believes that this material of bacterial origin ultimately could blend with the cellulose of the linen so well that it cannot be detected by testing, or separated chemically. In an email to me he wrote that:

> Bacterial cell wall peptidoglycan, as well as fungal cell wall chitin, resemble cellulose in that both are built on beta-1,4 glucose polymers. They are acetylated and in the case of peptidoglycan, have attached amino acids. I can envision that time and the second law of thermodynamics may have knocked off the acetyl groups and amino acids and we are left with bacterial and fungal cellulose laid down on linen cellulose. You won't be able to tell them apart. However, enzymatic treatments with lysozyme and chitinase may remove those remaining polymers that the enzymes still recognize.

Rogers and other chemists do not believe that such deposits would amount to anything more than a very tiny proportion of the mass of each fiber, and that they probably could still be identified and removed physically. But the question remains open whether this kind of microbiological residue could contaminate and skew a radiocarbon date.

Regarding the third scenario, the idea of heat-induced isotope exchange or other C-14 enrichment suffered a major blow with the disgrace of Kouznetsov. Of course his actions in the arena of con artistry have no direct bearing on the scientific merits of the hypothesis, but they do cast a shadow. Rogers has specialized in pyrolysis chemistry, and denies that such a carbon exchange is possible, though Adler believed it was, in the fire or even at ordinary temperatures over a long period of time. The possibility continues to be investigated by Jackson and his colleagues, and by Moroni. Both have achieved small apparent shifts of 100-200 years in experimental heating of old linen samples, but the results are far from the 1300 years required if carbon exchange is the true cause of an incorrect dating for the Shroud. They have focused mainly on exchange between

CO_2 in the air and cellulose, rather than between substances that might have been on the linen as contaminants, although Moroni also observed an unexplained backward shift in the radiocarbon age by boiling an old textile fragment in olive oil.

Bryan Walsh (2000) makes a very good case that the variation in the results obtained by the three labs may reflect a "thermal gradient" due to enrichment by the 1532 fire. His statistical analysis indicated a non-homogeneity in the published results, a factor downplayed and not explained in the published report. Taken at face value, the statistical variation indicates that the three samples were not consistent regarding their C-14 content. However, when the position of each sample is considered, Walsh believes:

> it is possible that the location of the sample was directly related to the radiocarbon measurement observed. This finding is supportive of the hypothesis that the exposure of the Shroud of Turin to a thermal event in 1532 enhanced the number of 14C atoms in the linen, possibly by thermally induced isotopic fractionation, or by other processes that have yet to be identified. It may be that the three labs ... actually measured the effects of this enhancement phenomenon.

And so the debate continues. In most other areas of research, new data from fresh samples would have been obtained long ago. But, as we have discussed already, the Church, alas, has failed to authorize any new tests. To paraphrase Galileo: *eppur non si muove* (but still, it doesn't move). Perhaps one of the reasons why this backward, anti-science position has become entrenched in the Turin Curia is the view expressed by Piero Savarino, the current scientific adviser to the Archbishop, that no new C-14 dating should be considered until it is established what went wrong with the previous one. This is not the way science usually works, and it is certainly not the way archaeological dating is done; one might never know what factor caused an aberrant date. The correct approach would be first to find out if the radiocarbon content is uniform over the cloth, by measuring three or four more samples from different sites. Savarino unfortunately follows in the footsteps of Gonella, prone to make uninformed judgments far from his area of expertise, instead of taking advice from those who are experienced in the field.

It was very disturbing to hear this same view being espoused by two prominent Shroud scholars at the Turin conference at Villa Gualino in 2000. Remarks such as "it is premature to conduct new C-14 dating" or "there is much research that needs to be done before any further dating is contemplated" were made by Ian Wilson and John Jackson, respectively. I had a lengthy argument with Jackson over this; he felt that the mechanism of isotope exchange or C-14 enrichment needed to be identified before any new dating was done on Shroud samples. He seemed strangely uninterested in obtaining the basic data regarding what the actual radiocarbon content of the rest of the cloth is. Rather, he seems more intent on being the first to crack the code than learning what the message says. Ian Wilson seems to be parroting the view of Savarino and the Turin Centro. As recently as 2004 he was still claiming that it is far from clear in what way the previous dating of the Shroud had erred, and that any new dating would basically be a shot in the dark. This he thought could further damage the Shroud's credibility in the eyes of the public, while the true age of the Shroud remained obscured.

These sorts of objections are little more than foot-dragging, and there is a variety of possible motivations. Some may simply dovetail their views to agree with Turin. Others may harbor the desire to keep the situation as it is, with an element of doubt about whether the carbon dating is correct; the Shroud can thus remain, at least in the minds of a few, a possible relic of Christ. Still others wish to delay any new round of C-14 dating as long as possible, while conducting a kind of alchemist quest for the solution. It is incredible that this foot-dragging has gone on for so long, that Turin has done nothing in the nearly two decades that have passed since the date was announced, and continues to procrastinate at present. The possible problems and issues posed by the carbon dating results of 1988 have been more than adequately addressed, and it is crystal clear how the issue can be advanced by further measurements.

The main issues are well defined. It is undeniable that the 1532 fire might have caused a shift in the C-14 content of the Shroud, but no one will ever be able to duplicate exactly the conditions inside the casket during the fire. And I doubt that anyone will ever be able to prove that the Shroud's C-14 content was augmented by the fire. All the experimenting in the world will only result in a hypothesis to be tested, against new carbon dating of Shroud samples. Further C-14 measurements along the lines proposed above would enable us to establish whether the radiocarbon age of the entire cloth is or is not consistent, and if variable whether such variations can be seen in charred-to-scorched-to-unscorched segments. It is clear where the samples need to be taken from in order to reach this goal. Establishing these facts would be of great significance in assessing the extent to which the C-14 age of the cloth might have been altered by the fire.

Furthermore, in spite of the very large body of evidence and strong arguments against it, the issue of microbiological residue or other contamination raised by Garza-Valdes and supported by Mattingly is not entirely disproved, and it cannot ever be resolved by continuing to examine samples that happen now to be in someone's hands. However, it will not be difficult to determine the existence or extent of the problem with new samples taken from the Shroud. This matter would have been encountered and probably resolved in 1988 if only a proper screening program had been carried out by the labs. In 2003, Frank DeBlase, a specialist in spectroscopy, said he thought the best physical test for a bioplastic coating would be Raman microprobe. In my 1985 paper, I wrote:

> The main contamination possibility is that of carbon from organic materials ... [from] mold, mildew or fungal growths ... bacterial or insect residues ... All samples should be subjected to elaborate pretreatment, SEM screening and testing (microchemical, mass spectrometry, micro-Raman) ...

The first step in a new round of C-14 testing of the Shroud must be to deal exhaustively and conclusively with the issue of possible contamination. If three samples are taken for C-14 dating, three 5mm snippets of threads from these samples should first be sent for examination and testing by three chosen institutions. Such an examination would undoubtedly be sufficient to settle this issue once and for all. If there is indeed a substantial bioplastic coating, or other foreign substance, then existing methods can be perfected either to extract the cellulose or to remove the contaminant. All of this could be achieved within a few weeks, and new dating results could be in hand soon after.

At the Turin meeting in 2000, the radiocarbon scientists Jacques Evin and Robert Otlet made a proposal for further testing in order, as they rather prejudicially put it, "to obtain additional confidence in the radiocarbon dating results for the Shroud." First, they said that chemical and physical tests should be done "to investigate possible spurious C-14 from whatever cause occurring in the linen of the Shroud (with confirmation that pretreatment could remove it)." These tests "should be carried out on the remnant of that cut for the radiocarbon samples," that is, the "reserve" piece. And in their view, only after these tests were completed and the results agreed by peer group review, should further radiocarbon measurements be made.

There are several basic problems with this approach, notably the fact that the so-called "reserve" has been separated from the Shroud for so many years, that it has been in various hands and storage conditions, and cannot be said any longer to represent even the samples that were dated. If exhaustive tests were done and no contamination was found, would this prove that the C-14 samples from the other end of the strip were not contaminated? No. And of course this piece comes from the non-representative area that has caused so much controversy, and may have been subjected to repair in medieval times. Finally, its chain of evidence is broken, and Vercelli (2000) has done a service by reminding us how easy it is to produce a linen that very closely resembles the Shroud. This is not to say that any stock whatsoever should be put in the conspiracy theories that have been floated, which are patent nonsense. But chain of evidence is important, to insure and be seen to insure that no tampering could have taken place. This is a point on which radiocarbon scientists seem to run afoul, as we have seen: the Gove/Harbottle proposal of 1979 (at first supported by STURP) called for the Raes piece to be used. An attempt was made to obtain it surreptitiously from Prof. Raes, who had the sample "kept in what looked like an old scrapbook for postage stamps." Eventually Gove and Harbottle accepted that credibility and chain of evidence required a fresh sample to be taken from the Shroud.

Evin and Otlet went on to suggest the following C-14 measurements be done:

    1. on the fragment already cut
    2. on a sample of scorched material taken from under one of the patches
    3. on a sample of the thread used to sew together the lateral bank and the main shroud piece.
    4. on a newly cut sample from another corner

After the conference, I wrote to the Turin Archbishop and Centro to register my strong support in principle for these proposals. While the details obviously need close scrutiny and in my view some amendments, it is clear that this is the right direction and the right attitude.

My first reaction was to reject number 1 on the basis of the chain of evidence and non-representativeness considerations discussed above. At the stage where we are today, it is useless to do a repeat measurement on this sample. A sample of scorched material is an obvious choice, and one that I argued vehemently **against** during the Turin conference of 1986 if there was to be only one sampling site. As a second sampling site the charred material makes perfect sense, as there is a relatively large amount, although most of it was reduced to fluff by the disastrous "restoration" of 2002. The carbon fluff could also be used as a sample, and a very small segment could be cut immediately adjacent to where the charred was scraped from, in order to obtain a gradient of charred-scorched-unscorched that might shed light on any disparity in C-14 content that might be due to the fire.

Number 3 of Evin and Otlet is an odd choice, and unnecessary if the objective is to determine the radiocarbon age of the cloth. It is an interesting side question, but should be left to future investigations. I would suggest in its place a weft thread teased out from the middle of the cloth, between the front and back head images. This thread would probably need to be 5 to 6 cm long to satisfy the minimum AMS sample size. Removal of such a thread would not leave any visible mark on the cloth.

A newly cut sample from another part of the cloth is also highly desirable, but emphatically **not** from another corner, to avoid places that have been subject to the greatest handling. Better to cut a small segment from one of the odd-shaped holes in the middle of the cloth to remove some projection or small tongue of material which detracts from the visual impact of the relic as a whole.

The carbonized edges and deeply scorched material around the burnholes that were under the patches have already been removed in the disastrous "restoration." The other samples can be removed with such an insignificant impact on the appearance and integrity of the Shroud as a relic and artifact that it is hard to imagine any objection on those grounds. The amount of material given up for testing would be tiny; the value of knowledge gained could be enormous.

Conclusion

It was extremely painful to see the demise of the Shroud on account of such poorly planned C-14 dating. And it has been torment added to the pain to see the Turin authorities do nothing to support investigation of the dated sample, not to mention allowing new carbon dating to be done.

It is undeniable that the time has come, nay is long overdue, for a complete and proper C-14 dating of the cloth. If the Shroud is to be universally relegated to the status of a medieval oddity or forgery, at least let it be on the basis of solid and unassailable measurements of the C-14 content of the entire cloth, based on samples from several sites chosen specifically to address the issues and scenarios that have been raised.

One must acknowledge that, at the end of the day, when all the measurements have been done, it is possible the C-14 age of the cloth will be confirmed as generally what the first measurement indicated. This would still not be proof in any ineluctable sense that the Shroud was medieval in age, as it is only an assumption not capable of proof that the carbon content of the linen today is the same as it was when the flax was harvested. But it would obviously be very strong evidence pointing to a medieval date for the Shroud. There is equally strong evidence pointing toward antiquity. The choice would therefore be stark; neither choice fits the data. The Shroud would be left as an enigma without explanation.

On the other hand, if any of the three scenarios are shown to have influenced the C-14 date of 1988, and if a new carbon dating were to indicate an age older than say the 10th century, then a dramatic new era in the saga of this intriguing cloth will have begun. If the date turns out to be first century, it would be powerful evidence that the Shroud really was the burial cloth of Christ. The impact on the public would be enormous. It is very difficult to understand why the Turin authorities continue to refuse a new dating; clearly there is no **legitimate** reason for this.

There were new, even more compelling circumstances for another round of carbon dating, arising out of the "restoration" of 2002. The struggle to obtain another C-14 measurement on the Shroud continues to the present (see Part IV). It is inextricably bound up with the new archbishop of Turin, Cardinal Poletto, the new personalities and new order of things in Turin, and the disaster of the "restoration." That sad tale must be told before we can come up to the present in the ongoing saga of the drive to reach a definitive carbon dating.

Part III – The Desecration

9. Road to Disaster

In His Acknowledgements Of The Proceedings of the Richmond Shroud studies conference in 1999, Bryan Walsh rightly paid tribute to "all those who, through the centuries, have protected and cared for the world's most unusual artifact." The story of how the relic has been "conserved" in the last two decades is by contrast a particularly sad one. Like the C-14 dating fiasco, it is marked by ignorance, incompetence, stubbornness and opportunism, but its results are far worse. The damage done is permanent, and the data lost is irretrievable.

The first conservation folly – thymol

Known only to a handful of people in Turin, a very strange and dangerous "conservation" effort was carried out immediately after the removal of the C-14 sample in 1988. According to Riggi, the Turin Polytechnic lecturer invited by Gonella to cut the C-14 sample: "The presence of humidity, dust, fungi, etc., was combatted during the 21 April 1988 session by a highly complicated and ingenious application of thymol to the reliquary." The reliquary was a silver casket with a wood lining; several satin and padded cloth "accessories" were also treated with thymol. This operation was of such staggering stupidity that the mind boggles. It was a precursor of what was to come in 2002.

From a study of his previous vacuuming samples, Riggi had developed the idea that the reliquary might be infested with tiny insects the size of dust mites, invisible to the eye. He wrote:

> In view of the existence of this doubt [about the presence of live microfauna inside the reliquary], a part of the work program was to

examine the fabric of the Shroud to ascertain the presence of living acarian mites and to tackle the problem with a weak anti-parasitic in order to eliminate them. In examining various chemical substances to use, my attention fell on thymol, a substance particularly useful in fumigating libraries and paper storage facilities owing to the fact that this product posed no danger to cellulose or to inks ... After reconsidering the issue, it was decided only to fumigate the reliquary and the accessories while the Shroud was outside. This was done by sealing several grams of thymol with the reliquary inside a polyethylene sack for ten hours, then allowing about three hours for it to be aired before the Shroud was returned.

Franco Testore was the other participant in this operation. He wrote that "the airing lasted for two hours so that all trace of thymol would be eliminated, as it evaporates very rapidly in the air. Thus the Shroud was not at any risk, and the objects in direct contact with it were fumigated."

One can only wonder in amazement that such an operation could take place. It seems that Gonella, Riggi and Testore had determined to their satisfaction, but with no outside consultation, that no risks were involved if the Shroud was not directly exposed to the thymol. According to Riggi, it was the unknown represented by the image that inhibited their use of thymol on the relic itself (and one can only thank God for that!): "Since the image forming process is still unknown and there was no way to predict the consequences of an interaction between the image and the thymol vapor, we decided not to introduce the thymol into the reliquary with the Shroud present."

Testore however wrote of the possibility of a reaction with the cellulose of the linen:

> The problem of the fumigation of the relic was considered, and after a series of inquiries and consultations on the basis of a vast specialist bibliography, it was concluded that the best product was ... thymol. This substance, which passes directly by sublimation from the solid state to the aerian, has however the serious inconvenience of combining with cellulose (important component of linen) and in large amounts can turn the fibers yellowish thus reducing the contrast between the image and the background.

Unfortunately, they had not investigated in depth the possible after-effects of this fumigation procedure. Ray Rogers was horrified to learn of it, years after it had taken place. He knew all about thymol, which is also called "thyme camphor." It is obtained by steam distillation of different species of plants of the genus *Thymus* or *Ajowan*. He wrote:

> As a 'phenol' thymol is a very polar compound, and it adsorbs strongly to any surface. While the thymol bags were in the reliquary, there was an adsorbed concentration on the surface. Wood and cloth both have a huge surface area, and lots will adsorb. When thymol is immobilized by adsorption, you do not smell it commensurate with the amount present. But adsorption is only the first step.
>
> When a gas is strongly adsorbed like thymol, the surface is practically completely covered with a film of thymol at all times. Rates between thymol and any reactant (e.g. wood) will be high, because the thymol is a continuous, adsorbed film. The molecules are hub to hub. Considerable thymol will be expected to react with the wood. The thymol that reacts with the wood will require time and energy to be removed. You won't smell it, because it is in new solid compounds. But there can be lots there, and they can do damage later.
>
> Phenols are compounds that have a -OH group attached to a benzene-type ring. The aromatic ring makes them more strongly acid than the alcohols. Most phenols give intense colors with iron compounds, and the Shroud contains a significant amount of iron throughout the entire cloth. Similar reactions are used to detect microscopic amounts of iron. One reason thymol is effective as an antiseptic is that it reacts with amino groups ($-NH_2$). It can be expected to react with the proteins of the blood on the Shroud. Among other things, it will denature the blood, making any genetic tests or blood-typing impossible.
>
> Given enough time, phenols will form ethers with other -OH groups. Where are there lots and lots of -OH groups? On linen (cellulose): it is made of sugar units. These ethers are very stable (that's why they form, even under unfavorable conditions), and you cannot reverse their formation without destroying the cellulose. Phenols also form esters with organic acids. There may be acid groups on the image (Adler claimed to have found some). They would react with thymol.
>
> There are lots of specific reactions of individual phenols. The bottom line is that **Thymol will react with the Shroud**. Nobody can guarantee that foreign carbon has **not** been grafted to the chemical structure of the Shroud. Its incorporation into the Shroud

would reduce the apparent C-14 age of the cloth, and it could not be removed by any safe method.

The use of thymol shows a complete irresponsible ignorance of chemistry. Many superbly qualified chemists live in Europe and the United States, and some of them have had years of experience with the Shroud. They care about the Shroud. Why were none asked about the long-term effects of thymol on cellulose (linen)? On iron compounds? On proteins?

Even though only traces of thymol might have remained in the reliquary and the accessory cloths after they were aired and the Shroud returned to contact with them, some damage such as described above may have taken place. A scientist member of STURP said about the fumigation exercise: "a hurried, stupid, thoughtless, secretive action ... a disaster." Another such action, of monumental proportions, was in the making, basically for the same reasons and lapses.

Paving the road to hell

In the years that followed the announcement of the C-14 dating, in addition to the debate over the date and the drastic decline in interest in the Shroud, research in other areas continued quietly. Conferences were held on average once a year, and very few Shroud researchers actually withdrew because of the medieval dating. A much more important reason for the loss of researcher enthusiasm was the continuing lack of access to the cloth for study. STURP gradually unraveled as the prospect of future testing grew more and more remote; by 1990 it existed in name only. STURP had been shoved aside in the brouhaha over the C-14 results. Gonella lost some or most of his influence after the dating was announced, or perhaps he did not push very hard for the second-round testing proposals. STURP was formally dissolved in 1993. My own interest was frustrated by the on-going refusal of the Church authorities to allow a properly constituted C-14 dating. Ballestrero's retirement in 1990 and the appointment of Monsignor Giovanni Saldarini as the new archbishop of Turin signaled a new era. Saldarini quickly let it be known that he was in no hurry to do anything regarding the Shroud, that there would be no scientific testing in the immediate future, and that conservation would be the priority.

In 1992, a conservation committee was formed, consisting of five textile experts: Jan Cardamone of the US, Sheila Landi from England,

ROAD TO DISASTER

Mechthild Flury-Lemberg of Switzerland, Silvio Diana and Gian Luigi Nicola of Italy. A report in *La Voce del Popolo* on Sunday 13 September, 1992 with the headline "The Shroud is to be Conserved" described the first meeting:

> A summary of conclusions of the meeting will be delivered to the Holy See and to the Guardian of the Shroud. Meanwhile the same group proposes to keep in touch and to work together in the next few years ... The significance of the event lies not so much in the exposition in itself as in the new direction that is now being given to studies on the Shroud. The question of the conservation of the Shroud in the best conditions possible has not been given priority. Until now very little has been done as far as the study of its conservation is concerned. It is however necessary to set in motion a complete cycle of studies on the fabric and on the best conditions possible for its conservation, for example, as far as temperature, humidity, chemical composition of the air, etc. are concerned. The private exposition last Monday was a 'study seminar' in which the experts who had been called could meet and exchange their opinions. They have set in motion a program of work that is destined to proceed in the next few months as well.

Cardamone describes the meeting as very positive, with the main objective to discover any risk of damage and to suggest what should be done to avoid this risk. There were round-table discussions with Cardinal Saldarini to lay out some ideas and then, as requested, after due consideration, the group drew up proposals for "the most suitable way to guarantee the Shroud's conservation in the future. During the exposition, the Shroud was never touched, nor was any fragment removed, nor were any instruments applied." The conservators observed that the Shroud was stored rolled up on a large spool, and had to be unrolled for viewing or display and re-rolled for storage. This sometimes resulted in new wrinkles appearing. For example, after the C-14 sample removal on April 21, 1988, two layers of cloth may have shifted when rolled back on the spool, resulting in three new wrinkles forming on the Shroud fabric. Cardamone wrote:

> The easing of these new wrinkles was an important topic in our discussions. I recommended that if the Shroud were to lie flat and remain undisturbed, there would be no need for a backing cloth. Specifically, I advised the following in my proposal: 'releasing the stitches which affix all other fabrics to the Shroud fabric would

release tension and prevent the formation of new wrinkles. Existing wrinkles could relax and become less pronounced. Because of the historical significance of the adjoining fabrics, they could be kept in place without the stitches that join them to the Shroud. The patches should remain as they are, stitched to the Shroud because they are in isolated, discrete areas which do not exert overall tension and because of their great historical significance.' It is generally agreed however, that older wrinkles have historical significance.

Although the formation and initial functioning of this conservation committee seemed perfectly reasonable and laudable at the time, the seeds of the 2002 tragedy were already being planted. Don Ghiberti (who was assuming prominence in the archdiocese for Shroud matters) relates that Cardinal Saldarini had been instructed to steer clear of the heated polemics surrounding the carbon dating and other analyses, and to focus on the question of conservation. Ghiberti apparently attended the initial meetings of the group of conservators, and writes:

> We were all new to this approach and greatly influenced by a past that hung like a millstone. Strict secrecy in all our doings had to be maintained from the beginning. [Among the conservation issues] Removal of the patches – seemingly a utopian idea – was also brought up ...

This is a very odd account. What exactly was the past "that hung like a millstone?" If he was referring to the "strict secrecy in all our dealings [that] had to be maintained from the beginning" mentioned in the next sentence, then instead of casting this millstone off he later embraced it with great gusto. But if his notion was that somehow the millstone of the past was the conservatism regarding any change in the way the Shroud was kept, that this had to be thrown off, and the process needed to be shrouded (!) in strictest secrecy, then these are extremely significant initial symptoms of the horrendous malady that would later afflict the conservation effort. The mindset was already in place, apparently, in 1991, to operate in secrecy. It is difficult to fathom why this was thought to be necessary when open discussion would have benefited immensely from the input of other experts, and there was no particularly sensitive topic involved at first. However, if one is contemplating something so radical that there will be a great public outcry, then secrecy is required until the deed is done. This is of course exactly what happened in 2002.

Ghiberti also described the removal of the patches as "a seemingly utopian idea." This is a totally bizarre notion – where on earth did this attitude come from? It is clear that it did **not** come from modern professional conservation, which would treat the patches as part of the object to be preserved, only to be removed as a last resort to deal with a clearly defined threat. If Ghiberti's account is accurate, and does not extrapolate an attitude that came much later, then it is clear that a major conservation error had entered into the thinking of the person who would later become, without the slightest qualification or experience in the subject, the chairman of the Commission for Conservation and one of the prime movers in the 2002 intervention.

Another person who gradually became a dominating force on this committee was Flury-Lemberg. The conservation committee began to recruit scientists with expertise in relevant fields other than textiles, and then in fields totally unrelated to conservation such as mathematics and engineering. One person who attended the meetings remarked that Al Adler became another dominating and rather bullying force after his appointment to the committee in 1994. Finally, non-scientists were also recruited, possibly owing to their degree of influence within Turin ecclesiastical circles. According to Sheila Landi, who attended several meetings of the committee in the 1990s, the atmosphere was characterized increasingly by manipulation: "All they wanted was people who said what they wanted to hear." This led to her decision to withdraw in 1997. It is not clear what happened to Silvio Diana and Gian Luigi Nicola; Jan Cardamone remained available but was not invited to attend further meetings. By 1999 Flury-Lemberg was the only textile expert left in the group, which had been re-christened formally as the "Commission for Conservation." Its membership at that time was published and consisted of the following:

- Mons. Giuseppe Ghiberti – priest and vice-president of the Diocesan Commission for the Exhibition of the Shroud
- Prof. Piero Savarino – organic chemist and scientific adviser to the Archbishop of Turin
- Prof. Alan Adler – inorganic chemist and member of STURP
- Engineer Gian Luigi Ardoino – civil engineer in Turin
- Prof. Pier Luigi Baima Bollone – forensics specialist and president of the Centro
- Prof. Bruno Barberis – mathematician and director of the Centro
- Prof. Karlheinz Dietz – historian at Warburg University
- Mechthild Flury-Lemberg – retired textile expert
- Prof. Silvano Scannerini – microbiologist at Turin University

- Prof. Paolo Soardo – of the National Electrotechnical Institute of Turin
- Prof. Carla Enrica Spantigati – superintendent of cultural heritage in Piedmont

It is unclear whether any other appointments were made after this list was published. Gian Maria Zaccone of the Turin Centro was deeply involved in the "restoration" and might have also become a member. With the loss of Adler, there were thus ten or eleven members when the "restoration" was decided. According to Flury-Lemberg, Ghiberti was the chairman of the Commission, and when questioned as to why a non-scientist and non-conservator should be chairman, she stated that he was a good organizer. The "past that hung like a millstone" was soon to be cut away.

The disastrous fire in the Royal Chapel in 1997 and the Shroud's removal during the fire-fighting operation led to an inspection of the cloth a few days later. Three experts were invited to examine the relic and determine whether it had been affected in any way by the fire. These were: Baima Bollone, Flury-Lemberg, and Dr. Rosalia Piazza, a prominent textile restorer from the Central Restoration Institute of Rome. It is not clear why Piazza was brought in, and she does not appear to have figured in any previous or subsequent deliberations on the conservation question.

Thus far there was nothing ostensibly sinister about the functioning of the committee/commission, as the interpersonal dynamics described above are quite commonplace. Certain individuals invariably become major players, others take on a less prominent role, while others for various reasons drop out. The Chinese say, "a mountain can only have one tiger," and the Conservation Commission could apparently only have one textile expert. The fact, however, that what began as a group of textile conservation experts transformed itself into a something entirely different consisting mainly of people with little or no knowledge of conservation, may be seen (in retrospect) as a dangerous turn of events. Combined with the irrational obsession with secrecy and pursuit of ill-advised "utopian ideas," it was to prove tragic. The final piece of the tragedy was the Commission's failure to heed its own recommendation. According to Barberis, in February 1996, the Commission issued a "conclusive report" on the conservation of the Shroud; one of the four suggestions in this report was "an in-depth study of the possible removal of the backing cloth and patches." It is clear that no such in-depth study was ever carried out.

No one in the world of Shroud research knew very much about these developments on the Commission. Most researchers including me assumed that the conservation group would be considering various methods of keeping the Shroud intact, e.g. protecting it from the harmful effects of air pollution in Turin, and that the presence of a scientist of the caliber of

Adler would keep the Commission on the straight and narrow path. Several purely conservation decisions were made in the late 1990s that did not arose any concern and indeed were quite advisable: the cloth would no longer be rolled up on a spool, but would be kept lying flat and unfolded; it would be housed in an inert gas atmosphere. Further, the silk border and cover cloth sewn on by Princess Clothilde in 1868 were removed. This action was less justified on conservation grounds, and should have been a foreshadowing of what might be in store for the Shroud, but no alarm was raised. The assumption was still widespread that the conservation of the Shroud was in capable hands. If anyone suspected that something was amiss or that the Commission was beginning to be dominated by a few personalities, such concerns did not get onto the grapevine. Sheila Landi's withdrawal from the Commission in 1997 went unannounced and unnoticed; Jan Cardamone was unaware that the conservation working group had taken on a more formal structure and had several new members appointed after 1992. She herself was not listed as a member of the Commission. A potentially dangerous situation was developing, but no one was aware of it. The crucial factor that would lead to the tragedy that was visited upon the Shroud was the sudden death of Adler in June 2000.

Calm and harmony before the storm

On the surface, research on the Shroud as well as its public cult seemed to be continuing as it had in previous decades, except that no direct testing was done on the cloth. 1998 saw an international conference and the first public exhibition of the relic since 1978. This exhibition was held to mark the 100th anniversary of Secondo Pia's first photographs of the image, which revealed its eerie lifelike appearance in the negative. Another exhibition was suggested by the Pope to mark the Holy Year of 2000, and two conferences were being planned for that year. In June 1999 I received a letter from the organizers of a conference that was going to be sponsored by the "Turin Diocese Committee for the Exposition of the Shroud." This conference was to prove a milestone in the impending disaster, but at the time my reaction to the invitation was a decided lack of interest. The date for the conference was March, whilst the dates for the public exhibition of the Shroud were July and August. It seemed odd that there would be an international conference several months before the Shroud was going to be put on display. This impression was shared by Emanuela Marinelli of Rome, who thought it best to arrange a conference during the summer when researchers would have the rare opportunity to see the Shroud. Her plan was not well received by the Turinese and led to some friction. The thought then occurred to me that the Turin conference was scheduled well in advance in order to be able to publish the proceedings in time for the exposition. The reality may have been far more sinister, or it may have been simply an extraordinary coincidence that gives the appearance of having been cunningly planned.

I declined the invitation, stating that I planned to visit Turin in the summer to see the Shroud on display, and could not justify another trip to Europe. In December, I received another letter from the organizers, this time with some intriguing information. It defined the objective of the symposium as bringing together "speakers and discussants whose scientific reputation is generally acknowledged" in order to "identify and examine in depth ... any questions which may become the subject of future theoretical and experimental research ... in view of a possible future campaign of studies and research." An email from the symposium chairman, Prof. Scannerini, encouraged me to attend as the event would be "an important one," and he noted that "Prof. Adler says that you must come." I knew that Adler had been deeply involved with the Turin Commission, and it began to dawn on me that this was a consultation being arranged by Turin for a new round of scientific testing. The symposium was by invitation only, and they offered to pay all travel and accommodation expenses – a significant fact not mentioned in the first invitation (!) Furthermore, in the preliminary program a 3-hour visit was scheduled to the Turin Cathedral where the Shroud is kept, which could only mean one thing: a private viewing of the Shroud. This of course clinched the matter for me, and I wrote back to accept their kind offer. I did not mention that I would have gladly paid my own way to be afforded a private view of the precious relic!

The symposium took place at Villa Gualino, a moderately well furnished hotel on a hill outside the city. It was certainly a high water mark of sorts, a brief Camelot in the history of Shroud politicking and factionalism characterized by all manner of Byzantine intrigues. There seemed to be a new spirit in the air, which had taken hold of the Centro and the various Turin personalities, perhaps owing to the dynamic new Archbishop, Monsignor (soon to be Cardinal) Severino Poletto. An affable and outgoing man, he speaks only Italian but manages to communicate his energy and feeling despite the language barrier. He visited the symposium on the second day to welcome all the guests, and as he went down the line shaking hands, all the foreigners said 'hello' or 'pleased to meet you'. When he got to me I said *'sono archaeologo di hong kong'* (I am an archaeologist from Hong Kong) at which point his eyes lit up and we conversed for a few seconds. This was not merely the old 'use-a-bit-of-the-native-language' ploy; I had studied at the Gregorian University in Rome for a year in graduate school and knew Italian well, back in 1969 that is. I explained to him that it had been a long time since I had spoken Italian, and we seemed to hit it off. He visited the symposium twice more, and each time was very friendly to me. I came away with the strong feeling that he would take some decisive action and we would soon see further testing of the cloth, and particularly C-14 dating. Never in a million years would I have imagined what was to come.

The conference was a well-run affair, and had interesting papers and discussion. Nothing earth-shaking was unveiled, such as a plan to emasculate the Shroud! Al Adler was his usual self – intelligent, vocal, domineering, friendly, bull-in-a-chinashop. One moment stands vividly in my mind, and saddens me to recall. Ian Wilson and I were arguing with Al about the bio-plastic hypothesis, which he adamantly denied. I raised the possibility that the microbial presence on the Shroud might be altered by storing it in an inert atmosphere, and that someone like Mattingly should be consulted for the conservation aspects of the microbiology. He got very defensive and a bit stroppy, and said that they had a textile conservator on the Commission in the form of Mechthild Flury-Lemberg. I asked if a second opinion had been sought, and he shot back "Yeah, Sheila Landi." She had withdrawn from the Commission in 1997, and Al certainly knew that.

The truly memorable moment during the conference was the visit to the Turin Cathedral. Everyone guessed that this would be a viewing of the Shroud, but it was not officially announced until we set off on a bus to the city. We were told that Archbishop Poletto would be there, and that we were not allowed to take photographs. Before entering the room where the Shroud was kept, there were a few further introductory comments, and then we were ushered in. It was a heart-stopping moment for me. There, mounted on a long board was the Shroud, **not** in its usual glass display case; windows high up in the room provided quite adequate natural lighting. A red silk cordon about one yard away was all that separated people from the relic.

To see the Shroud for the first time in such a setting was an unexpected joy, and something of a shock. In spite of all I had read about it, and all the photos I had seen of it, the real thing is haunting. The first glance tells you that this object is extraordinary, that it is most unlike any late medieval painting, or painting of any sort. The blood fascinated me as much as the image. For the first hour my feelings were all archaeological and historical curiosity about this intriguing object, intermingled with an emotional/religious response. As I inched my way from the feet of the frontal side to the other end, all sorts of strange detail caught my eye and occupied my mind in addition to the obvious image and blood stains: the odd stitching that accompanied some of the 1534 patches, the random bits of dirt or stain, the scorch mark patterns, how the burns had (miraculously many said) missed all the important parts of the image.

These reveries were interrupted when one of the Italians came up and said that the Archbishop wanted to speak with me. I had been aware of an animated conversation going on behind me, but realized then that it was a group gathered around Poletto. He and several Centro people were probing Evin and another French scientist on the issue of C-14. Evin believed it proved the Shroud medieval, and I was asked to give my view. I started out in Italian, but faltered after a couple of sentences. Zaccone then started translating, both for me and for the French. I then switched to French myself (as I speak it better than Italian) and was surprised to note that Poletto still needed translation. Turin and Piedmont are close to France and French is widely spoken in the area, but I guessed Poletto was not a Piedmont native. He seemed genuinely interested in the issues, and looked pleased when I finally got Evin to admit that it was possible, even though he thought it very unlikely, that an isotope exchange could have been induced by the fire. And again Evin had to admit that it was possible that the area sampled for C-14 could have been anomalous. As I went back to viewing the Shroud, I thought to myself that this archbishop will eventually permit another C-14 dating, and perhaps in the not-too-distant future.

I picked up the viewing where I had left off, but after ten minutes or so was summoned back to the Archbishop's discussion group. This time I really felt like I was being forced to make Sophie's choice – to my right was the Archbishop of Turin requesting my presence in his lively discussion on the study of the Shroud, to the left was the object itself an arm's length away, outside of its case and naturally lit. Each of these opportunities were irresistible, but I opted out of the conversation as soon as I could diplomatically exit, to have more time in front of the cloth.

As I got back into the viewing, I saw Poletto and the gaggle of people around him move up to the cordon. Suddenly, a flash bulb exploded and I turned around to see a fellow in an ill-fitting suit with an old-fashioned press camera. Horrified, I went over to Adler and asked him how in the world they could be using flash photography. He shrugged his shoulders, saying it was the official archdiocese photographer. I then asked him to try to stop it, as he was on the Commission. He said there was no way he was going to interfere with the arrangements, as this viewing was very special. It bothered me that this simple issue had not been considered beforehand. A tripod-mounted camera would have given perfectly good photographs without the use of a flash, and spared the cloth that extra unnecessary exposure to bright light.

Worse was to come shortly. A heavily built delegate was energetically pointing out some feature on the Shroud to Poletto, and they both stepped over the cordon to get a closer view. The delegate suddenly pulled out his ballpoint pen and pointed at the feature. The tip of the pen was an inch away from the surface of the cloth. Aghast, I started to intervene, when he lowered the pen. I was determined this time not to sit idly by, and if he raised the pen again I was going to remonstrate with him. Instead, he put it away and continued to gesture toward the Shroud with his hand. Several other people were watching the proceedings, and no one seemed bothered by the fact that a possible ink stain was a mere hand tremble away. When I recalled that many archives do not even allow ballpoint pens to be brought inside, I shuddered at the thought of how poor was the state of awareness in Turin concerning the Shroud's conservation.

At the end of the viewing there was a short devotional type speech made by Poletto, and then a reading from the Old Testament in Hebrew by Avinoam Danin, a botanist from Israel, accompanied by Adler in English. A quite amazing moment for me, a Methodist from the South, to be standing before this great Catholic relic and listening to the words of Isaiah in Hebrew.

Another conservation issue was raised by John Jackson, who has been particularly interested in the old creases and "foldmark patterns" (as he calls them) preserved on the Shroud. One of the last items done in STURP's 1978 examination of the Shroud was raking (or oblique) light photography, which showed dozens of creases, some barely visible. Jackson has spun an interesting theory about how the Shroud was folded in its early period, while it was believed to be in Constantinople in the 12th and early 13th centuries. He was very upset after leaving the viewing of the Shroud, over the manner in which the Shroud was stretched on the board. It was so taut that hardly any of the creases could be seen, and were obviously under considerable pressure. Writing about this viewing later, Jackson commented:

> In March 2000 when I saw the Shroud during a special showing, I saw, much to my dismay, that the Shroud was then being maintained in a stretched configuration!! ... I can state that storing the Shroud in this condition for a long period of time **will** destroy forever the precious fold mark pattern, if it has not already done so.

Jackson raised the question in a later session at Villa Gualino; he was told that the stretching for mounting on the board was only a temporary arrangement. This was apparently not true. Zaccone and Barberis, writing in an appendix in Flury-Lemberg's (2003) book, state: "in 2000 it was decided that new measurements [of the length and width of the cloth] should be taken, above all in view of the fact that, unlike in the past, the Shroud was stretched and fixed in a practically definitive position. This meant that measurements could be obtained that were independent from variations in traction on the Shroud." This last sentence certainly implies that the Shroud was stretched taut during the exhibition and was going to be kept that way. The issue of the creases would arise again after the "restoration," when, incredibly, a deliberate attempt was made to remove them.

The conference concluded on a very strange note. In the last session, Ghiberti and Scannerini announced that a summary statement should be agreed upon to release to the press. There were murmurings against this, as there had been no discussion of such a document. Ghiberti happened to have a text prepared, which he read out and discussion followed. This became rather heated when the subject of C-14 arose, and several people wanted to insert their strong disapproval of the way it was done, and their doubts about whether real Shroud samples were dated. Ghiberti suddenly became agitated, and sternly declared that he was not going to get into this area. Scannerini stated that they merely wanted to reflect the range of opinions and not to reach any consensus view. Almost unnoticed in the heat of the moment was this innocent line in the summary statement: "A series of experiments specifically directed at improving our knowledge for the purposes of conservation is essential, especially in view of the considerable development of instruments and improvements in non-invasive analytical methods." This struck me at the time as odd, since there had hardly been any discussion during the meeting of conservation matters, but the statement seemed innocuous enough. Despite some misgivings expressed by a few delegates, the summary statement was adopted. It would return to haunt the organizers of the conference.

What did strike a very positive chord with everyone present was the suggestion that a databank be established, and that proposals or ideas for future research and testing should be submitted by a deadline of October 30, for coordination and review in a process of consultation. The exact parameters of this process were left vague, a omission which ultimately proved fatal for the new-found spirit of harmony and cooperation. But at the time the developments seemed so promising that it was assumed the details would be worked out later.

In retrospect, it is very difficult to understand what the true intention of this conference was. It espoused lofty ideals of international cooperation, careful scientific investigation, multi-disciplinary approach, peer review, dialogue and the exchange of ideas; participants were invited to submit proposals or ideas for future research, measurement, testing and conservation of the Shroud; and a future review process for the proposals was discussed. And yet, no less than eight members of the Commission, which two years later visited the tragic "restoration" on the Shroud, organized this conference, attended all three days, read papers and took part in the discussions. **Not once** was there any mention of any radical conservation plan. On balance, the evidence does suggest that at that stage the plan had not yet been conceived. But other stealth was definitely afoot.

I shared a taxi with Al Adler and Bob Otlet to the Turin airport. A spirited conversation took place about C-14 and new testing of the Shroud. Adler was confident that things were moving along, and he felt that another round of C-14 dating was in the cards, but he thought it would still take time to bring the Turin people round to it – months rather than years, he said. As we left to find our respective check-in counters, I thanked Al for getting me invited to the conference, and he said he was glad that I was "back on the scene." It was the last time I would see him. He died quietly in his sleep on June 12, 2000 at the age of 68. When I saw an email with the subject line that simply stated "Al Adler" I had a cold shiver, and my worst fear was confirmed. His passing was a great tragedy for the study of the Shroud, as he still had much to give and knew the science better than anyone else. It was to be an even greater tragedy because of what would be done in his name, something he would never have allowed to happen.

Shortly after the conference, a letter was sent to all participants by Ghiberti, fairly gushing with nostalgia for the time just spent together:

> Two weeks ago we were all together at Villa Gualino and we experienced the truth of Psalm 132 (133) which in the Vulgate version says '*ecce quam bonum et quam jucumdum habitare fraters in unum*', or in English 'how good, how delightful it is to live as brothers all together.' We parted with some nostalgia and I can assure you that the Archbishop, Mon. Severino Poletto, also remembers those days of joy ...

He went on to describe the progress and cooperation that had been achieved, and the limitations of various disciplines, the need for harmony and synthesis, etc. He spoke of future communication to be sustained, and the distinct possibility of future symposia. He closed with words that now, in the light of what happened, seem most hypocritical and preposterous: "Meanwhile we have undertaken not to interrupt contact between us ... the memory and the various mail options now available will keep us united." But at the time it sounded so promising. Verily, it seemed that a new era of Shroud research and community had begun. The conference organizers, Piero Savarino and Silvano Scannerini, sent a letter accompanying Ghiberti's in which they reminded all participants to submit their proposals and ideas: "The sooner your proposals arrive the sooner we can work on them. We will send you a synthesis of the proposals which will keep the dialogue open." Alas, these things did not happen, and the "brotherhood," harmony and cooperative spirit would be very short-lived indeed.

The conference secretariat also wrote and emailed several times, seeking the finalized texts of papers for the proceedings, which were obviously being given a very high priority in order to be published in time for the public exhibition of the Shroud, due to open August 12. They succeeded in publishing the volume in time for the opening, and a very nicely prepared book *The Turin Shroud: Past, Present, and Future* was sent to all conference delegates in September. In the Preface by Savarino and Scannerini, the summary statement prepared at the end of the conference was included, followed by these words:

> We consider that these works provide an incentive to accept and compare new research proposals, with the limitation that they should be formulated with rigorous methodological correctness and conducted with the absolute guarantee of conservation without damage to the Shroud cloth. The presidency of the Congress wishes to point out that research proposals respecting these standards should be sent to the Exposition Committee not later than 30 October 2000.

The word got around quickly that new proposals for testing the Shroud were being accepted, and by the end of October quite a few researchers had made submissions.

Just a few days after this deadline passed, the most incredible thing happened. Unbeknownst to the world at large, a group of Turinese was allowed to conduct their own project on the Shroud. Ghiberti would describe it later in these terms: "in November 2000 came the grand exploration of the underside of the Shroud through scanning." The coterie around Cardinal Poletto had clearly put their own pet project at the head of the queue, and given it the green light without any international discussion or "peer review" whatever. And the fact that it started within days of the so-called deadline for submission of proposals was most deplorable. To invert Ghiberti's quote from the psalmist, "how bad, how repugnant it is, when people who have appeared to be so open and so gracious, plot secretly to achieve their own selfish ends." It was however some time before these events became known.

From Camelot to catastrophe

The 2000 exhibition of the Shroud was scheduled to end on October 22, but it was extended for a few extra days due to serious flooding in north Italy that prevented some tourists and pilgrims from attending on the last days. Shortly thereafter, in the first week of November 2000, in total secrecy, the weeklong "grand exploration" began with the aim of recording the underside of the Shroud. Since the cloth is sewn onto a backing cloth for support, the scanning was achieved by unstitching one section at a time and manipulating a portable scanner with long handle. The resultant scans were then merged digitally to form a complete picture of the underside. Paolo Soardo, a member of the Conservation Commission, designed and conducted the project.

The operation was kept secret for quite some time after it was completed, while a coffee table book *The Two Faces Of The Shroud* was prepared for publication. It was written principally by Gian Maria Zaccone of the Turin Centro, and described the operation in considerable detail, with many large color photographs. A press release issued in May 2001 by the Turin Archdiocese described the work in somewhat over-dramatic terms as follows:

> The Shroud of Turin has bloodstains on its reverse side, indicating that the image of the man it bears was not copied, a new study indicates. The shroud, widely believed to have been the burial cloth of Jesus, was subjected to new scanning techniques last November, and results of the tests were first scrutinized by a symposium of scientists. Cardinal Severino Poletto, archbishop of Turin, released the news of the tests ...
>
> The recent examination, carried out with a scanner, revealed bloodstains on the reverse side, indicating that the image was not copied. 'This is a confirmation of the unfounded character of the hypothesis formulated in the past, according to which the image of the Holy Shroud was formed by combustion, namely, by the warming of an image wrapped in the cloth,' explained Monsignor Giuseppe Ghiberti, vice president of the Commission for the Exposition of the Shroud ...

Paolo Soardo of the Galileo Ferraris Italian Institute carried out the scanning of the reverse of the shroud, which no one had seen in more than 450 years. In the one-week study, done in the sacristy of the new cathedral, a flat scanner was introduced between the shroud and the linen lining.

This news stunned the worldwide community of Shroud researchers, but there was scant protest. It was inexplicable that a project simply for data acquisition was allowed to proceed apparently with no peer review and no consultation, and so far ahead of all other proposals. One assumed that it must have been handpicked and given instant approval because of personal connections. And because the preparations must have taken weeks, the project would have been approved long before the deadline of October 30 that had been set at the Villa Gualino conference and re-affirmed in the conference proceedings published in August. This seemed nothing more than rank cronyism, a clear violation of the procedures that had been established with such fanfare and bonhomie just a few months earlier. What the devil was going on?

My reaction on learning of this breach in the protocols was, I now regret, fairly mild. It struck me as the kind of pet project that a few individuals with connections in Turin wanted to do, and it was given the go-ahead prior to the other more serious research proposals that had been submitted. I recall thinking that although it was certainly a violation of the "spirit of Villa Gualino," it did not seem too serious and it was hopefully only a small blip in the larger process of scientific inquiry that had been set in motion. I could not have been more wrong.

One person who did not see it that way was Barrie Schwortz, photographer for STURP and creator of the premier Shroud website www.shroud.com. He spoke out boldly and forthrightly, knowing full well that in doing so he would incur the wrath of the Turin clique. He ran an editorial on his website in June 2001 that was highly critical of the scanning operation. It is quoted extensively here because of its importance and his insight at that early stage into the mindset prevalent in Turin:

> I rarely use this website as a forum for my personal opinions, but I feel compelled to speak out in response to the above article [press release concerning the scanning of the underside]. It makes several points about Shroud research that I believe need clarification.
>
> As most of you know, the Shroud of Turin Research Project (STURP), spent 120 hours in October 1978 performing an in-depth examination of the cloth. Working alongside STURP were a number of Italian researchers. One of these, Professor Giovanni Riggi, used

an endoscopic camera system to look at and photograph the underside of the Shroud. Prof. Riggi's resulting photographs clearly showed the blood had soaked through the cloth. To accommodate his experiment, a small section of the Shroud was separated from its backing cloth by a Poor Clare nun, giving the researchers the first look at the underside of the Shroud in 400 years. In fact, one of my most well known and often published photographs from 1978 is of the precise moment this 'first look' occurred (it can be viewed on this website at http://www.shroud.com/78strp4.htm) ...

The article also states that this new research disputes the theory that the Shroud was 'formed by combustion.' However, the actual scientific evidence that excludes heat as the image formation mechanism of the Shroud is the ultraviolet fluorescence photography done in 1978 by Vernon Miller. ...

However, my purpose in writing this is not to argue who did what first or criticize the recently performed experiment and its results. I think it is wonderful that 21st century technology is being applied to Shroud research and have personally lobbied for further research using new digital imaging technologies myself. My criticism is that the Turin authorities took an important opportunity to gather new data from the Shroud and applied it to questions that had been answered long ago.

Last year the Turin authorities sent out an urgent call to Sindonologists worldwide to submit proposals for future research and set a deadline of October 31, 2000. I am told they received dozens, if not hundreds of responses and many of these were from top researchers around the world. The plan was that these would be reviewed and evaluated and certain groups and individuals would be chosen to perform the tests at some later date. In spite of this, and almost immediately after the deadline expired, the scanning tests mentioned in the above article were performed. Interestingly, none of the researchers who submitted proposals that included this type of scanning were ever contacted or consulted prior to the November tests.

It is my hope that the Turin authorities proceed with the evaluation of the proposals they received as originally planned, and select appropriate, qualified researchers to perform new data gathering tests on the Shroud based on the quality of their proposals, experience, technology and credentials. But I strongly believe it is necessary to select tests that will help us gather new data and not put the Shroud at risk (from exposure to light, handling and the polluted air in Turin) in the wasted effort of redoing experiments that have already been done or reproving science that has already been proved.

After the news of the scanning broke, there were a number of rumors and suspicions that the October 30 deadline had deliberately been chosen so that all proposals could be reviewed prior to proceeding with this scanning operation (and perhaps future projects that were still kept secret) and any useful elements cherry-picked. This was rather harsh, I thought, but the timing of the scanning did lend itself to such suspicions. What was not clear at the time was how the Turin clique justified the violation of the procedures agreed at Villa Gualino. There was no response to Schwortz's editorial. But several people with close links to those in Turin reported that Schwortz had indeed become *persona non grata* for his criticisms.

Of course the reality was far worse than Schwortz or anyone else could have imagined, and at the conclusion of the scanning operation an extraordinary series of events took place in rapid succession, again totally unknown to the outside world but reconstructible now from later accounts.

When the "restoration" was first announced in August 2002, the feeling shared by many of those who had attended the Villa Gualino conference was one of betrayal. I also held this view. All the lofty ideals of cooperation and peer review and cautious, responsible science seemed nullified by this radical, ill-advised and unnecessary intervention in the name of conservation. What made matters worse was that initial statements claimed that the intervention "had been under consideration for a long time." It seemed nothing short of outrageous that eight members of the Commission could join a congress of worldwide experts and conceal the fact that such radical plan was brewing. It appeared that the conference had been nothing but a sham, and a façade behind which a course of action was being plotted that would have been universally condemned had it been known. Ultimately, this was probably the main reason why the Commission made its deliberations in secret and consulted no one about the plan.

The published accounts of how the "restoration" came to be decided now make it abundantly clear that it was not being planned at the time of the conference. Although both Ghiberti and Flury-Lemberg write that it was an option that had been considered for a long time, Ghiberti states flatly that it was going nowhere: "This idea remained as a dead letter until the official photos taken in [early November] 2000 revealed how much pulverous material had accumulated between the patches and the backing cloth." Flury-Lemberg specifies:

> When the central part of the reverse of the Shroud was scanned in November 2000 we did not foresee that the Holland cloth was to be removed one day. Only the thorough investigation carried out on the Holland cloth on that occasion revealed the whole dramatic meaning of the staining ... This clear evidence finally made it possible to come to a decision about whether to remove the Holland cloth or not.

Therefore, during the early days of November, while the scanning was being conducted, members of the Conservation Commission suddenly and without outside consultation took it upon themselves to decide that a major intervention was required for the Shroud. A dead letter became a hot proposal almost overnight, and by noon was approved by acclimation. Ghiberti writes:

> ... there were well founded reasons for thinking that a substantial advantage for conservation would be conferred on the Shroud by the removal of its patches and Holland cloth ... All the members of the Committee agreed with this line of reasoning. A document was drawn up and signed by all, and presented to Cardinal Poletto ... The text [was] drawn up on November 10, 2000 ...

The dubious reasons for this decision will be scrutinized later, along with the possible damage to the Shroud, lost data, lost opportunities, and the motivations of the Commission members. It is clear that it was a precipitous and totally unwarranted decision, one that will go down in history as a tragedy for the Shroud. What is most difficult to understand is how the members could take such a momentous decision in such haste. Could they have genuinely believed that it was so terribly urgent that there was no time to discuss the matter with the scientific and conservation community? Or was it their intention to keep the decision secret so that it could be executed before any discussion and dissent arose? The answer seems obvious.

The unanimous recommendation of the Commission was endorsed by Cardinal Poletto, apparently without further consultation or independent evaluation. It was then sent to the Vatican for consideration. One year later, on November 3, 2001, the Secretary of State for the Vatican, Cardinal Sodano, granted permission to proceed. Again, it appears that no independent evaluation or peer review was conducted by the Vatican, and so far as can be determined today, no scientist or conservator who was familiar with the Shroud was consulted on the matter. It is not clear why the approval took one year to be granted; it is possible that the Vatican was considering the matter from a religious perspective. One would like to think that the Vatican Museum or Pontifical Academy of Sciences were consulted, but there is no evidence to suggest that this occurred. According to statements issued by the Turin archdiocese, the only condition imposed by the Vatican was that the Commission should be unanimous in its recommendation. But as reported by Ghiberti this was the case already, as the initial letter was signed by all members on November 10, 2000.

Most likely what happened during the year that the proposal was under consideration at the Vatican was that a faction supporting Poletto was mustering its forces and pushing through the recommendation from the Conservation Commission, which was of course appointed entirely by Poletto. One can imagine that there might have been opposition from certain quarters arising out of conservatism (actually a very good principle to follow in conservation!). In the opinion of Prof. Daniel Scavone, Emeritus Professor of History at the University of Southern Indiana:

> Many scholars, therefore, have found it outrageous that a small group of well-intentioned persons [the Commission] who had the attention of the official curator of the Shroud [Poletto] should have used his influence at the papal court to gain permission to perform such radical and invasive surgery on the cloth. They did so with absolutely no discussion with experts and knowledgeable scholars who are also vitally concerned about all matters relating to the precious Shroud – but who were taken by surprise by the announcements only when the operation was a fait accompli. Whatever could have been the unspoken motives of the interventionists that moved them to such secrecy, haste, and the consequent carelessness?

When approval from the Vatican came in November 2001, the terrorist attack on the World Trade Center and Pentagon in the USA was of course still very fresh in everyone's mind, and this certainly was the major factor for keeping the operation secret. Ghiberti wrote that once permission was obtained, they considered it advisable to proceed without delay. After discussion with city officials and police, it was decided to conduct the work in the new sacristy adjacent to the Cathedral. Every necessary precaution was taken, and foremost among these was silence: "it was decided to tell all those who might seek information that nothing at all was going on."

Security concerns were later cited as a reason for not carrying out a wide-ranging consultation and peer review process of the proposed intervention. This was nonsense. While no one disputes the need for secrecy regarding the actual time and place of such a large operation on the Shroud, there is no justification for the veil of total secrecy which was kept over the perceived need for this radical intervention. As long-time Shroud researcher Emanuela Marinelli of Rome observed:

> The decision to carry out such an operation has been taken by a very narrow group of people, without a wider consultation among the scientists and the historians, who have been interested in this Relic for many years. In fact, nobody had proposed any intervention of the sort at any of the eight international conferences held in the last four years (Turin 1998, Richmond 1999, Rio de Janeiro 1999, Turin 2000, Orvieto 2000, Dallas 2001, Paris 2002, Rio de Janeiro 2002). Not even those convened by the Turin International Center of Sindonology (Turin 1998) and by the Archbishop of Turin (Turin 2000) included such a proposal.

The road to the catastrophic "restoration" was thus set in place from November 2000 to June 2002. It may have been paved with good intentions, but its path was bulldozed by the most hypocritical and machiavellian maneuvering. Could the people involved in the planning of this operation during those 20 months not have been aware of and disturbed by the fact that to the outside world the spirit of Villa Gualino still seemed alive? Did they have no misgivings in pursuing a plan that was certain to destroy all the good will and harmony that was established at that conference? Perhaps they had gotten so swept up in the "historic task" they were undertaking that they simply lost touch with the outside world. As Ghiberti wrote later: "it was the greatest and most significant intervention on the Shroud in 500 years, since that of the Clarisse nuns of Chambery in 1534." Another interpretation would be that they simply did not care about what the rest of the world would think, since their inside position and access to power had gone to their heads.

The final act in the Villa Gualino farce was played out on April 4, 2001, just a few weeks before the secret "restoration" was due to begin. A rather badly written email was sent to all participants in the conference, and others who had also been welcomed to submit proposals. It read:

> Dear contributors, in keeping with the conclusions of 'Shroud 2000 – Past, present and future, Torino, Villa Gualino march 2-5, 2000,' your future research proposals have been collected in the files of Congress Scientific Committee just after the end of the Congress. So to avoid any mistake in our files as well as any misunderstanding or trouble in communication and/or in research

program time courses we are kindly asking you to duly check this list of research program leaders and coworkers. Please remind that the dead line to confirm, by first class Mail, your programmes or to set up a claim to your presence in the list is imperatively to be present in Torino before May 2, 2002. The final list of your research proposals will be submitted by Professors Silvano Scannerini, President of Shroud 2000, and Piero Savarino, Torino Archbishop Advisor to the Holy Shroud Custodian (as the representative of the Holy Shroud lawful owner, the Holy See) on May 5. Thank you very much for your attention. Best regards. Prof. Silvano Scannerini, Prof. Piero Savarino.

All the scientific proposals, from researchers all over the world, were going to be formally presented to Poletto on May 5. A massive month-long invasive operation on the Shroud was due to begin in June. Was cherry-picking the aim once again? Or was the collecting of these proposals a mere sideshow, a diversion, to distract the world from the real task at hand? Perhaps to feign that "nothing at all was going on," as Ghiberti put it? Or all of the above? We will probably never know.

10. The "Restoration" and its Aftermath

On June 20, 2002 The Shroud Was Removed from its casket and carried to the newly renovated sacristy adjacent to Turin's main cathedral. For the next five weeks the relic was subject to a number of surgical operations and data-gathering projects. As described by Ghiberti, the work was carried out in three stages:

1) removal of the old backing-cloth (the "Holland cloth") and patches, and stretching the wrinkles on the backside of the Shroud (21-25 June);

2) photography, spectrophotometry and scanning of front and back (26 June-15 July);

3) attachment of the new backing-cloth, photographs, and measurements (16-23 July).

The people most involved in this large-scale operation were mainly members of the Conservation Commission:
- Ghiberti – spokesman for and general overseer of the operation
- Flury-Lemberg – "restorer"/ seamstress
- Savarino – directed scientific measurements
- Baima Bollone – conducted sampling
- Soardo – conducted scanning
- Ardoino – designed instrument for measurements
- Dietz – took photomicrographs
- Barberis – made measurements.

Among the other main participants were Irene Tomedi (a textile restorer trained by Flury-Lemberg), Gian Maria Zaccone and Nello Balossino, officers of the Centro, and Gino Moretti. The involvement of other Commission members (Spantigati, Scannerini) is not known. Ghiberti remarks: "The final stage of the restoration was entirely in the hands of the seamstresses and left most of the members of the Committee

[Conservation Commission] disoccupied." Clearly it was a Commission-led effort.

A number of teams and individuals was also involved, mostly in data gathering and photography; in such a large undertaking there were numerous other tasks to be organized. The various teams were: Sister Maria Clara Antonini and her assistants (recording and daily reporting), Turin police team (fluorescence photography), Laser Point team (reflectance and fluorescence measurement), Renishaw team (Raman spectroscopy), Soardo's team (scanning), Giandurante's team (photography), ADL team (gantry for measurement instruments), Marchisciano's team (photography), two TV crews, security guards, various archdiocesan personnel.

From this welter of scientific and recording personnel, probably 40 to 50 persons in total, one might have the impression that the operation was similar to STURP's weeklong scientific investigation of the Shroud in 1978. Nothing could be further from the truth. STURP was an extremely well planned, multi-disciplinary project that recruited experts from across the entire USA. It held planning sessions, de-briefing and interpretation sessions, and published its results in peer-reviewed academic journals. The various teams of the "restoration" were all assembled from Turin and vicinity, recruited by Savarino; they went in and did their thing, then handed the data over the Poletto. There was no peer review, there was no coordinated planning, there were no clearly formulated research objectives, and it is doubtful many of them even knew why they were recording the data they were requested to do. It is doubtful if any of them will publish their work. Some of the participants may be excellent in their area of expertise, others not, but what is most important in a scientific project is a sense of purpose, understanding of the mission, integrated methodology and common objective. In a multi-disciplinary project additional elements needed are cross-coordination and comparison. All of these appear to have been lacking in the provincial Turinese measurement and data recording of 2002. The achievements of STURP are very well documented, "and this, sir, was no STURP!"

As one American Shroud researcher put it:

> One hates to think that Turin's pride was so threatened by the accomplishments of the STURP team in 1978 that the constituency of the present investigators was limited to Turin's 'favorites', but it is certainly both a concern and conclusion already being voiced by many in the international community. Even more troubling is the complaint that some of the procedures carried out recently were originally submitted by other scientists in proposals requested by the

Turin authorities – international scientists who were neither consulted nor included in these 'secret' investigations.

Ghiberti writes oddly about the end of the work: "The procession that was to accompany the Shroud back to its chapel was formed. ... It seemed like a funeral cortège." And indeed in many respects it was! The Shroud that had been preserved intact for more than four centuries was no more.

The secrecy that had enveloped the operation would soon be pierced, however. In August 2002, the Rome newspaper *Il Messaggero* ran a story by its Vatican reporter Orazio Petrosillo that the Shroud had undergone a radical intervention. As details emerged from the Turin archdiocese, it was confirmed that the patches and backing cloth had been removed, and "dusts and residues" had been cleared away. The worldwide community of Shroud researchers was stunned, unable to believe that such an invasive procedure could have been allowed to take place when there had been so much emphasis in recent decades on the need for non-intrusive, non-destructive testing. Rumors abounded, and it was feared that all scorched portions of cloth had been cut away, that the entire relic had been vacuumed, and even that the burn holes had been repaired or rewoven.

There were confusing and outrageous statements by a spokesman for the archdiocese. At first it was claimed that the "restoration" was in line with the consensus of opinion at the Villa Gualino conference. Then it was "clarified" that this conference had dealt only with scientific studies and "conservation has nothing to do with scientific analysis." Incredibly, it was also claimed that Prof. Adler had stated that an intervention such as this was necessary.

Most of the news was reported in the Italian press, and precious little was carried by the international agencies. An AP story reported that Flury-Lemberg was undertaking a study of Shroud specimens, and quoted her as saying that she was carrying out tests on the Shroud of Turin, but she would not explain what she was studying or what the tests consisted of. She said that everything would be described in detail at the press conference that had already been planned for September by the Turin archdiocese, when the "new-look Shroud" would be presented to the world. The press in Italy was buzzing with stories, gossip and speculation about what had been done to the Shroud. Emanuela Marinelli and her sister Roberta worked tirelessly while on holiday to translate the news reports and keep the Shroud community informed. Discussion was raging in the Italian media; a very senior political and academic figure, Francesco Sissini, wrote an important piece asking:

Did this important object, on whose material and historical authenticity scholars from every part of the world have worked tirelessly, and, above all, in front of which millions of faithful from all over the world have kneeled, really need to have undergone such a massive intervention? In spite of the widespread prohibition of 'do not touch' as far as the relics are concerned, dictated not by mere conservatism, but by the accumulated wisdom of preservationism, that admonishes us to have the due respect not only for the object in itself, but also for what the history has left on it, with signs which are testimonies to be conserved as well. For example, today who would dare remove the Renaissance and baroque integrations (and not only Bernini's famous ones) from the statues which have reached us mutilated from the Greco-Roman Classical Age? Nevertheless, those statues are not 'unique', whereas the Shroud is.

Meanwhile, the pace of email exchange and telephone conversations was rising to a fever pitch amongst sindonologists and Shroud devotees. Emanuela was encouraging people to write to the Pope, and many did. She was also encouraging the participants of the Villa Gualino conference to write a joint letter countering the statements that had appeared in the media and setting the record straight on what that congress did and did not decide. I had numerous discussions via email and telephone with John Jackson and Fred Zugibe, who were both outraged and deeply disturbed by what had apparently been done. Jackson circulated a letter that condemned the intervention in rather strong terms. He wrote:

> I am greatly concerned that the world scientific community apparently wasn't consulted before attempting the removal of the backing cloth and patches. This [consultation] did **not** occur during the March 2000 meeting in Turin. This is important because it is essential that scientific information resident on the Shroud be preserved. The only people qualified to know what that information is are people who have spent years, if not their lifetimes, thinking about the Shroud in a scientific sense.

He expressed particular concern over what he feared might have occurred to the fold mark information on the Shroud; he wondered why such an operation was done in secret, and lamented the lost opportunity for obtaining new scientific information from the back side of the Shroud in a spirit of collaboration. He was worried that the operation may have damaged the Shroud as an archaeological object. Jackson concluded by

THE "RESTORATION" AND ITS AFTERMATH

appealing to the Turin authorities to involve responsible scientists from around the world before making important decisions.

Strangely, the writer Ian Wilson displayed an uncharacteristic sympathy for the "authorities" in Turin. This was especially odd since he had not very long before written a "farewell editorial" in the newsletter of the British Society for the Turin Shroud, ranting and raving at an American Shroud organization (AMSTAR), and in particular at its board member artist Isabel Piczek, for not taking his advice on who to invite to a forthcoming conference that AMSTAR was organizing. Terms such as "American-led Shroud oligarchy" were tossed about.

Just months before this petulant outburst from Wilson, I had been invited to serve on the executive board of AMSTAR. The four other members of the board were also deeply disturbed about the "restoration," but divided on how to deal with the issue. Some people said that loyalty to the Church encouraged "moderation." Emanuela and I had spoken earlier of a hoped-for unity amongst all researchers, but it began to dawn on me that this issue was going to split the Shroud world. The cracks had begun to appear already, dividing those who were indignant from those who wanted relations with the Turin people to "remain harmonious." Lurking behind these latter sentiments was the inevitable desire on the part of some people to curry favor with those in power, regardless of considerations of truth or morality. This lamentable side of human nature would be seen, in a most surprising manifestation, on Sept. 21 in Turin.

The immediate reaction of most people to the announcement from Turin that a press conference would be held soon and photographs made available was to withhold any criticism until the situation was clarified and more information was at hand. This was my initial feeling as well, although it was clear that the "restoration" was a terrible mistake and an unforgivable violation of the broad agreement and process set out at Villa Gualino. What bothered me most was the increasing awareness that there had been no outside consultation or peer review of this intervention. I attempted to find out if this was indeed the case. Jan Cardamone was on holiday in New Jersey, and when I finally was able to contact her she was surprised and shocked at the news. Sheila Landi in England had the same reaction. The textile specialist Vercelli, a resident of Turin, was not consulted either. It was becoming clear that there had been no consultation with other textile conservators or indeed with other scientists outside Turin who were familiar with the Shroud. This realization, combined with Emanuela's urging that pressure was needed in order to force Turin to reveal more and answer hard questions, led me to draft a letter to circulate to other participants of Villa Gualino.

One of the participants that I met at that conference for the first time was Karlheinz Dietz, a German historian/archaeologist and a likeable chap. He, Flury-Lemberg, Fr. Heinrech Pfeiffer and I had lunch together several times during the conference. I fired off an email to Dietz full of fury at what had been done to the Shroud, asking how our colleague Flury-Lemberg could have been involved in such a reprehensible operation and how the Turinese could have plotted such a thing. The next day I learned that Dietz himself was a member of the Conservation Committee, so I fired off another email asking how **he** could have been involved in this operation. His response surprised me for the nonsense it contained, and the vehemence with which he expressed it. He claimed they had done:

> ... an indispensable work for the conservation of the famous object. This measure of conservation was always demanded from the late Alan D. Adler who was a member of the conservation committee ... Those who are acting now in a nervous way are acting irresponsible on account of an indiscreet announcement of a journalist and obviously know nothing precise. Those [people] neither saw photographs nor have authorized first hand information. However, in my opinion a scientist never should judge and act in a precipitated manner but provide for certainty ... In my opinion the greatest damage for the Shroud is that bad rumor which was caused. I wonder if 'those' really want the best for the Shroud or only the best for their own vanity ..."

I marveled at how someone seemingly so intelligent could utter such utter rubbish. My reply set out what I thought would force him to deal with the issue more deeply:

> I would gladly withdraw every criticism and strong word I have written or spoken if you or anyone can demonstrate to me that the action was justified. Will you do the same? If the operation is shown to be unwarranted, will you apologize to the world and resign from the Commission?
>
> I know already the conclusion however, because even if your Commission had discovered a new species of rapidly spreading, cellulose-eating bacteria on the Shroud and had to take urgent action, it would not be justified unless the world's experts in bacteriology and cellulose chemistry were consulted. Jan Cardamone was at the March 2000 Villa Gualino meeting, and she knew nothing of this 'conservation' nor did Sheila Landi, so I already know that it has been carried out recklessly, unscientifically,

without proper peer review, not even with a second opinion from the two conservators above who knew the Shroud very well and had been involved in the study of its conservation. This is simply a disgrace, an absolute disgrace.

There is talk of the 'betrayal of Villa Gualino' ... and all the high-sounding idealistic words of international cooperation, careful scientific investigation, peer review, openness, dialogue and the exchange of ideas, plus the invitation to submit proposals for future research, measurement, testing and conservation of the Shroud, plus the review process that was outlined ... making people feel that something had changed, that now there really would be openness and dialogue and peer-review. It pains me now to think of it. ...

You and the Commission have made a big mistake, and Al Adler is partly to blame because he had a big mouth which was a loose cannon. But he was very careful about what he wrote. Why was his **last written word** on conservation not followed? This is found in his paper in the published proceedings of Villa Gualino, in which Adler included a section on 'Conservation Issues' (page 70) . He describes the problems and certain steps that had been taken, and he concludes the section with this important sentence: 'To continue to further this work, more data acquired by further testing on the Shroud itself is required.' He did not say 'is desirable'. He said it was required. And, he was a porphyrin chemist, not a textile chemist. I asked Mechthild what textile chemist was consulted and she only mentioned Adler, so again I know that a terrible mistake was made. Further, Adler also said many times that direct testing and monitoring should be done; he would never have consented to such an operation without assurance that the best scientists that could be found would be involved to insure that no data was lost when alterations were made to the Shroud.

Conservation was discussed at Villa Gualino, and there is a recommendation in the conference summation. This was not followed either. Those who are deeply disturbed about the news that has come out, from Poletto's own mouth or that of his spokesman, are acting very responsibly, but with indignation that such radical measures were taken without lengthy, careful and open consideration.

... a simple internet search turned up many references to [Flury-Lemberg's] book and her work, and led me also to the fact that she is considered an 'old guard' aggressive textile repairer/restorer with a fixation on cleaning and neatness. She is quite far from the mainstream of modern archaeological textile conservation. That she would be allowed to mount a cleaning and refixing operation on the Shroud without overview and consultation with other conservators demonstrates a dangerous carelessness on the part of the Commission which authorized it and an incredible over-confidence on her part.

Let me ask you, Karlheinz, if you were invited by the Israeli government to go there and excavate a tomb that was world famous with solid evidence that it might be the tomb of Christ, would you not assemble a team of archaeologists? Would you not seek out the best geologist for the kind of rock and soil it was situated in, the best civil engineer who had experience with the rock, the best specialist in 1st century Jewish burial customs and artifacts, the best forensics specialist for a detailed investigation of the *in situ* evidence found in and around it, the best epigrapher, etc, etc. I think you would. And not a bunch of cronies from Wurzburg and vicinity. Mechthild had a comparable task, and she did not do this. **Far, far** from it. Which international scientist who has worked on the Shroud was present?

The Holy Shroud of Turin is not St. Anthony's tunic; it does not belong to some provincial Italian archdiocese; it belongs to the world.

His response, sadly, did not address the major issues, and after a rather more bitter exchange, communication between us ceased. This would happen several times more, with people for whom I had considerable respect until the crisis brought on by the "restoration" showed their true colors.

For the draft letter to be circulated to Villa Gualino participants, several of us decided that the focus should be on the process, and the promising vision prevalent at the conference, contrasted with the harsh reality of what had happened. There would be no direct criticism of the "restoration" as that could only be addressed after the forthcoming press conference. We felt also that it was very important that Adler's name and stature not be used to justify the intervention, unless Turin could produce solid evidence that he had endorsed the measures that were taken. I felt very confident that they would not be able to do this, and indeed they never did. The draft was circulated to a small group, revised and translated into Italian, then sent out to all 39 participants at Villa Gualino – 19 Italians and 20 non-Italian; Adler had died a few months after the conference and we learned later that another, Ron Jenkins, had also passed away. The letter was eventually signed by ten people, and the textile expert Testore indicated his agreement in general but said that he had already written directly to Poletto so there was no need to add his name. The letter read:

> Dear Cardinal Poletto, and Profs. Savarino and Scannerini,
>
> We the undersigned participants of the March 2000 conference held at Villa Gualino in Turin were shocked to read newspaper accounts of the recent 'conservation' operation conducted on the Shroud. In the light of the official press conference planned for mid-September, and desiring first to have all the facts and the full official statement, we will refrain from any comments on the conservation works that have been done.
>
> However, certain statements made in the press by officials regarding the conference at Villa Gualino need to be corrected, and we call upon the conference organizers, profs. Savarino and Scannerini, to issue a public statement rectifying the erroneous information which has been disseminated in the media.
>
> Firstly, a statement was made that the operation of June and July was conducted 'on the basis of directions which emerged from the world-wide symposium of experts of March 2000.' This is categorically untrue, as everyone who attended the conference knows full well. In fact, the exact opposite is the truth. Not only was there no mention at all of any such radical invasive 'conservation' measure at the conference, but a specific recommendation regarding a program of non-invasive scientific testing to further understand the conservation issues was agreed.
>
> Secondly, a general summation agreed by conference participants was published on pages 16-17 in the conference proceedings (which appeared as the book *The Turin Shroud: Past, Present, and Future*). The last two paragraphs of that summation state:
>
> 'A series of experiments specifically directed at improving our knowledge for the purposes of conservation is essential, especially in view of the considerable development of instruments and improvements in non-invasive analytical methods.'
>
> 'We therefore recommend the co-ordination of those experts interested in the Shroud as a subject of research and in the methods and instruments which may be used for this purpose.'
>
> To our knowledge, there has been no such series of experiments made since March 2000, nor has there been any 'co-ordination of experts interested in the Shroud as a subject of research.'
>
> Thirdly, it has been claimed in the media that Prof. Alan Adler supported the type of the operation which was carried out in June-

July. We feel that it is very important that the truth be made known. In his last statements on the subject, and especially in his last written article, Prof. Adler made a strong recommendation identical to that quoted above in the summation of the conference. This is found in his paper in the published proceedings, in which Prof. Adler included a section on 'Conservation Issues' (page 70) . He describes the problems and certain steps that had been taken, and he concludes the section with this important sentence: 'To continue to further this work, more data acquired by further testing on the Shroud itself is required.' It is vital to note that he did not say 'is desirable' or 'would be of considerable assistance.' His statement is very clear – to take conservation any further, direct testing on the Shroud was **required**. This testing has not been carried out, to our knowledge, and therefore no progress has been made since March 2000 in understanding the conservation issues.

Fourthly, the following statement was made in the media by an official representing the archdiocese of Turin: 'The conservation [of the Shroud] has nothing to do with the scientific research, which is another issue. The conference [at Villa Gualino] dealt with other things, not with this, with the conservation.' Of course, one cannot expect a diocesan spokesman to understand the complicated issues involved in conservation. Nonetheless, a correction must be made to this statement, and we call upon Profs. Savarino and Scannerini to do so. Scientific research, testing, measuring and monitoring are an absolutely essential part of conservation, as the above statements from the conference summation and from Prof. Adler's paper so clearly demonstrate.

Finally, and sadly, we must express our disappointment at the final outcome of the gathering at Villa Gualino in March 2000. It was a wonderful conference and ended with such promise. The ideals of international cooperation, careful scientific investigation, peer review, openness, dialogue and the exchange of ideas were all affirmed. Proposals or ideas for future research, measurement, testing and conservation of the Shroud were invited, and a review process was outlined.

After the conference, in their letter of March 18, 2000, the conference chairman and vice-chairman reminded all participants to submit their proposals or ideas. This letter further stated: 'We will send you a synthesis of the proposals which will keep the dialogue open.' No synthesis of proposals has ever been sent, and no dialogue has taken place. We understand that a large amount of work is involved, and no one has been unduly impatient about this.

But the shocking news of Aug. 9 puts things in a very different perspective.
Sincerely,

Dr. Jeannette Cardamone, Prof. Avinoam Danin, Dr. Frank DeBlase, Prof. John P. Jackson, Prof. William Meacham, Dr. Robert L. Otlet, Prof. Sam Pellicori, Fr. Heinrich Pfeiffer SJ, Dr. Alan D. Whanger, Dr. Fredrick Zugibe

Fr. Pfeiffer, an expert on Christian art, was on vacation in Mexico when the draft reached him. His immediate comment was: "When someone in Italy wants to do something sly or announce something bad, they do it in August, when the whole country is on holiday." Dietz wrote back in a very hostile manner asking why, since I knew Flury-Lemberg well, I had not spoken with her directly. I had presumed she would not be at liberty to say anything until the press conference, but I went ahead and called her anyway. She was not at liberty to say anything. I asked her what experts had been consulted, and she said 'many', but when pressed for names she only mentioned Adler and other members of the Commission.

I also wrote a personal letter to Poletto, to let him know the depth of feeling about what he had authorized:

Dear Cardinal Poletto,
Please forgive me for writing in English, but I have no one to help prepare a translation, and my Italian, from the year I spent at the Gregorian University in Rome in 1969, is now too poor to write a serious letter.
And please pardon me for speaking freely, bluntly and without polite niceties. 'To speak the truth, in love.'
My dear brother in Christ, you have made a terrible mistake; you have allowed a horrendous thing to be done to the Holy Shroud. I have no doubt that you have been grievously ill advised and misled by the Commission for Preservation. It saddens me to recall that when I met you in March 2000, I had the strong feeling that you were a dynamic leader and that you would do good things for the Shroud. Others at that meeting had the same impression of you. Never in our wildest dreams would we have imagined that you would allow such a tragedy to befall the Shroud. Never could we have imagined that you would be so completely misled by a small group of people, possibly motivated by their own vanity or overwhelmed by the historic misadventure they were about to undertake on the Shroud.

The Commission has strayed from what should have been their sole task – to preserve the Shroud intact, as it is, with no deterioration. Instead, they embarked on a confused and ill-informed mission to beautify or improve the appearance of the Shroud, in an outrageous 'restoration.'

Unfortunately they will not go down in history as the main culprit, although they do bear much responsibility. But it is you, Cardinal, who will forever be linked to this. A senior Shroud researcher has already labeled it the 'Poletto desecration.' **Everyone** that I have spoken with feels anger, bitterness, sadness, betrayal, or all of these emotions. Especially feeling betrayed are those who attended the conference at Villa Gualino, which upheld the noble ideals of international cooperation and dialogue. And yet, the very people who were planning this terrible, ignorant and confused mission to beautify the Shroud participated for three days in the conference, read papers and entered in the discussions, and **not once** was there mention of this radical intervention, this major alteration of the relic.

You will certainly receive extensive and worldwide criticisms for allowing this intervention. Many people will explain more eloquently and precisely than I why it was unnecessary, why it was a violation of the stewardship of the precious relic, handed down from one generation to the next since 1534 intact and **without** major alteration. Conservators will tell you that what was done was totally unnecessary and put great stress on the cloth. Researchers will tell you that it was organized improperly, without peer review. And worst of all, scientists will tell you that vital information contained in the cloth has been irretrievably lost. If the Holy Shroud really is the burial cloth of Christ, then it is the only physical evidence we have about His passion, and burial. To lose **any** information that the precious relic has carried down through the centuries, due to an ill-considered 'restoration,' can only be described as a tragedy.

The reason that I write to you, however, is not to bewail or mourn something that has already been done, no matter how appalling. Rather, it is to plead with you **to take some action now** that will give new hope to those who love the Shroud and seek the truth about it. The shock and horror at what has been done can be partly soothed and dispelled by decisive actions that will open new horizons for the precious relic, so the world can look beyond the outrageous 'restoration' to something positive.

The most important thing that I urge you to consider authorizing, as soon as possible, is a new radiocarbon dating ... Further, please

THE "RESTORATION" AND ITS AFTERMATH

consider authorizing another international scientific study of the Shroud. It would take several months to review and select the best protocols and teams, and several months more for them to get organized, but the mere fact that this program of research was starting would also do much to dispel the horror and dismay now felt all over the world.

All of the above actions would give new hope where there is now despair and a sense of betrayal. These actions would show you to be a dynamic leader of the Church, and would help to erase the memories of the terrible 'restoration.' And above all, they would advance the cause of the Church.

I did not expect much by way of a reply, and I did not get much of one. It was curt and self-confident. It made me wonder if he was really misled by the Commission, or rather if he was out there in front egging them on, to be involved in the "historic task"!

> Dear Doctor Meacham,
> [Concerning an article I sent to him previously] this will be taken into consideration along with all the other proposals, when the Holy Father directs us to move from the phase of commitment to conservation on to that of new experimental research relative to the Shroud.
> Concerning what you have written [about the recent intervention], I want to tell you that I was seeking only to promote initiatives for the conservation of the Shroud and to be able to draw help therefrom in the evangelical and pastoral action of the Church. I thus cannot accept your reasoning and your negative opinions. A basic criterion in scientific discourse says that before judging it is necessary to know, to see and to hear. Now you do not know how things were done, you have not seen the results achieved by our artisans, and you have not heard what those who were asked to give their views have said – views which were endorsed by the Pope himself – and the views of those who did the intervention. I hope that you can acknowledge this deficiency. ...
> With salutations,
> Severino Cardinal Poletto

The point he made about moving from the conservation phase to the research phase is interesting in clarifying perhaps how the "Turin Group" (as Poletto would later refer to it) could separate or try to justify in their own minds, albeit erroneously, the functions they were taking upon themselves to do, without peer review or outside consultation, whereas "all the scientific proposals" needed to be subjected to such review. This was another indication that they had made terrible mistakes in 1) believing that there was a clear-cut distinction between the two; 2) failing to recognize the potential dangers of the former; and 3) thinking that this distinction would be acceptable to the world of scholarship. It is of course debatable to what extent if any they cared about the last item, as the manner in which the intervention was planned certainly appeared cavalier.

Poletto and his "Turin Group" obviously **did** care very much about the media and how their alteration of the relic would be portrayed to the world. The fact that certain Italian sindonologists like Emanuela were raising such a ruckus, that letters were being sent to the Pope, and that ten of their own selected "international experts" had expressed dismay (though not yet publicly) – all must have reached a critical mass in the first week of September. On the 8th of that month, I and several others received an urgent email from Ghiberti saying he had been authorized by Cardinal Poletto to invite us to attend a private briefing and viewing of the Shroud on the 20th, and the press conference on the next day. No expenses could be covered, however. I was attending an archaeological conference in Taiwan at the time, and spent much of the next two days on the telephone and internet discussing with others, deciding finally to go (after considering asking if the private viewing for international invitees could be delayed until October), then sorting out travel arrangements. It transpired that all participants of Villa Gualino had been invited, and about half of the foreign ones were planning to come. The executive board of AMSTAR was also invited, and all five planned to come. I thought their participation would give added strength to the rising dismay and criticism that had been unleashed. Sadly, in this regard I had not fully appreciated the attraction of power, and the desperate desire of some people to get closer to it.

From the outset it was clear that this invitation from Turin was a maneuver to moderate any criticism that might be expressed. I believed (wrongly as it turned out) that it might backfire, gathering together all those who were so stung by what had happened, with a big press conference planned. I thought the media would get an earful from many of these critics, even if not for citation by name. Emanuela felt differently, and proposed that the opposition should hold their own separate press conference two days later, in Rome. She felt that Turin was Poletto's turf, and people would be reluctant to speak their minds as guests, so it would be more appropriate to comment at a different venue. She said three others had agreed and pressed for a commitment from me; I insisted on making the decision in Turin after the preview and after speaking with the others who had confirmed their plan to attend – Cardamone, Jackson,

Zugibe, Fr. Pfeiffer. It seemed that it might be possible for us to arrange a meeting with the media in Turin, perhaps the next day. Certainly, a drama was about to be played out.

11. Altered Shroud Unveiled

On September 18, 2002 I Arrived In Turin, and immediately met the other members of the AMSTAR board for lunch. Dorothy Crispino, an American Shroud researcher retired and living near Turin, was there as well. Unlike the previous board meetings I had attended in Dallas, this one seemed cooler and more formal. It was a bad portent. We decided to meet later that afternoon with several of the other foreign invitees, and messages were left at various hotels for people arriving. We installed ourselves in the reception area of the dining room at the Dogana Vecchia Hotel, which had appropriately an old world charm with old sofas and creaking wooden floor. By early evening, the numbers swelled to about 15. Among the first to arrive was Ian Wilson, who breathlessly announced that he had just spoken with two members of the Centro and they assured him that no scorched or charred material had been cut away from the Shroud. This had been one of the biggest fears, so a mood of somewhat guarded optimism prevailed and the atmosphere was generally jovial. There were still of course many areas of concern. A group from Rome including Emanuela and Fr. Pfeiffer arrived, and conversation turned to what damage might have been done and what information possibly lost. Emanuela cautioned everyone quite pointedly not to believe what Wilson had been told by the Centro members. Alas, this warning proved to be correct.

By the time we all set out for the private briefing, which was to begin at 7pm, everyone seemed to be agreed that hard questions needed to be raised, and no punches should be pulled. Even Ian Wilson, who had hitherto been sympathetic to the "restoration," told me before we entered the room where the briefing would be held that he was in agreement with me and the others, and "there was no need for daggers at dawn." His forecast was wrong, and daggers would be out soon enough.

Entering the gate of the old seminary building was, to borrow the immortal words of Yogi Berra, "déjà vu all over again". I had walked through this door 16 years before, almost to the day, for the beginning of the C-14 conference. Then, there was a great feeling that progress was imminent, and that we were on the verge of a major breakthrough. This time however there was a foreboding and a sense that nothing positive could come from this gathering. The atmosphere in the courtyard was cordial, and everyone exchanged pleasantries. We were handed the large format Ghiberti publication ("a coffee table booklet" I called it) and another one of the same size (10.5 by 12 inches) entitled *Shroud Images 2000* which contained photographs and digital images of the Shroud taken in November 2000. It had a very long (38 inches) centerfold color photograph of the Shroud which matched exactly one in the Ghiberti booklet, constituting a "before" and "after" record of the relic. I took a seat next to Karlheinz Dietz and the first thing he said to me was "You are not a good person. You have been causing a lot of trouble." I replied that *au contraire*, he and his associates were the ones that had caused the trouble, and whatever could they have been thinking. As we sat in the meeting room waiting for the proceedings to begin, John Jackson came over to me with a very angry look on his face. He asked if I remembered the old crease he had described that ran into a charred area under a patch. "Well, they cut it away." He walked back to his seat looking miserable and indignant. A quick perusal of the two "centerfolds" revealed several more areas that had changed: two small holes had been merged with larger adjacent ones, and other small holes were enlarged. Clearly material had been removed in some manner if not by cutting. Emanuela had been right.

Poletto, Ghiberti and another priest who I learned later was the foot-in-mouth spokesman for the Turin archdiocese were seated at the podium. The room was quiet and someone was fooling with the notebook computer and projector for what seemed like a very long time. Finally, an image appeared on the screen to a small chorus of '*ecco*' and '*va bene*'. The show was underway, describing the "conservation measures" that were taken to "protect the Shroud." At the third or fourth slide someone took a photograph with flash. Ghiberti stood up and shook his index finger from side to side: "No fotographia, no photographs." His tone and look were stern, authoritarian. I bit my lip to refrain from asking why not – have we not had enough of this secrecy? I had seen this sudden attitude shift in him once before, at Villa Gualino when the conference summary was being discussed and a diversion came up. But better not to antagonize over this, when there were much more important fish to fry.

After opening remarks by Poletto and Ghiberti, Piero Savarino, scientific adviser to Poletto, gave the main presentation. He stated:

> In the course of these [earlier] works, the Shroud was the object of a series of careful observations. As an example, it was found that

under the patch situated near the foot, a considerable amount of foreign substances was present. Therefore, the possible presence of polluting systems under the central patches as well was feared. The decision to intervene, backed by the Holy See, was taken with the will to proceed by degrees and intervene with means proportioned to the situation that, moreover, had to be verified moment by moment.

In fact, the imagination had not succeeded in previewing the real situation. ... on the edge of [another] patch, a worrisome presence of the very fine dust of carbon. A microscopic observation, carried out with the equipment provided by Dr. Tomedi, has demonstrated that the carbonized material is present on the Holland cloth and also on Shroud sites far from the burns. ... On the Shroud sites not closely adjacent to the burns no intervention has been carried out, in order to avoid alteration and hindrance to future research.

The intervention has followed these criteria:

a) Improvement of the conservation conditions removing the polluting parts on the edges of the burns, avoiding obviously any damage to the Shroud.

b) Collection, cataloguing (on the basis of the position) and delivery to the Papal Custodian of the parts removed on the edges of the burns and without making any cuts.

c) Replacement of the backing cloth in order to supply an adequate mechanical support to the Shroud.

d) Carrying out of observations and measurements (on the posterior part) which would be difficult to do later. The surveys have been executed using a purpose-built apparatus which carried the various sensors of the instruments to the sites for measurement. These measurements have been delivered to His Eminence Cardinal Poletto, Papal Custodian of the Shroud, to be made available for later research.

e) On sites of spectrophotometric measures on the back of the Shroud, sampling was done by means of suction and adhesive tape. The samples, taken in the presence of the Chancellor of the Curia, have been sealed and held by the same Chancellor. The choice of the sites was made by Prof. Baima Bollone with the approval of the entire commission. Prof. Baima Bollone did furthermore carry out the sampling in the presence of the same commission.

f) Carrying out a series of microscopic surveys with the use of the equipment supplied by Dr. Tomedi.

The particulars and techniques concerned more specifically with the conservation operation will be later described by Dr. Flury-

Lemberg in response to any questions of those present. Here we only describe the most important operations that Dr. Flury-Lemberg has executed with the aid of Dr. Tomedi. The Shroud was first supported on neutral rice paper with the image side down. Then, the Holland cloth was unstitched and after that the patches. All the carbonized material was removed from the sites under the patches. Such material consisted of a very fine dust. Without any cutting, the material still weakly connected to the cloth was removed. Subsequently, the abovementioned surveys took place. At the end of these surveys, the operation of sewing the Shroud onto the new backing cloth began. The operation was carried out by turning the Shroud (without ever raising it extended) by a careful series of position variations that have guaranteed its absolute safety. We are not going into technical details, even though interesting, but we want to emphasize here the absolutely very high level of professionalism shown by Dr. Lemberg and Tomedi who carried out their task with dedication, ability and respect for the Shroud. The results obtained are noticeable in the photographs of the Shroud before and after the intervention. Therefore, the comparison leaves no doubt about the positive quality of the work carried out.

His conclusion says a lot about what the motivation for the "restoration" really was. It was to improve the appearance of the relic. All the speakers made constant reference to the "sullied", "dirty", "filthy" situation under the patches and on the corresponding inner side of the backing cloth. One of the things Savarino remarked off the cuff was very telling. Summing up the Shroud's condition, he said: "It was filthy. I wouldn't sleep in a sheet in that condition." At this there was a smattering of nervous laughter, but most did not know whether to laugh or cry. To the layman, and obviously to the aggressive textile restorer as well, cleaning must always seem a good thing. This is not necessarily the case. Modern conservators say that dirt is not the problem; **cleaning** is the problem, and a real challenge, often not undertaken. Another remark Savarino made was equally shocking. He said that an attempt was made to smooth out the creases, but "unfortunately it was not entirely successful." I said the Italian word *purtroppo* (unfortunately) out loud with the inflection of a question, and he nodded. He apparently was unaware of their historical value; they merely detracted from the Shroud's appearance.

The presentation lasted for nearly two hours, as there was staggered translation from Italian into English. According to the schedule it was supposed to be followed by questions and discussion, then a viewing of the Shroud, then dinner. When the formal presentation finished, there was a long question of several parts from one of the Italians, and by the time Poletto and Ghiberti answered it all, it was approaching 9:30pm. Looking at his watch repeatedly, Ghiberti suggested that, due to the late hour, the discussion be postponed until after dinner, and we should proceed directly to view the Shroud. There was a brief discussion about this, but it seemed completely pointless to oppose it since, as Poletto had said in his letter to me, we still had not seen the object itself. It occurred to me that the discussion session after dinner might be cut short, or even might not take place at all. When I recounted the sequence of events later to an old Shroud hand in the US, he was in no doubt that the entire evening was planned, from the 7pm scheduled start to the actual 7:40, followed by the long presentation, the looming visit to view the Shroud, and dinner – so that the hard question-and-answer and open discussion session simply would not happen.

The entire party of about 60 people assembled in the main cathedral. Groups of 8 to 10 at a time were admitted into the small chapel where the Shroud is now kept, lying flat in a glass case. Some prayed at a railing outside before going in. I was in a somber mood, wondering how bad the damage might be. The viewing this time was totally different from the one at Villa Gualino. There it had been a part of an academic conference, but for me seeing this object for the first time was equally a moving emotional and religious experience. This time the atmosphere was decidedly religious, but my mood was in opposition to the atmosphere. I wanted to examine the object for alteration and damage. The glass case allowed inspection from eight inches away, but the image looked fainter and less impressive than it had in natural light. My eyes kept coming back to the blood and noticing details that I had not seen the first time, while I kept trying to focus on the changes. After a minute or so, a priest began to read out a meditation, which I found annoying. A woman was crying, and I moved away. Definitely not a wondrous experience this time.

When everyone had seen it, Poletto assembled the entire group in front of the main altar, announcing that he would not be joining us for dinner, but before he left he wanted to hear some reactions and opinions. The first speaker seemed to me to have been planted – he spoke of "feeling closer to the holy relic." He droned on and on, pausing for every sentence to be translated. Several others praised the fine work of Flury-Lemberg and Tomedi, even Isabel Piczek spoke positively of the fine sewing and the "reversibility" of the stitching (how could it not be?). I was surprised, having heard previously the depth of her negative feelings toward the "restoration." Fred Zugibe was the first to make an adverse comment, saying that he was disappointed to see that gloves were not being worn while the cloth was handled, resulting no doubt in some contamination. Fr.

Pfeiffer said that a valuable archaeological object would not be treated in this manner, but he was interrupted by Dietz who was then interrupted by me. I said that the entire operation was unnecessary and scientific data had been lost, but did not go into much detail. It was 10:30pm and people were shifting about impatiently, most not having eaten anything since early afternoon. Dinner was served. Ironically, it was in the sacristy where the "restoration" had been performed.

Poletto did come into the dining area to say a prayer, and as the food was being served he stood around talking to a clutch of people. Hungry and tired, I nonetheless went over and told him I had to point out that he had been badly advised. He asked what I would have done, and I started to make an analogy: "If you had an infection on your foot, and your doctor told you it would have to be amputated ..." Ghiberti interjected at this point: "But we didn't amputate anything." I replied: "Yes you did." And to Poletto: "But what would you do if the doctor told you this?" Poletto shrugged and before he could reply I told him I knew what he would do. He would get a taxi and be off immediately to see another doctor for a second opinion. He laughed and said I should have been on the Conservation Commission. I laughed and lied, saying it was not for nothing that he had been made cardinal, as he could see right through to the crux of the matter. All very cordial, but I felt that, just maybe, the fact had gotten through to him that the process had been flawed.

Dinner lasted until almost midnight, and sure enough, there was no discussion. Ghiberti reminded us of the press conference the next day and suggested that perhaps certain groups might want to nominate a spokesman to make statements at the press conference. I presumed that this was more planting of favorable comment, and didn't give it another thought. By this time, it was clear to me that Emanuela had been right, and the turf was Poletto's. We were his guests, and it would be bad form to bite the hand that had just fed us and given us a rare opportunity to see the Shroud again. The veteran US Shroudie thought that this too was the devilishly sly intention of the Turin group from the beginning.

As everyone left the sacristy, I was speaking with someone on the steps and saw Isabel go by, eyes straight ahead and in a hurry. I didn't give this much thought either, as it had been a long day. I looked for Jackson but he had disappeared. When I got back to my hotel, an old style (i.e. cheap) *pensione* that Emanuela had booked for me, she knocked on my door and asked if the Shroud was dead. She and a number of others had not been invited to the briefing, but were accredited to attend the press conference. I told her the situation was as bad as we had feared, and she asked if I now agreed to participate in the press conference she had planned for two days later in Rome. "Absolutely!" She had already printed up flyers with the title: "The Shroud – Restored or Manipulated?" Somehow one of these flyers managed to get to Poletto, and he made it a point the next day to lash out at the planned Rome press conference, taking serious exception to the title. It was of course good publicity for the opposition.

The press conference the next morning was in the same hall as the briefing had been the night before. I took a seat next to Tom d'Muhala, president of AMSTAR. He asked me if I wanted to say anything after the main presentation, and I said no, whereupon he told me that "they" had decided that Mike Minor would give a short speech. Minor was a board member and vice-president of AMSTAR. This was disturbing, and I was going to protest but thought it useless as the meeting would start in a few minutes. Things would just play themselves out here; reactions would come later.

The entire press conference was in Italian, with no translation, so only I and Isabel among the foreign guests were able to follow. It was however almost exactly a re-run from the briefing, with Ghiberti and Savarino making basically the same statements. Poletto surprised me from the very beginning. His look was hostile and his tone was harsh. His first remarks were very sharp and aimed at Orazio Petrosillo, Vatican reporter of the Rome daily *Il Messaggero*, who had broken the story of the Shroud's "restoration" and was seated in the front row. Poletto returned to the subject twice in his remarks, and could be seen to get agitated each time. This was very puzzling to me, since Petrosillo was only doing his job, which is to find out what is going on and to let the public know. Governments and other institutions that want secrecy have to find ways to prevent leaks, limiting the number of people who know the secret, etc. But to lash out against a reporter seemed unjustified. Poletto made the curious statement that the reporter should have called him to get the facts straight before publishing the story. When a scoop is involved, the priority is to break the news first, and then publish the comments of officials like Poletto the next day. If Poletto's suggested course of action had been followed, the reporter would risk loosing the scoop (if the news is then given to a more friendly media outlet), possibly even the story (if highly placed officials chose to lean on the editor). Petrosillo spoke brilliantly in his defence at the Rome news conference two days later. He remarked that he had never seen a prince of the Church launch such an attack on a lowly reporter. The episode left me with the impression that Poletto was not well advised and behaved vis-à-vis the media, since his normal manner is friendly and outgoing.

The conclusion of the official press conference held some surprises. When all the officials had finished their presentations, they announced that some of the foreign guests would speak. First up was Raffard de Brienne from France, who repeatedly and in the most glowing terms praised the Cardinal and the Commission on doing a fine job in "restoring" the Shroud. My reaction was mild nausea, but it was obvious that this fellow was engaged in mere sycophancy and knew nothing about conservation. The next speaker was Minor, who introduced himself as the vice-president of AMSTAR. The next few sentences left me in shock. He offered "congratulations on a fine job." And he continued: "We had heard many rumors and we're pleased to see that they are not true ... The removal of the potentially damaging acidic carbon is a very positive thing ... also positive is that the stitching is reversible and less invasive than that done in 1534." As AMSTAR had to my knowledge taken no position on the issue, his speech struck me as highly objectionable. Of course he is a lawyer and as such could not be expected to know anything about the science of conservation, but it certainly appeared to give the impression, especially with the use of 'we,' that he was speaking for AMSTAR. I learned later that other board members had been up until past 2am the night before discussing whether he should speak and if so what he should say. I had not been informed of the meeting. This and a similar incident of deception the next day led to my resignation from AMSTAR.

But worse was yet to come. Ian Wilson gave an even more nauseatingly sweet speech, gushing with compliments:

> ... I read with alarm the reports of what seemed to be damage done to the Shroud in this recent conservation. Having seen the results of that conservation, as I did last night, and heard of the careful attention to detail that was done by Mechthild Flury-Lemberg and others in the course of that work, I can only say that I have the deepest admiration for everything that was done. ... In my time of studying the Shroud, I have known four cardinals [in charge of the Shroud] and I can honestly say that now there is greater openness in Turin. ... I can only re-iterate the commendations of Mike Minor and to say thank you very much indeed to Mechthild and her assistant for this wonderful work.

This was turning into a really disgusting kissing-up fest. Wilson seemed to have undergone "a mind-blowing conversion in order to become Turin's mouthpiece" (paraphrasing something he once said about his British colleague David Sox). The press conference was turning into a re-run of the emperor's new clothes, with all the courtiers and sycophants daring not to risk displeasure by telling the truth. I had already made my views known quite clearly to Cardinal Poletto and his advisers at the briefing the night before. But in view of the Cardinal's visible agitation at the start of the press conference, and my status as a guest in these live televised proceedings, I decided that I would not speak unless invited by the chair to do so. This did not happen, and the show played out according to the prepared script. I later wrote to Poletto setting out my views in some detail, and explaining that out of consideration for him I did not speak at the press conference.

The story about the emperor's new clothes has a wonderful message, and those in positions of considerable power need to be constantly reminded of it – people will tell you what they think you want to hear in order not to risk falling from favor. Poletto genuinely seemed to want to know what people felt after seeing the Shroud "in its new condition," but many of the guests both Italian and foreign were certainly praising the "restoration" in the belief that doing so would be beneficial to their own standing and future Shroud endeavors.

Worst of all, however, was the last speaker. When the name of John Jackson was read out, I thought "ok, here we go." It was a huge shock to hear what he had to say:

> I first learned of the conservation operation through a news conference about one month ago. Naturally I became concerned if the conservation action had affected any characteristics of scientific value on the Shroud. For over 30 years, I have wanted to learn what the back side of the Shroud looked like. The complete visualization required the removal of the backing cloth. Once this was done, removal of the patches would logically follow. This would then expose the charred regions under the patches due to the 1532 fire. This material would then logically have to have been removed so as not to contaminate the rest of the Shroud. Hence the price to be paid in order to see the back side of the Shroud completely translates ultimately into the removal of this charred material. ... Our 1978 radiographs show that the historical foldmark pattern on the Shroud propagated into the charred material. This clearly shows that the foldmark pattern predates 1532. ... But we do have the radiographs that show this, so the loss is not that significant. I want to conclude by saying I think that the conservation repair, from what I can tell, seems to be of a very high quality.

I have not spoken with Jackson since, but wrote him a few weeks later:

> Dear John,
>   I am dismayed that you did not respond to my last email. Does this mean that you are going to wimp out and keep silent about the

desecration of the Shroud? Before going to Turin, we spoke about a strategy to respond in a professional and scientific manner, taking the high road of focusing on the facts and building sound arguments, avoiding accusations, personalities and emotive diversions. What happened to that?

... others are saying that you want to keep silent in the hope that your proposals for testing will receive eventual approval from Turin. If this is true I am extremely disappointed, as I have always had respect for what you and STURP did in 1978, and that will not change. But the way you go down in Shroud history is going to be determined to a not insignificant degree by the way you react to this desecration. Future generations will look back with absolute and unmitigated horror at what was done in the summer of 2002, and at the toadying, sycophantic reactions of those who tried to curry favor with the Turin inner circle. I don't think that is the way you want to be seen.

I thought you would remain silent in Turin, and that would have been vastly preferable. As it happened you offered praise and justification, which they continue to make use of. You have been repeatedly quoted in print by Ghiberti and others in Italy since Sept. 21 as supporting the "restoration" right alongside the truly opportunistic [names and expletives deleted!]. I reviewed the tape of your remarks at the press conference and found them even worse than I remembered. Much of what you said is utter rubbish which you should be ashamed of. No scientist worth his salt would approve of the irretrievable destruction of data just to satisfy his curiosity about a feature. Yet this is what you said on Sept 21. No archaeologist or museum curator of any caliber would allow the destruction of part of a priceless artifact in order to see the underside or interior. Yet this is what you said.

Have you read the detailed descriptions by Paul Maloney and me of the types of data that have been destroyed? Have you seen the video clips that I put up on my HKU website? There, in three seconds, you see the full barbarity of the operation, as one of the seamstresses scrapes away the deposit around a poker hole. When I think of all the thought, word, and deed over the last 30 years that have gone into the conservation of the Shroud and its data intact, esp. on the need to limit the invasive and destructive type testing to the absolute minimum, and so forth – all to be negated in such a stupid and unscientific operation. It makes me sick, as it should you.

This 'restoration' is the defining event in the existence of the Shroud for perhaps the next 470 years, just like the fire at Chambery has been for the last 470. Someone from STURP needs to condemn, in the strongest terms, the unnecessary and unjustified alteration to the relic and loss of data. All there is so far for the record, as I wrote to Larry and Ray, is John Jackson saying how happy he is that we now have photos and scans of the backside of the cloth, and that the foldmarks he is so interested in are still there (not for lack of trying to get rid of them) ... And you actually praise the quality of the conservation work!!!!

If this is how you want to go down for posterity on the 'restoration,' so be it. I will proceed to publish these remarks and treat them with the contempt they deserve, right alongside Ian Wilson's. But I have a feeling that you do not want it to go this way, that you want to set the record straight by publishing your considered reaction to the 'restoration.' I know that Jan Cardamone, Larry Schwalbe, Bryan Walsh, Dan Scavone and others have submitted or are preparing comments for Barrie's website. I hope you will do so as well.

His reply was a one-sentence haughty rebuke saying that my letter lacked professional respect. Aye, that it did! One can never know what goes on inside someone else's head, but one has to wonder if the speech Jackson made at the press conference represents his real view. The speech however goes down for posterity. The Turin group embraced it, naturally, saying that the leading STURP scientist Jackson was concerned and skeptical about the intervention "until he saw the Shroud" and *mirabile dictu* this changed his mind. Others were saying that it had something to do with positive vibes that Jackson supposedly received from brief eye contact with Poletto. I had also seen something in Poletto's eyes, and it was not pretty. His stinging attack on Petrosillo showed instead a certain ugliness.

Following this flurry of activity in Turin, I had time to go through the papers that were handed out at the private briefing and press conference. A curious one was a statement issued by Silvano Scannerini, chairman of the Villa Gualino conference. It was obviously a response to the letter from ten participants that I had drafted and circulated, but strangely it was only in Italian and it was only handed out at the briefing. It read:

> The president of the Congress Shroud 2000, in conjunction with the co-president Prof. Piero Savarino, have the duty to rectify erroneous information that appeared in the media, re-asserting with this declaration the truth of the facts:

1. In the Congress there was no mention of any specific intervention for conservation, given the brief time, but non-invasive scientific tests were discussed which could shed light on problems related to the conservation of the Shroud.
2. The Congress stated in its conclusions that, to accord with point one above, various proposals for research should be invited without excluding those not related to conservation. To this end all the proposals received were submitted by us to the Custodian of the Shroud, His Eminence Cardinal Severino Poletto, on July 18, 2002. ...
3. If it is undeniable that Prof. Adler did, during the Congress, propose that research on conservation was essential, it is equally true that he did, in his capacity as a member of the Commission for Conservation, sustain the necessity of that intervention which was discussed by the Commission to stabilize a situation which could result in damage also brought about as a result of the presence of semi-combusted or strongly oxidized particles between the Holland cloth and the Shroud, or on the Shroud itself. But it must be stressed that those interventions, though important, are aimed, like the conservation [of the Shroud] in the new case, at stabilizing the situation of the cloth; they leave unchanged the need for deeper research to optimize the conservation.
4. The statement which appeared in the press that 'conservation has nothing to do with scientific research' is untenable and absurd, surely the fruit of misunderstanding. Unfortunately, errors and misunderstandings abound in the publicizing of Shroud matters, and one can only regret this.

Prof. Silvano Scannerini
President of Shroud 2000

The fact that this was not in English and that it was not handed out at the press conference was puzzling. It was as though it was directed only at the Italian participants of Villa Gualino. No reply was ever sent to the ten who wrote the original letter. This struck me as strange, and after a while I wrote to Scannerini, who is a very mild-mannered and likeable chap.

> Dear Silvano,
> It was a pleasure to see you again in Turin last month. And I was pleased to receive, at the briefing on Friday evening, a copy of your declaration regarding the Congress 'Shroud 2000' at Villa Gualino. It addressed some of the points made in the letter to you by nine participants at that Congress. (A tenth participant, Dr. F.J. DeBlase,

asked that his name be added, but the letter to you and Prof. Savarino had already been sent by that time.)

Several things puzzled me, however, about the declaration:

1) it was only in Italian, but

2) it was not handed out at the official press conference the next day, and

3) it was not sent to the nine signatories of the original letter.

... I have translated the declaration and sent it out to all signatories plus Dr. DeBlase with a copy of this letter to you. The questions that remain in everyone's mind, unanswered to this day, are:

a) why there was no mention of this planned intervention at Villa Gualino, and especially,

b) why there was no wide consultation with the experts who attended Villa Gualino, before such an aggressive and invasive intervention was conducted on the Shroud.

It is this failure to engage in peer review and dialogue that brought about 'our disappointment at the final outcome of the gathering at Villa Gualino in March 2000.'

His reply consisted of a bit of platitude about being desirous of insuring the future conservation of the Shroud. So at least one of "the questions that remain in everyone's mind, unanswered to this day" still has not been answered – the failure to consult widely. It is now abundantly clear that the "restoration" was not mentioned at Villa Gualino because it was not planned at that time; its conception was the result of a hasty and particularly sordid affair during the first week of November 2000.

Early on Sunday morning I left Turin with Fr. Pfeiffer, Prof. Giulio Fanti of the University of Padova, Emanuela and her brother Maurizio for the day-long drive to Rome. The "opposition" press conference was largely planned in the car during the trip, and opening statements were written, amidst exchanging views on various Shroud issues and gossip on various personalities.

The next day in Rome, in a room packed with reporters and others interested in the Shroud, each of us made our statements. Mine was translated into Italian. It was fairly brief; I laid out the basic objections to the "restoration" while acknowledging (perhaps too charitably) the good intentions of the Conservation Commission. I concluded with a response to Poletto's reported dismay over the controversy:

> Cardinal Poletto has expressed concern over the 'polemics' that have arisen as a result of this ill-advised action. It would of course

have been infinitely better if there had been discussion **before** deciding to alter forever the precious relic. Now it is inevitable that there will be discussion, for a long time, about what has been done. But we must endeavor to be professional, to focus on the facts and the empirical reality, and to avoid as far as possible personal attacks and accusations. I know that Cardinal Poletto will recall that we are advised by the Apostle Paul to be honest with each other and 'speak the truth in love.'

Fr. Pfeiffer made a very impressive presentation focusing on the reasons why the Shroud needed to be conserved, properly. Fanti focused on further scientific research that needs to be done. Petrosillo spoke eloquently about his role as a reporter and his duty to the public. Emanuela summed up our concern that the Shroud had been treated badly, and whether the present authorities could be trusted to preserve it in the future.

A response from Turin was not long in coming, and it took the form of personal attack and accusation. Ghiberti wrote an article a few days later in a Catholic newspaper making a "sour grapes" allegation, that those who were criticizing the "restoration" were annoyed that they had not been included in the operation. What total rubbish! The truth is that the small group comprising the Commission had decided in secret to make a place for themselves in history by embarking on a monumental "restoration" of the sacred relic, without even minimal consultation with experts. Certainly, there was a degree of opportunism, perhaps subconscious, and several degrees of extreme over-confidence and self-delusion.

That there was a conflict of interest is indisputable. Access to the Shroud for first hand observation and research is a valuable commodity; very few have had the opportunity. "Restoring" the Shroud would be perceived as a great important and historic task, as Ghiberti himself stated. Those who carry out these functions would acquire significant status and importance, nay a place in history, as a result. Clearly they should **not** be the same ones who make the decision about whether the work is necessary. When one translates the situation into monetary terms it becomes crystal clear: if a million-dollar project was being considered then it is painfully obvious that a committee would raise instant questions if it awarded the contract to its own members.

Apparently all Commission members were directly involved in the operation, in one capacity or another. And of course there was the previous secret scanning of the underside also carried out by Commission members. Thus far, three coffee table books have been written by Commission members about the "restoration," and others are said to be in preparation. Rather highly-priced photographs, postcards and a DVD of the "new-look"

Shroud are being marketed by the Archdiocese. Ghiberti concluded his account thus: "Those who took part in this round of operations are grateful for the gift they have received from the Lord." Whether through divine blessing or insider dealing, they have certainly left their mark on the Shroud.

12. Impact on the Relic

In July of 2003, a well-illustrated trilingual coffee table book written by Flury-Lemberg was published by the Turin archdiocese. While this volume is far from the full documentation that was expected, it is now possible to render a more complete and informed judgement concerning the radical and invasive intervention on the relic. What was done to the Shroud may have been well intentioned, but these intentions paved the road to hell for the preservation of the relic and the data it contained.

According to the official press release issued by Turin:

> Dr Flury-Lemberg is considered an authority in the methodology of restoration, and she is above the debates of recent decades. The author is moreover a firm supporter of the criterion of reversibility, considering it an inalienable component of the methodology of restoration of an ancient piece. The book describes the conservation work in minute detail with the aid of precise photographic documentation [and] the various stages of work for the purpose of the conservation of the cloth: the removal of the patches, the Holland cloth and the material that was the source of the pollution. In the text it is demonstrated how no invasive intervention was conducted and how material that was already flaking off was collected and accurately catalogued for future research.

Alas, almost all of these claims were demonstrably and patently untrue. Practically the only statement that can be accepted from the above blurb is that Flury-Lemberg is an authority on restoration. As we shall see, most conservators today abhor aggressive restoration methods, and keep restorers well away from any valuable historical item.

The basic premise for the entire operation was the claim that the present condition of the Shroud posed a threat to its preservation. In explaining how this threat was perceived, Flury-Lemberg makes a telling statement: "The linen fabric of the Shroud, though marked by damaging events in the past, has survived until today without special measures for its protection." This fact alone would lead most modern conservators to apply the "protect-do-not-treat" rule, the rule of thumb for important pieces. In the popular expression this could be translated as "even if it is broke, don't try to fix it." But Flury-Lemberg and the Conservation Commission mistakenly believed that the situation was dangerous. She wrote:

> The fibers of the linen as such are in a very healthy condition and there would be no cause for concern if not for the image of a crucified man. The Shroud of Turin is a unique relic the meaning of which solely relies [resides?] in this image ... All efforts regarding the conservation of the Shroud must therefore aim at the preservation of this image.

So far so good. STURP pointed out on numerous occasions the importance of the scientific studies for conservation, since it is necessary to define precisely and accurately what is to be preserved. Flury-Lemberg begins to get in over her head as she proceeds to describe the image: "The phenomenon of the image on the linen fabric is due to an as yet unrecognized process which affected only the topmost layer of the fibers. ... The image – also the product of some kind of oxidation ..." She should have stayed with an "as yet unrecognized process."

There are several competing hypotheses regarding what caused the image and even what it consists of. STURP proposed that it was due to a dehydration, degradation or oxidation of the topmost fibrils, and although there is much to commend it, this was far from being conclusively proven. Another hypothesis, proposed by the microscopist McCrone based on his examination of sticky tape samples, was that the image consisted of fine particles of iron oxide. A recent proposal from Ray Rogers, re-studying the sticky tape samples, is that the image resulted from a Maillard-type reaction between naturally occurring impurities on the surface of the fibers and vapors emitted from the body. None of these hypotheses can be considered as proven or disproven, though McCrone's is certainly very close to the latter category; it was a grievous error to proceed with a radical intervention on the assumption that the image was "the product of some kind of oxidation."

Even assuming that the STURP hypothesis is correct, it was totally unjustified and a huge mistake to make the huge leap to a final conservation solution:

IMPACT ON THE RELIC

> ... to avoid the possible absorption of the relatively delicate lines of the image into the darkening color of the background, thus rendering the image unrecognizable, [it] is therefore urgent to find effective measures to counteract the oxidation process.

If this was an appeal for further study and collaborative research over the next few years, as Adler was urging, one could not find fault with it. However, as a licence or a justification that the Conservation Commission gave themselves for immediate, invasive surgery without outside consultation, it is outrageous. What expertise did they gather before deciding on "effective measures" to counter what they wrongly perceived as an urgent problem? There was absolutely no scientific data or basis for these measures, despite what Flury-Lemberg went on to argue:

> The possibility that residues of burnt material in the areas of the holes caused by the fire could be trapped in between the Holland cloth and the patches was soon recognized as a danger. As these substances can considerably accelerate oxidation ...

These substances are inert carbon. They have been on the cloth since 1532, principally around the perimeter of some burnholes. In the course of handling over the years, some of the carbonized cloth has been abraded down to dust-sized particles. There is no evidence at all that the carbonized edges accelerated oxidation around the burnholes, nor is there any known chemical process by which it could. Nor is there any evidence to suggest or any reason to suppose that it would accelerate oxidation in the form of accumulations of loose particles. As if one red herring were not enough, Flury-Lemberg tosses in another one: "and as the consequences of future water damage would be devastating for the Shroud – as the combination of water and burnt residue would produce a black dye ..." This can only be described as sheer fantasy and total nonsense. In order to produce a dye on the Shroud from the carbon dust under the patches, one would have to add an organic binder and thoroughly mix the carbon, binder and water. Yes, perhaps if someone with greasy hands rubbed the dust into the wet cloth it might produce a dye, of sorts. It is simply ludicrous to suggest that a dye might be produced simply from the Shroud getting wet. I tried a simple experiment by burning some linen to carbon, grinding it to fine particles (mimicking the process of abrasion to the charred edges of the burnholes over 470 years), and then mixing it with water. Carbon does not dissolve in water, and it was difficult to get all of it into suspension. I poured the resulting black liquid on an old shirt, and let it dry. Most of the carbon brushed off easily. All that remained was a very slight grayish discoloration. This was probably caused by the smallest particles in a dispersal, not a dye at all. It came out with simple rinsing. Hardly devastating for my shirt.

Flury-Lemberg goes on to relate how the Commission's reluctance to remove the patches and backing cloth was "finally overridden by the proven danger." Her use of the word 'proven' shows how far she had strayed from the path of proper scientific investigation. Her account takes a strange turn as she then introduces a new aspect – the supposed "staining" of the Shroud due to the burn residues. She states that up to November 2000 there was no plan to remove the patches and backing cloth, but then:

> Only the thorough investigation carried out on the Holland cloth on that occasion [the scanning of the underside] revealed the whole dramatic meaning of the staining. ... Now it turned out that all the holes caused by the fire showed as dark gray stains on that lining at the reverse of the Shroud. Under the microscope these stains turned out to be carbon dust embedded in between the fibers. Thus it became obvious that residues from the fire were present in the areas of the holes between the Holland cloth and the patches. This clear evidence finally made it possible to come to a decision ...

In other words, the presence of particulate carbon embedded in the fibers of the backing cloth (not a stain in the true chemical sense) was the final proof of the some imminent danger to the Shroud. This is so absurd it is hard to imagine anyone taking it seriously. How does carbon dust embedded **in the backing cloth** threaten the Shroud itself? How does it accelerate the oxidation process on the main cloth if it is only in contact with the patch directly facing it? And yet, this was the final straw as far as the Commission was concerned, and within a few days all of its members had signed the letter recommending the "restoration" to Poletto. Absolutely incredible, mind-blowing stuff!

Sensing perhaps that the arguments presented thus far are less than persuasive, Flury-Lemberg describes how "after the restoration began it became abundantly clear how necessary this decision had been." She cites the "great amount of carbon dust" that was found under the patches, and "piles of black soot [actually merely carbon particles, not soot which usually means an oily, grimy substance deposited by smoke] embedded in between all the healthy fibers of the areas around the holes." She believes that this finding, "even up to a teaspoon full" in places, justified the urgency of the intervention. One can only marvel at this attitude that is exacerbated by an obsession with neatness and cleanliness. One wonders if she had never heard the old saying among archaeological conservators: "dirt is not the problem; **cleaning** is the problem." To quote from Turin's press conference, she was "above the debates of recent decades." But in the final analysis, the fault was not hers, but the Commission's, for failing to conduct a proper review. If an articulate launderer had also been a member of the Commission, one wonders if they would have dry-cleaned the Shroud!

Flury-Lemberg also believed that an "autocatalytic" (self-propelling) process of oxidation had been continuing in the centuries since the fire:

> All the fragile threads that we found would undoubtedly have disintegrated during any work done [in 1534] as today they fall apart at the merest touch. ... That would mean that the burnt, brown parts were still strong enough at that time to survive the restoration work without disintegrating. They became blacker through oxidation and finally disintegrated into soot.

There are several things wrong with this notion, not the least of which is that it is a phenomenon unknown to science. Autocatalytic reactions such as she is describing do not proceed at normal air temperatures, and partly carbonized textiles will survive much longer than uncharred ones. The fire damage does not continue to spread long after the smoldering has died out. This is simply wrong, and she makes a number of erroneous assumptions to arrive at the fiction of spreading oxidation. There is no reason to believe that the cloth repaired by the nuns in 1534 was not in essentially the same condition as it was in 2002. There is every reason to doubt the claim that the charred cloth near the edge of the burnholes falls apart "at the merest touch." More than a century of handling since 1898 when the first photographs were taken has not produced any visible deterioration around the patches or around the smaller burn holes that are not covered. Perhaps it does give way under the heavy-handed tugging or scraping of the restorer, but apparently this "fragile" material survived at least eight exhibitions and many more private viewings in the twentieth century, being unrolled and then rolled back up each time, without disintegrating. And even if this material has become weaker over time there are other factors that might be the cause: mechanical stress and chemical residues from frequent handling being the two most likely candidates.

In addition to Adler (whose role in the fateful process leading to the "restoration" is discussed below), only one other reference (Hofenk de Graaff 1994) is cited by Flury-Lemberg to support the case for the supposed deterioration process. This reference however pertains to the cause of browning in old paper mounted on mats, in relation to changes in temperature and humidity causing repeated evaporation. This is another red herring, totally unrelated to the Shroud. Paper is made by a different process, it has different qualities and any suggestion of comparability between the two materials is spurious and mischievous. Furthermore, the browning effect studied by Hofenk has nothing whatever to do with oxidation from contiguous carbonized materials or carbon dust. Citing this article is a laughable attempt to add a thin veneer of scientific legitimacy to a series of unnecessary invasive procedures.

Flury-Lemberg implies that the deposition of carbon dust residues on the backing cloth was brought about by a transfer made possible by changes in temperature and humidity. This is highly debatable, but even allowing it there was still no justification for the radical intervention, since the Shroud is now kept at constant temperature and humidity, and it is not unrolled for viewing and rolled back up afterwards. The processes that led to the transport of carbon particles are no longer operative, and the carbonized edges of the burnholes will not be producing more carbon dust through movement and abrasion. If fluctuations in temperature and humidity played any role, they have now been eliminated. The roots of the problem were thus eradicated when it was decided in 1997 to keep the Shroud stored flat; the residual effects could have been dealt with in a well planned, sampled and recorded vacuuming, including under the patches and between Shroud and backing cloth, if the loose debris posed even the remotest threat. Partial unstitching would have provided access, and there was absolutely no need for the patches and original backing cloth to be removed.

To follow the logic of the "restoration," the most important condition that should have been addressed is the charred areas nearest the image, particularly the upper arms and shoulders on both frontal and dorsal body images. If oxidation were spreading out from the burn residues and posing a threat to the image, these areas should have been treated first. Of course the argument is entirely unfounded: these charred areas are not covered by patches and can be clearly seen in the 1898 photographs to be identical to the 2002 photographs. Another treatment that should have been considered, deriving from the views that led to the "restoration," was a complete vacuuming of the image side of the Shroud. (If done properly this would not be a bad idea, after a microscopic search for particles of interest that could be collected by micromanipulator.) Particulate carbon has been spread over cloth during the centuries since the fire and can be found all over the image side, in small quantities. If this matter posed a threat of increased oxidation, why was all of it not removed?

IMPACT ON THE RELIC

In fact, however, there was no such danger of accelerated oxidation from these loose carbon particles, as consultation with experts would have easily revealed. Ray Rogers of the Los Alamos National Laboratory is one of the foremost pyrolysis chemists in the world, and was involved in the STURP investigations. He is unequivocal that there is **absolutely** no threat from the charred material or carbon dust in any chemical sense and especially not from autocatalysis (Rogers 2002). The carbonized areas and the carbon dust posed no immediate or even mid-term threat to the cloth, witnessed by the simple fact that they have been on the cloth for 471 years. The coup de grace for this bizarre notion is that photographic documentation exists since 1898, and very detailed photographs since 1933. Extensive scientific measurements were made in 1978. None of this wealth of data reveals any shred of evidence to suggest that the charred areas were spreading or that any degradative process was occurring adjacent to those areas. And, no oxidation or degradation is reported for the patches and opposing areas of the backing cloth, which (as we are told many times in the book) were infiltrated with large quantities of carbon dust.

From both Ghiberti's and Flury-Lemberg's accounts, the impression one gains is that one of the prime motivations to conduct the intervention was a deep aversion to the constantly mentioned "sullied", "dirty", "filthy" situation under the patches and on the corresponding inner side of the backing cloth. As we have seen, Savarino, the official archdiocese scientific adviser, aptly summed up this attitude when he remarked at the unveiling: "It was filthy. I wouldn't sleep in a sheet in that condition." Such was the fixation with this accumulation of carbon dust that a most incongruous photograph, of an odd-shaped burn hole with patch removed showing black powdery material, was chosen for the cover of Flury-Lemberg's book. Most people would not know what it represents, and even after reading the caption on the inside title page would **still** not understand what the cover photo was meant to convey. The Conservation Commission clearly became fixated on the "dirt" and "dust," and acted precipitously without conducting even minimal research on the issue.

Finally, to an archaeologist, it is very odd to read of carbon having destructive properties on a textile. If such oxidation processes as Flury-Lemberg imagined do continue long after the initial burning, one wonders how any of the charred textile fragments could have survived from Pompeii, not to mention from the Neolithic. Some small fragments of textile several thousand years old are partly charred. Are we to suppose that they were once much bigger, but have been disappearing through Flury-Lemberg's "gradual combustion" over the centuries. This is of course complete and utter nonsense, unknown to science, just as is the paranormal claim of spontaneous human combustion. The reality is exactly the opposite; it is often the partial charring of textiles that allows them to survive even thousands of years in harsh environments, by burning off the organic components and leaving a carbonized skeleton. The textile expert John Tyrer (1983:39) wrote that "the fire at Chambery would have sterilized the Shroud and helped with its preservation." Left alone, the charred areas around the burnholes on the Shroud would have survived long after the main body of the cloth had decayed and disappeared. Yet they have been scraped away by the "restorers" – this would be an enormously comical irony if it were not so tragic.

Modern conservation principles violated

If even minimal consultation had been conducted, the Vatican, Poletto and the Commission would have learned that the radical invasive procedures employed during this "restoration" are very rarely conducted on important pieces by museum conservators today. Such procedures would only be authorized after careful consultation with scientists and other practicing conservators had established clear and indisputable danger to the object itself. The overwhelming emphasis in conservation is on passive preservation, "as is", with minimal intervention. In an article discussing modern textile conservation methods relating to "objects of awe," two American conservators (Orlofsky and Trupin, 1993) wrote in the *Journal of the American Institute of Conservation*:

> As illustrated by the Shroud of Turin, awe probably plays the strongest role in religious and reliquary objects ... Awe severely limits a conservator's options; it is the greatest inhibitor of choice. Sometimes religious textiles like a saint's tunic have come to be considered so precious that their dust is not seen as detritus but as treasure. It seems to follow that the greater the awe with which the conservators behold the textile object, the more likely they are to preserve every stain, thread, and historic dirt particle. In such cases, all concerned instinctively recoil from intrusive treatment because they understand that any action may negatively affect the future significance of the object. ... Most textile conservators now consider only preventative conservation in the form of passive mounts, developed in a variety of creative styles, and upgraded storage for archaeological and ethnographic pieces. It is hard for the textile conservator to justify elaborate sewing on these pieces, let alone

incorporating any restoration work. ... Invasive treatment is no longer considered appropriate for textiles of unique significance. ... It is universally acknowledged that overambitious treatment may prejudice artistic or cultural significance. ... The race to distance conservation from restoration became a strong characteristic of our field from the 1960s to the mid-1990s.

The "restoration" of the Shroud was thus diametrically opposed to modern conservation practice. The word restoration as applied to this operation deserves to be in quotation marks because it was not a true restoration either, but a series of radical, invasive alterations and cleaning operations for cosmetic and misinformed conservation purposes. The cloth was handled every day for a month by the "seamstresses" (Ghiberti's term) without gloves; no gowns, lab coats or hair nets were worn; no clean room controls were instituted; visitors, photographers, teams of technicians and TV crews trooped through; the cloth was illuminated by lamps without filters, shining for long periods directly on the cloth at close range; the relic was subjected to considerable stresses in the removal of patches and backing cloth, and addition of a new backing cloth.

Even if the cloth were a proven medieval relic, with no image at all, the 1534 repairs should have been retained. Flury-Lemberg discusses this issue in very strange terms:

> The conservation of the poor Clare sisters from 1534 is certainly of historical interest and therefore needs to be analyzed and noted for future research, but it does not present a value in its own right. The same is true for the conservation measures of 2002.

It is nothing short of amazing to equate repairs nearly five hundred years old with those of last year. The patches and backing cloth were visible elements of a rich heritage that had intrinsic value as part of the history and commonly recognized identity of the relic. Ancient additions to or repairs of an object become part of the object to be preserved unless 1) they pose a definite threat to it, or 2) they seriously detract from the appreciation of the original. There would be little disagreement among conservators on this point. It would be a very foolish conservator who would erase medieval graffiti from a Roman temple in the name of return to the pristine original. Even on cosmetic criteria, retention of the patches would have been sensible; Flury-Lemberg herself wrote that the patches covered "big ugly holes left by the fire."

The argument has been made before that even with a backing cloth on the Shroud it was hazardous to mount the relic in a vertical position for display. As the Shroud is now stored laid out flat in a glass case, this would also be the best manner to exhibit it, according to Jeanette Cardamone (personal communication), i.e. with observers moving around it in small groups, or on a walkway above it. To remove the existing backing cloth only to replace it with another seems to be the height of folly, or as one Shroud researcher remarked, no real advance on the repair work of 1534. Further, the whiteness of this new lining detracts from the image. The eye is struck by the stark contrast of white spots (lining visible through the holes) on straw colored ground (the Shroud) that makes the sepia body image seem even more faint. These factors clearly were not considered.

It is hard to understand why no outside expert was consulted. Ghiberti explains it this way:

> ... the consultation was ample and careful, even if done by the group appointed by the Custodian and by the Holy See and not by others. But that group consisted of university professors, and specialists in chemistry, textile science, botany, forensics, mathematics, information technology, heritage conservation, history ...

While one can understand that none of these local luminaries would know anything about textile conservation, one would certainly have expected at least some of them to know about the normal process of determining the validity of a scientific or academic proposal. This is of course the process of peer review. For an operation as radical and invasive as the "restoration" program proposed by Flury-Lemberg (who was their colleague on the same commission), one would have expected **at the very least** that two or three independent textile conservators would have been formally consulted. That this was not done reflects extremely badly on all ten (or eleven) members of the Commission, on Cardinal Poletto, and on the Vatican. The Commission members and perhaps Poletto too were obviously eager to get on with the historic task they had anointed themselves to do. At the end of the day, the Vatican owns the relic, and it has immense resources in the form of a world-renowned museum, a Pontifical Academy of Sciences, and numerous pontifical commissions for church heritage, relics and archaeology. The fact that (apparently) it did not consult any of these bodies, nor did it mandate independent expert review, relying instead on a provincial committee to make such a monumental decision regarding what could well be the burial cloth of Christ, brings nothing but shame on those in the Vatican who approved it.

Data destroyed

Ever since the first scientific examination of the Shroud in 1933, there has been a great and entirely proper emphasis on non-invasive techniques. Modern conservation shares this emphasis, as noted above, and for important archaeological objects there would be extreme reluctance to employ invasive methods, e.g. for cleaning, that would put information at risk. Ideally, there should be close collaboration between the archaeologist or museum curator and the conservator. In the case of the Shroud, this should have meant direct consultation with the experts from various fields who have studied the cloth and know the types of data it contains, and most importantly, how this data needs to be collected, extracted or preserved.

Savarino stated at the unveiling in Turin that "nothing was lost or thrown away, everything was kept." I tried in a one minute aside to explain to him why it is not simply retaining every particle of debris and dust that is important, but it is above all the structure of the evidence that must not be lost, and the manner in which samples are collected is vital. It would be useless to present an archaeologist with all the objects from a site in a giant bag, with all stratigraphic and contextual information lost. Along the same line, Ghiberti wrote later in detail to refute the notion that data was lost:

> Some objections were heard that the restoration caused the loss of information that could have been useful. The contrary is true: everything that was removed was saved in containers, catalogued and authenticated by ... a notary, and will be at the disposition of scientists when the Pope gives approval for a new stage of experimental research.

It is simply incredible that such an attitude could be found after the intensive research on the Shroud of the last three decades, which has shown so dramatically that the most important information is in the context and the structure of the materials, not simply the materials themselves. Archaeologists know this in their bones, and it is amazing that Dietz did not raise any red flags about this destruction of in situ evidence and simple "collecting" of the remnants in little glass bottles. Microbiologists know the importance of sample purity, so how could Scannerini not have been attuned to the potential for mixing up of materials in the "restoration." It would be interesting to know their response; so far neither has written in defence of the "restoration."

We are told that the fiber bits, dust and debris was collected and saved in glass vials. It seems that the most ad hoc arrangements were made for sample taking. Ghiberti's account is perplexing:

> ... when the patches were unstitched, [they were found to be] pockets of carbonaceous residues and dusty detritus. ... But now there was the problem of the collection of all this material. ... Piero Savarino, scientific advisor to the Papal Custodian, provided an army of little glass containers ...

This sounds as if they were woefully unprepared for "pockets of carbonaceous residues," yet it was precisely the presence of such residues that was the main justification for the intervention. Baima Bollone was also given the task of sampling the underside by taking sticky tape and aspirated samples from various locations decided on a "visual findings" criterion; these samples too were handed over to Poletto and went straight into the archbishopric safe.

From what I can gather, and surmise, with a little pinch of hope thrown in, all the aspirated materials were stored by patch/burn hole area, plus the four areas of so-called "poker holes." The reason for assuming so is as follows: 29 patches were removed, and the four areas of poker holes were worked over and scraped. Ghiberti said on Italian TV on Sept. 21 (and this just happens to be in the short video clip I have on my website www.hku.hk/hkprehis/shrdvid2.htm): "We saved all this [removed] material ... we have more than 30 small glass containers." This indicates less than 40, so it would appear to be the 29 patch areas plus 4 poker hole areas plus some other areas selected for sampling on the underside. This makes it clear that a tremendous amount of information has been lost, since the perimeters of all 29 burn holes under the patches plus the four sets of poker holes were vacuumed, front and back. There should have been several hundred divisions of this material for rigorous study. To cite a single example, pollen from the Middle East has been identified from the Shroud, apparently in clusters, but previous collection techniques have been faulty.

Presumably material from the front and back of the cloth were lumped together for each patch area, and no other subdivision was made, as for example between the area which had been covered by the patch and that which was already exposed. Loose adventitious material and scraped carbonized fabric appear to have been collected together. And there do not appear to have been any subdivisions within each burnhole area; each large one should **at the minimum** have been divided into quadrants, both front and back. There are 19 large burnhole areas, thus sampled properly there should have 19 x 4 x 2 or 152 collection units for these alone. There are 10 small holes, thus 10 x 2 or 20 collection units for them, plus at least one for each of the four small holes in the four poker hole sets, also separating front and back, so 4 x 4 x 2 or 32. Special collection units should also have been reserved for any area of the image side covered by a patch and thus protected since 1534, plus any area where image or bloodstain intersected the edge of the burnhole. The total number of collection units should have been at least 250-300 rather than 30 odd. In sum, the sampling was a disaster. I made this point to Savarino and his reaction was: "what difference does it make whether the material came from the front or back side of the Shroud?" I said: "We'll never know now." He looked puzzled; I almost said: If you have to ask, you shouldn't be involved in this kind of work. Of course most of this material should not have been removed at all, so it was a double disaster.

Besides pollen, other particulate material – plant and insect debris, traces of natron, aloes, etc – has also been identified from the Shroud as important for study. And yet, the vacuuming was done all around the edges of the burn holes, with no microscopic search of the areas carried out beforehand. Microremains that could have been identified and extracted by micromanipulator with precise provenance were instead aspirated along with all the other debris from that general area. Larry Schwalbe of STURP commented that this general vacuuming was "a barbaric method."

Worse still is the destruction of the charred edges of the burn holes. Here the structure of evidence is crucial, and it was deliberately reduced to fluff. The Commission was said to have decided that no cutting would take place, and this would have moderated somewhat the loss of data if that decision had been strictly adhered to, and only loose particles were aspirated away. It was thus shocking to discover that intact segments between or around the edges of burn holes had gone. Ghiberti states:

> Cutting away the charred parts to get back to the undamaged cloth would have produced an unnatural and devastating effect. It was decided to use tweezers to remove material which tended to give way when pulled and to reach the brownish borders ...

This is a new method for preserving ancient textiles – material which tends to "give way" when pulled is removed! This description does not however agree with the published evidence: a photograph in Flury-Lemberg's book shows a scraping tool lying beside a pile of tiny bits of charred fiber in front of the "brownish border" which had become the new man-made edge of the burnhole. When this slide was shown at the unveiling its effect was indeed "devastating." Unfortunately, instead of cutting, the "restorers" chose to scrape away charred cloth around the edges of the burn holes. Since they wanted the frayed look, it would have been better for science if they had cut the small segment first, and then done the scraping.

The brutal nature of this operation was seen even more clearly in a scene shown on Italian television which shows a few seconds of the scraping around one of the so-called "poker holes" – small burns which are known to pre-date the 1534 fire. It was quite violent and clearly not the gentle tugging one imagines when reading Ghiberti's account. It is also crystal clear from the TV video that this material was not "about to fall off" as Flury-Lemberg is reported to have said. This was an aggressive operation aimed at removing the charred fabric which presumably was brittle and crumbled under the pressure of a scraping tool.

There are several categories of evidence that might have existed in the structure of the charred material at the edges of the burn holes and poker holes that was scraped away and pulverized. The small poker holes for example are often thought to have been the result of burning pitch, or some acidic substance, being dropped onto the cloth and eating through four layers. Any residues that might have been on the inner edges of the holes is now dust residing in a container, the structure of their original in situ deposit destroyed, and the possibility open that their presence is due to contamination or human error during the "restoration." Further, the intersection of the body image and bloodstains with the charred area was, in the view of several STURP scientists, crucial for the study of those phenomena, especially if any paint, pigment or other substance was used to create or touchup the image or bloodstain. The physical and chemical changes that the deposits would have undergone in the thermal gradient to charring would be most important, and diagnostic pyrolysis products might remain in trace amounts. Whatever evidence there was is now jumbled together with the carbon dust and bits of fiber. Rogers termed this "a terrible, discouraging loss." To make matters worse, Savarino relates without comment that the scientific measurements on the underside – reflectance, fluorescence and Raman spectra – were made **after** the carbonized deposits and brittle brown fibers around the edges of the holes had been scraped away. Clearly no one on the Commission realized what important evidence they were destroying, and no one considered that it might be advisable to take these scientific measurements before the "restorers" had wreaked their havoc.

There are several other types of data that have been lost. One is the particulate evidence on narrow ledges of cloth beneath the patches that were effectively sealed since 1534. There was general vacuuming and mixing of material from the sealed and adjacent open areas. The ultrasonic vaporizer (mentioned by Ghiberti) may have disturbed and dispersed particulate deposits. Further, sophisticated measurements should have been made to compare the degree of oxidation of the linen in and outside the sealed areas, and on the underside of the cloth, to quantify how much the exposed area has degraded from exposure to light over the last 468 years.

Old creases weakened

Finally, there are the old foldmarks and creases, important for studying how the Shroud was stored in earlier times. One prominent crease below the neck area is believed by some to date to the 7th century, from similar lines in an image of that period thought to have been copied from the Shroud. During the "restoration" an attempt was made to smooth these creases by applying weights onto the cloth. Savarino's remarked at the briefing in Turin that "weights were used in attempting to remove the various creases and wrinkles, but unfortunately not all of them could be smoothed out." His word was *purtroppo* (unfortunately) which several of us were astounded to hear. It was clearly the intention to get rid of all the creases, wrinkles, old foldmarks, etc. Ghiberti mentions the use of an ultrasonic vaporizer, which sprays a fine water mist under high pressure and apparently can be used to weaken creases and wrinkles in textiles. Flury-Lemberg does not describe using it, and says the weights were put on the cloth only to "ease" the creases that remain visible. How much longer they will survive is anyone's guess. Some creases are not visible in normal light but were revealed when photographed in raking light in 1978. It is not known if raking light photos were taken in 2002.

New sewing on each of the burn holes puts different tensions on the cloth, as does its new flat storage, and many of the old weaker creases may not be visible for much longer. It should be clear to any intelligent observer or researcher that the Shroud's data and features should **not** be experimented with on the relic itself. As an amateurish experiment, without peer review and with potentially huge damaging effects, the attempt to "ease" or to remove the creases suffers from lack of controls and thus obscurity in interpretation. Some of the oldest foldmarks could also be the weakest, as they have been on the cloth the longest time since their original formation. However, the strongest are not necessarily the most recent, but rather those that were formed in the most favorable conditions and not uncreased or deliberately counteracted. There are no doubt many other factors that enter into determining which creases/foldmarks survive and which don't. But it is clear that weights or stretching will put pressure on them all, and weaken them all. Previous exhibitions including that of 2000 of course have put stress and increased tension on the cloth. But that does not excuse what was done in 2002.

It is absurd for Ian Wilson and other cheerleaders for the "restoration" to claim that all the old creases are all still there. There are dozens, some of which are very faint and can only be seen in just the right oblique light. The ones that Jackson is most interested in do seem to survive, for now, but they were weakened by the month-long handling, and the stretching, and by the unstitching and re-stitching, and now they are under a new tension arrangement due to the unnecessary attachment of a new backing cloth. This is the opinion of Jan Cardamone and several other textile conservators that I spoke with. These creases will disappear when they reach a critical level of weakness.

I do not put a whole lot of stock in Jackson's interpretation of the "historical foldmark pattern," and it is ridiculous to claim as he does that this pattern provides evidence of an early medieval arrangement related to how the Shroud was displayed in Constantinople, thus challenging the C-14 date. But I do put enormous value in the preservation of this and all other evidence on the Shroud for all future researchers to have access to. Jackson made this very same point, with some vehemence (until, that is, he joined the others at the press conference to praise the emperor's new cloth). He was especially concerned about one foldmark which continues into a charred area and under a patch, as he had determined from the X-rays taken by STURP. This circumstance Jackson interpreted, reasonably I believe, as evidence that the foldmark pre-dated the 1532 fire.

Flury-Lemberg was quoted as saying she did not remove any material from the Shroud that was "about to fall off." Conservators are supposed to do their best to conserve, and that is the major difference that separates them from restorers. Removing important evidence that you think is going to fall off later makes no conservation sense; in this instance it has denied all future researchers the opportunity to verify for themselves, on the actual cloth, that there are pre-1532 foldmarks. The carbonized crease might even have survived the stretching and the vaporizer and the new tensions after the uncarbonized part of the crease disappeared. But now we will not know.

Opportunities lost

With the decision to remove the backing cloth, significant opportunities were created for sophisticated scientific research on the backside of the cloth. Instead of inviting proposals and considering the best that could be obtained, the Commission simply invited several teams of local Turinese technicians to do a series of measurements, without any peer review of the protocols and without any specific research objectives. Sites for sampling by sticky tape were decided on the spot. It is still not known whether a complete photographic record was made (including raking and transmitted light), on this once-in-500-years occasion.

To add insult to injury, the "restorers" deemed it necessary to sew on a new backing cloth immediately. The reason given by Flury-Lemberg was that the backing support was needed for when the Shroud would be mounted again on a vertical board for public display. The next such display of the Shroud is planned for 2025. The new backing fabric was described by Ghiberti as "a length of raw linen presented by Flury-Lemberg. Her father bought it ... for household uses that never materialized. She washed it several times to de-size and soften it, but did not bleach or dye it." To many this constituted a sacrilege: that the backing cloth of the poor Clares in 1534 should be removed and replaced by a piece of linen owned by Flury-Lemberg. To others it was an outrage that, having exposed the underside of the Shroud which had not been seen since 1534, it should then be sewn up again with such haste. As Ghiberti remarked, apparently unaware of the self-indicting nature of his words: "Once the new lining was in place, the back of the Shroud would again be invisible for who knows how long."

The charred material around the burnholes could have provided many excellent C-14 samples, several dozen in fact, but it was scrapped away and pulverized; the value of this powdered material for science was thereby much reduced. In some cases, one centimeter or more was removed. If these tiny segments had instead been cut and keep intact, they could have been examined for possible contaminants charred along with the linen cellulose, and subjected to a proper pretreatment procedure prior to C-14 dating. Segments with body image or bloodstain could have been studied with their deposits intact. As fluff they are of greatly reduced value for C-14 and other analyses, and their provenance cannot now be independently established. The removal of this material from the Shroud (if proven to be absolutely necessary) should have been done in a systematic manner, with proper controls and comprehensive recording. As it is, the pulverized material sits in little glass bottles in the Archbishopric's safe, and is of scant use to anyone for research purposes.

This ignorance of basic sampling strategy can only be explained by the lack of consultation and the lack of expertise on the Commission. It would have been infinitely preferable to have cut away the small segments intact instead of pulverizing them, for several reasons. Pretreatment by the C-14 labs is not the only thing that has been compromised by reducing the material to fluff. Even a segment as small as 0.25 sq cm would still retain idiosyncrasies and could be identified in the record photomicrographs taken (one would hope) before its removal, so that provenance could always be independently re-established. As it stands now, a little vial of powdered carbonized fabric could come from anywhere, and the fact that it has the Archbishopric seal on it does not carry any weight scientifically. For all the vial samples, the chain of evidence is broken and the samples are useless as primary C-14 samples. If they were to be used and a date came back of 1st century or anything significantly earlier than 1000 A.D., people would certainly cry foul and claim tampering, just as Bro. Bruno did with Tite's cryptic handling of the 1988 C-14 sampling.

My estimate is that about 15 to 20 square centimeters of cloth were scraped away by the "restorers." For comparison, it needs to be borne in mind that, before a small strip of about 8.1 x 1.6 cm (about 13 sq cm) was finally allowed to be cut for C-14 dating in 1988, there were several years of discussion and dispute, and a formal 3-day consultation for C-14 dating the Shroud was organized in 1986 by the Archbishop of Turin and the Pontifical Academy of Sciences, attended by 22 scientists and scholars, including me. The 1988 samples given to each lab were about 2 sq cm or 48 mg of cloth, representing final pure carbon of about 16 mg after pretreatment (a ratio of about 33% carbon yield for linen has been reported). Even at that time, this was enough sample for quite a number of C-14 measurements, depending on how rigorous the pretreatment was. In the 1986 conference, the minimum Shroud sample size for AMS dating was agreed amongst the AMS lab representatives at 0.6 sq cm or 15 mg of cloth, yielding 5 mg final carbon. AMS labs now routinely date samples of 1mg final carbon, corresponding to a Shroud sample of only 0.125 sq cm ! This is an amazingly small amount, even smaller than an average watermelon seed. It is about the size of a capital 'D' in 12 point type. To see for yourself: draw a 1 x 1 cm square, bisect it horizontally, vertically and diagonally both ways. Each section is 0.125 sq cm. When one recalls the unsuccessful struggle over the last 16 years to obtain a second C-14 run on a different part of the Shroud, and when the minuscule amount of material needed for that measurement is compared with the enormous amount wasted in this "restoration," the situation can only be described as comical and absurd.

"Full documentation"

The trilingual coffee table book by Flury-Lemberg (2003) with the riveting title *Sindone 2002 – L'intervento Conservativo – Preservation – Konser-*

vierung is certainly a lavish publication with large color photographs and nice line drawings. There is useful information on the history of the Shroud's mounting on the Holland cloth and its storage. Most of the photographs those of the water stains, scorch marks, creases, detail of the stitching, etc. would be of interest to the textile specialist; they would be familiar already to the Shroud researcher.

As mentioned above, there is a fixation with the presence of carbon dust under the patches and on the backing cloth. The "exchange of dirt" (transfer of particulate carbon) from the Shroud to the backing cloth is the subject of five photographs, while the "quantities of soot" (bits of carbonized linen) revealed when the patches were removed are illustrated by no less than 12 large photographs in addition to the very odd cover picture. In spite of all this attention, the case is unconvincing; the amounts of carbon dust are not overwhelming, rather as if a few pinches of black powder were sprinkled about. There is no evidence presented that this material had spread outside the area under the patches except to the corresponding area on the backing cloth.

Very little scientific documentation is provided in this book, but it is said that further publications are being planned. There is no list of sticky tape samples, although it is mentioned that ten sites were sampled by this method on the underside; there is a map apparently of these sites but it has no caption. There is no list of the collected samples of carbon dust and scraped material aspirated from the burn holes. There is a brief description of the scientific measurements made, and there is a list, with map, of protruding weft end threads that were cut away from the underside, but no lengths or weights are given. There is a very nice 90cm long foldout color photograph with front and back of the Shroud printed on opposite sides, and a grid laid over it for reference. For some strange reason the grid is in 4cm units. No photograph in the book has a scale or color chart, despite the fact that the editorial committee had a member (Karlheinz Dietz) who claims to be an archaeologist. A batch of videophotomicrographs was taken by Dietz. While these were also all mapped, there seems to have been no particular strategy designed, and it is doubtful that any improvement was made on the STURP photomicrographs. To the contrary, the quality of the images seems to be lower than that obtained by Pellicori and Evans of STURP.

As we have described in a previous chapter, the underside of the Shroud had already been scanned secretly in 2000, by working a long-handled portable scanner between Shroud and backing cloth, and a coffee table book was published later (Zaccone 2001) of the images obtained. Very large foldout color photographs of the underside were also published in Ghiberti's booklet. What should have been the most important documentation in Flury-Lemberg's book is the appearance of the burn holes under the patches. These had not been seen since 1534, except for one patch that was partially unstitched and lifted up for viewing in 1978. There is an entire section in the book entitled "Catalogue" devoted to documentation of the patches. Seven illustrations are given for each large patch or pair of smaller patches, showing:

    a) underside of the patches after their removal
    b) and c) position of the patches on the holes caused by the fire
    d) stitching of the patches seen on the backing cloth
    e) front of the Shroud with patches
    f) underside of the Shroud: "holes caused by the fire after the removal of the Holland cloth and the patches"
    g) front of the Shroud without patches

All were color photographs except (b) and (c) which were line drawings. One would think that with such a wealth of documentation, the actual size and shape of each burn hole would be quite clear. Incredibly, this is not the case, and the devil is in the details. One finds that the significant amount of charred material that was removed by the "restorers" has been obscured. Drawings (b) and (c) and photograph (f) are often misleading and false; they show the patches covering holes with the shape these holes had at the end of the "restoration," not at the moment when the patches were removed. Photograph (f) likewise does not show the "holes caused by the fire" but rather the holes as enlarged by the "restorers." This is a very basic and serious mistake, or it is an attempt to obscure how much material was scraped away.

    It is hard to understand why this might have been done, as contradicting evidence is sometimes found on the same page. In two cases, T9 and T10, it can be seen from photograph (e) that a small hole just outside the coverage of the patch has been merged by the "restorers" with the larger burn hole under the patch. Drawings (b) and (c) for these two are thus false, since the patches never covered holes of those shapes. From a comparison of the X-rays taken in 1978, four other burn holes are seen to have been significantly expanded in the "new-look" Shroud, and several others altered to a lesser extent. As the two small holes were outside the coverage of the patches, they can be seen on the 1898 and 1933 photographs, and there has been no loss of material since that time, despite the frequent handling and different storage methods over the intervening 69 years. Furthermore, among the abundant photographs of the "sullied" condition found when the patches were lifted, there is confirmation that no change had taken place since 1978 for T3, T5, and T11, but significant change is obvious after the "restorers" had finished.

As mentioned above, a rough estimate is that a total of 15 to 20 square centimeters of charred to partly charred cloth was scraped away. It is clear that this was most emphatically not "material that was flaking off" as claimed in the press release announcing the book. We can see five different areas that were exactly as they had been recorded by the 1978 X-rays, having survived being unrolled, handled, and rolled back up numerous times over the last 25 years. There is no evidence of any flaking or other deterioration in those areas.

Exactly how much intact Shroud material has been lost in the "restoration" is very difficult to establish, even with the large and very nice 'before' and 'after' photographs of the full-length Shroud taken from the same position and to the same scale, as published in Ghiberti's *Sindone Le Imagine 2002 Shroud Images* and the companion book *Shroud Images 2000*. Most of the scraping took place in areas formerly covered by the patches. Using the X-rays taken in 1978, I made several attempts to match the shapes of the burn holes before and after the "restoration," only to find that this was virtually impossible, even assuming some expansion of the holes due to scraping. If the sizes matched, the shapes did not, and vice-versa; the alignments were often different as well. As Barrie Schwortz has been at pains to point out, mechanically reproduced photographs have very limited value for detailed studies of this type. In addition, for wide shots of the full length Shroud, even spread over three slides, there is bound to be distortion depending on the distance from and angle to the lens of the camera. I understand that the X-rays were actual size "contact prints," as it were, so these should not suffer the same distortion problem. Clearly, when the higher resolution digital scans are available of the new-look Shroud, a much more accurate measurement can be made of the amount of material scraped away.

Flury-Lemberg's book is one that can be judged by its cover. The photograph on the cover ironically is the patch T11 area with the patch just removed. It is directly under the English title of the book: *Preservation*. A surviving remnant of cloth protrudes out from the main body into the hole and tapers down. It is similar in shape to the southern half of South America. After "preservation" half of Argentina and Chile are gone.

Damage to the relic

Of infinitely greater danger to the Shroud than its carbon dust, the invasive "restoration" put enormous stresses on the cloth, even with all the care in the world in handling it. It has been remarked that many ancient objects will last for centuries to come if we can just keep our hands off them. Alas, the temptation to improve or set things right is difficult to resist.

The lighting has been mentioned above. Apparently, ordinary desk lamps without filters were used at very close range, ca 30 to 40 cm. Instead of being bounced off walls or ceiling, the lighting was aimed directly at the cloth. Flash photography may also have been done. It will be recalled that at the private viewing of the Shroud arranged for the Turin congress in 2000, an official photographer from the archdiocese took about a dozen shots a few feet from the Shroud with a very powerful flash. One shudders to contemplate how often the cloth may have been exposed to light secretly in recent years.

Light is of course a great danger to the preservation of any historic textile, and especially for the Shroud whose image is composed of advanced yellowing similar to that produced by aging. One can only wonder to what degree the non-image surface fibers have been further aged by this month-long illumination during the "restoration." It was extremely painful to watch Mons. Ghiberti, chairman of the Conservation Commission, giving a television interview in front of the Shroud, while a lamp unattended shines at close range on the cloth. He was speaking about the measures being taken to conserve the Shroud.

Another danger may be posed by the new backing cloth. It was said to have been washed to de-size and soften, and tested for chemical residues by Prof. Savarino, but no other information is given. How sensitive were the tests, and for what chemicals? Flury-Lemberg writes that the cloth had not been bleached, but a textile expert attending the unveiling reported seeing small black specks or "neps" on the cloth (a nep is a small knot of entangled fibers), and opined that the material could be a bleached cotton. Introduction of a new material of whatever type, whether free of bleach and sizing or not, introduces new surface impurities and constitutes a radical change that will have an unforeseen impact on the relic over time.

The greatest damage may have come from handling without gloves. From the video clips that are available, it appears that the cloth was touched thousands of times during the course of the "restoration." Flury-Lemberg may be responding to this criticism when she writes:

> Anyone who has held these fine silk organzine threads and the corresponding needles in their hands will understand immediately that we could not wear gloves for the needlework. ... If the restorer cannot feel what he is doing with his fingertips he cannot do a good job.

While this is an excellent argument for keeping restorers well away from any historic textile, one can only wonder if sewing really does require more sense of touch than brain surgery. Dr. Frederick Zugibe, medical examiner for 30 years in New York, wrote: "I stressed the fact that there was no excuse for not wearing fine surgical gloves because even eye surgeons and micro surgeons wear them during extremely delicate surgical operations" (Zugibe 2003). The argument for sensitivity does not explain why the cloth was touched innumerable times simply to provide pressure, and during the vacuuming. Several close-up photographs and video clips reveal fingers often placed on the cloth to hold it steady.

If bare hands were truly required for stitching, was any consideration (impact assessment) given to the risk that this might pose to the cloth in the long term? Most of the sewing was for mounting the new backing cloth, which as we have seen was not urgently required and probably could have been dispensed with altogether. It appears that these factors were not weighed or even known by the Conservation Commission.

It is gospel among most textile conservators that gloves should be worn when handling any important or historic textile. Handbooks are full of cautions against the dangers of contact with the hands. To cite a few examples:

> Handling a textile causes deterioration and risks damage ... Acids, which are present on our hands and skin ... are also harmful. Wear cotton gloves or disposable vinyl household gloves whenever possible when handling. – United Kingdom Institute for Conservation's guidelines on 'Caring for Historic Textiles'

> Damage from touching however is usually gradual over time. Textiles absorb salts and fatty substances from skin and eventually they discolor, stiffen and weaken fibres ... – Scottish Museums Council's factsheet 'Caring for Textile Collections in Museums'

> Physical handling is ... often overlooked as a source of potential damage to museum objects ... cotton gloves should be used when handling museum objects. – US Dept of the Interior's Museum Property Handbook

> ... dust containing human hair and skin particles must be managed to prevent harm to the collection ... When handling fragile items wear thin cotton gloves to protect the items from naturally occurring oils in the human skin. – Tasmania State Library

It has been said that fingerprints serve as good culture media for moulds, fungi and bacteria. Even after washing, hands transmit dead skin cells, salts, urea, bacteria, dirt and slightly acidic skin oils. Touching doorknobs, chairs, lamps, etc (as seen often in the video clips) increases the dirt and bacteria transmitted. All of the five textile conservators I contacted expressed horror when informed that the "restorers" handled the Shroud without gloves for more than one month. Even though the growth of bacteria and fungi may be retarded by the inert gas atmosphere in which the Shroud is now stored, one shudders to contemplate the long-term implications, especially of the salts, oils, skin cells and bacteria that have been deposited.

In 1978, the STURP members who needed to touch the cloth were required to wear cotton gloves. The "restoration" would thus represent a regression in this regard. It is certainly true that the Shroud has often been handled throughout its history, but that fact cannot justify continued barehanded touching today when the contamination effects are known. It is quite possible that the Shroud was touched more times by bare hands, and exposed to more light, in one month of 2002 than in its entire history as a relic. In addition, the devout nuns in 1534 were careful to preserve every part of the precious cloth, even blackened remnants protruding into ugly holes. The 2002 "restoration" was, alas, a regression in this regard as well.

Nothing can insure that any object or the information it contains will survive, but conservation parameters are well known. Many of these were violated in the ill-considered "restoration" of the Shroud. Regardless of its age, the image on the Shroud presents a unique and very complicated conservation challenge, and it can only be met by the highest standard of scientific collaboration. This needs to be addressed in a methodical, scientific manner, subject to rigorous peer-review at an international level. Clearly the Vatican must exercise greater and more considered control over the relic.

The role of Adler

Seeking to justify the aggressive "restoration," Flury-Lemberg cited the words of the late Prof. Alan Adler: "If we are remiss in undertaking conservation/preservation studies and measures on the Shroud of Turin, future generations will have every right to castigate us for failing to meet our responsibilities. History will not be kind to us." Her emphasis was on undertaking "measures" but it is important to note that he stated quite clearly that **studies and** measures" needed to be done. In the same article Adler wrote that:

> A great deal is known about the preservation of cellulosic materials. While such experience is valuable in deciding on conservation measures for the Shroud, it is unfortunately insufficient. The images and marks on the cloth, and not the cloth itself, are what makes it worthy of preservation. Conservation of these cannot be undertaken until the chemical composition of their chromophores is unequivocably established. This will require further scientific testing.

Contrast this cautious and scientific approach with that of Flury-Lemberg who claimed to know what the image was composed of and what conservation it required. Adler's views were also cited by Ghiberti, Dietz, Savarino and other Commission members as crucial in leading to their decision to proceed with the "restoration." They seem to have heard what they wanted to hear, exactly as Sheila Landi remarked about the Commission. Ghiberti relates:

> Adler worried about the possibility of the damaging effects of material from the 1532 fire that was trapped under the patches applied by the nuns of Chambéry. When he spoke during the Committee meetings, he did not retreat from the most advanced hypotheses. One of these (certainly not new, as mentioned above, but backed now by the weight of his authority) was to remove the patches and the Holland cloth.

Adler was a brilliant scientist, and a friend. But it must be acknowledged that he was sometimes a loose cannon, and he may have said things in order to shock or to spur action. As one of his STURP colleagues put it:

> I am surprised and horrified by some of the statements I have seen attributed to Al. I still think he was trying to scare the immobile ignoranti in Turin into more studies. The greatest danger to the Shroud is the people deciding what can and will be done to study and 'preserve' it.

It is impossible to know what was really said in the private Commission meetings, but one thing seems crystal clear to those of us who knew Al – he would never have agreed to the "restoration" of 2002. He was far too good a scientist to allow himself to be associated with such an intellectually shoddy and ill-considered enterprise. If, and this is by no means certain, he thought that removing the patches and backing cloth might be the best solution, he most certainly would not have been a party to such a drastic action until there was a solid scientific basis for it. A close examination of his writing on the subject leaves absolutely no doubt that obtaining this data was his first priority, but it was twisted and mutated by the Commission after his death.

Flury-Lemberg states that "at the committee meeting in 1996 Alan D. Adler (1) already believed the removal of the patches to be the most effective way to reduce oxidation." This claim is not corroborated by any of the statements Adler made in print, and may not be accurate. Footnote (1) in the above quote refers to articles Adler published in 1991, 1993 and 2002; examining these articles does not reveal any such belief or proposal. In the conclusion of an article he co-authored in 1993 with Larry Schwalbe that was specifically focused on conservation, it was stated quite clearly and definitively: "Problems affecting the cloth itself are not really pressing ... the blood images present a different story [which] requires immediate attention." One has to wonder if he could have gone from this view of non-urgency in 1993 to belief in the drastic action on the linen as Flury-Lemberg alleges by 1996. Furthermore, in a personal communication to Dorothy Crispino, Adler wrote in June 1997, after seeing the Shroud for the first time: "The linen is very thin. I have changed my mind about removing the backing cloth."

What comes through very forcefully in Adler's writings is a cautious scientific approach, an eagerness for more data and a strong reluctance to make decisions without solid evidence. He did believe that the burn residues posed an oxidative threat over the long term, by autocatalysis. In the 1993 article cited above, he wrote:

> ... the acidic structures produced by previous oxidative activity can strongly promote various types of autocatalysis. As much of this material resides in the scorch marks, a very difficult problem is presented. Should they be removed or chemically treated in some fashion?

However, in the same section he also wrote that "a research program should be initiated to find an appropriate temperature" for storage of the Shroud to minimize this perceived threat. And he called attention to "the importance of unequivocally determining what these chemical materials really are before attempting to design an appropriate conservation program." This was typical of Al's approach – put forward ideas and

IMPACT ON THE RELIC

scenarios, state your hypothesis forcefully, with "shock and awe" sometimes, but put them all to the test of empirical, solid evidence **before** proceeding. In his last published paper, he devoted a brief section to conservation issues, and concluded it with these words:

> The various conservation and preservation issues and their possible resolution have been analyzed and reported in some detail ... To continue to further this work, more data acquired by further testing on the Shroud itself is required.

As we noted above, a very similar statement was included, somewhat strangely, in the Villa Gualino conference summation, and one suspects that it was at Adler's instigation. Note the similar choice of words "required" and "essential." It seems very likely that Adler was keen to obtain data that would confirm his hunches about the possible threat posed by substances from "previous oxidative activity" (i.e. charred cloth). Perhaps he knew that this claim would not be generally accepted without empirical evidence to back it up.

His death was not only a terrible loss to Shroud scholarship and to those who knew him personally, but it was a terrible blow to the Shroud itself. The conservation studies that he considered so vital were not done, yet the Commission (emasculated without the weight of his intellect) barged ahead with "measures" carried out in the most ill-conceived and poorly researched manner. His expressions of concern for the Shroud's future preservation mutated shortly after his demise into the monster that was unleashed in 2002. He must be turning over in his grave at what was done in his name. But history will be kinder to him than to those who misunderstood and twisted his intentions.

13. Reactions

After The Dramatic Events of September 2002, there was something of a lull as the magnitude of the intervention sank in and people contemplated what if anything could be done to improve the situation. Some adopted the attitude that what was done was done and there was no point in crying over spilt milk. Others felt that some pressure on the Vatican might be useful to help internationalize control over the Shroud. Barrie Schwortz began collecting comments to be published on a special page on his website. I was spurred to write again to Poletto in order to re-affirm my views on the "restoration," while at the same time urging him to take some positive step to counter the despair widespread in the Shroud community:

> Dear Cardinal Poletto,
> Thank you very much for another opportunity to see the Holy Shroud. Regrettably, this time the experience was tinged with sadness. As I wrote to you in my email of Sept. 3, a terrible mistake was made in carrying out the 'restoration,' and much valuable information has been needlessly lost.
> Members of the Commission for Preservation bear full responsibility. Apparently their desire for secrecy coupled with their desire to conduct this operation themselves are the main reasons for this tragedy for the Shroud. There was a clear conflict of interest, and the Commission served as judge, jury and executioner.
> At the official press conference of Sept. 21, the foreign researchers who spoke were motivated by opportunism. I know for certain that at least two of the speakers believed that the 'restoration' was ill advised and destructive of scientific information. ... But, during that official function, I did not want to be the one to say: 'The emperor is not wearing any clothes.' This

was only out of respect for you, to avoid causing you embarrassment or stress.

You are surely a dynamic church leader, and I still have hope that you will do great things for the Shroud. Many research proposals have recently been submitted, and an international panel needs to be created to review these proposals and advise you directly on their merits.

But clearly what the whole world wants is another C-14 dating, which is also scientifically justified. Analyses conducted by the widely respected chemist Dr. Ray Rogers indicate that the 1988 C-14 sample was not representative of the cloth as a whole. Please authorize another C-14 test to be done.

With best wishes to you and the Archdiocese of Turin, I hope to see you again some day in happier circumstances.

Ceterum, sindon carbone recomputanda est!

The last line translates as "And furthermore, the Shroud must be carbon-dated again" (with acknowledgements to Cato the Elder, who ended every speech in the Roman Senate, no matter what the subject, with the same exhortation: "And furthermore, Carthage must be destroyed!" Carthage was of course eventually destroyed.)

Poletto sent a fairly aggressive, obstinate and rather strange reply:

Esteemed Dr. Meacham,

... Since we had our encounter in Turin, at which we were able to speak with much serenity at the occasion of the dinner in the new sacristy of the Cathedral, I thought that no further response was necessary. Now your recent letter convinces me that our encounter did not accomplish anything. To this letter I want to respond with much firmness.

With the works carried out in the months of June and July 2002 to guarantee a better conservation of the Shroud, no terrible error was made, because no important information was lost, as you write, and the planned operation was totally successful.

Furthermore, the members of the Commission acted exclusively on my behalf, with the explicit permission of the Pope and under my surveillance. The climate of secrecy in which the works were carried out was desired by me and was not dictated by the desire, which you are wrong to suppose, of the members to conduct the operation themselves without my knowledge. Therefore, I can assure you that the Commission was neither judge nor jury nor executioner. The only thing that seems sure to me is the malevolence of whoever would make such an insinuation.

I know for certain that the people who spoke at the press conference of the 21st of September in favor of the works carried out for a better conservation of the Shroud, especially after having changed their mind as a result of seeing the perfection of the restoration. These same people have had the opportunity to state that their opposition arose from being badly informed by adverse propaganda.

I do not know what the Lord would have me do further for the Shroud, but for the proposals of research which have been submitted in recent years, I must listen first to the response of the peer review, as I promised the scientists, and then the decision of the Pope, the only person competent to establish the time and manner of future research. This goes also for C-14, concerning the scientific justification for which it seems to me however that your view is in the minority. I should also tell you that the view you attribute to Ray Rogers on the non-representativeness of the sample taken in 1988 has no foundation.

My response ends here and I hope that it can be definitive.
With greetings,

Severino Cardinal Poletto

This correspondence was all in Italian, so nothing was lost or misunderstood by him in translation. Reading this letter made me realize how easily Poletto must have been misled by the Commission. What was "definitive" in this letter was his lack of logical and reasoning powers. But having dug himself into a badly designed pit he was going to defend it to the death, and he was going to stamp all the authority of his position as cardinal on it. Of course this cuts no ice in science and scholarship, and his closing remark about being "definitive" suggested to me that he had a somewhat blinkered view of the world outside of the Roman Catholic ecclesiastical hierarchy. In addition, he missed my point entirely about "their desire for secrecy coupled with their desire to conduct this operation themselves." How could he possibly take this to mean that I was alleging that the Commission members wanted to conduct the operation without his knowledge? Such faulty reasoning on such a simple point makes one wonder. Likewise, he did not want to believe what I told him from my own personal experience, preferring to go along with some fairy tale about those who first had been subverted by "adverse propaganda," but then saw "the perfection of the restoration" and changed their minds. What a load of codswallop, as the British say for utter nonsense! And finally, he alleges malevolence, the last refuge of a weak argument. Where exactly is the malevolence in arguing that the Commission had no oversight, no peer review, no consultation with outside experts? It would be good to hear that Poletto **did** consult with other textile experts, or that the Vatican **did** consult with other Shroud experts. It is indisputable that the Commission made the decision that the intervention was necessary, then turned around and appointed themselves to conduct the "historic" work itself. The conflict of interest could not have been clearer if they had granted themselves a nice juicy million dollar project. The Vatican appears simply to have delegated the matter to Poletto, who in turn seems to have merely rubber-stamped the Commission's decision. Instead of refuting any of this, he resorts to the charge of malevolence.

A few weeks after the unveiling, a move was begun to organize a petition to the Vatican, urging that an international commission be appointed to manage the conservation and study of the Shroud. It read:

PETITION TO HIS HOLINESS POPE JOHN PAUL II

> In the light of recent alterations to the Shroud of Turin, we the undersigned are deeply concerned about the future scientific study of this precious object treasured by many people all over the world.
>
> We request that Your Holiness consider appointing an international commission of respected scientists and other knowledgeable persons, to advise on all matters relevant to the Shroud's conservation, scientific testing and long-term preservation as an object of study.
>
> Such a commission would, we hope, also include representatives of the Pontifical Academy of Sciences, the Vatican Museum, and the Pontifical Commission for the Heritage of the Church.
>
> We request further that the commission operate on the basis of peer-review prior to recommendation of any proposal, that it invite public comments on matters before it, and that its deliberations be published regularly.
>
> We believe that the appointment of such a commission will contribute significantly to progress in our understanding of this fascinating object.

After several months it had 52 signatories, many of them well-known Shroud researchers, and it was posted to the Vatican. No acknowledgement was ever received, but reverberations were felt very quickly. Within three weeks of it being submitted, one of the Italians who signed it was told by a close associate of Poletto that he would be blacklisted from future research on the Shroud unless he "repented" of his error. The petition was very mildly worded, making no direct criticism of the "restoration," but the intent was clear: the Shroud was too important to be left in the hands of a parochial committee selected by Poletto, or more probably recommended to Poletto by another parochial committee. Several people suggested that the number of signatories was too small to have any impact, but even if it had been in the hundreds or thousands, one doubts that the numbers would have carried much weight in the Vatican. The only hope was that the petition might find its way to a sympathetic person in a high position who might initiate a process of change. Thus far, there has been no indication of that happening.

Meanwhile, the comments on the "restoration" were published on www.shroud.com/restored.htm and with a few glaring exceptions they were highly critical. Selected extracts are given here.

Rev. Albert R. Dreisbach, Episcopal Priest and Shroud Historian – Turin has in reality assumed 'proprietary' control of who will have access to this burial cloth and what and by whom any future testing will be performed. I for one believe this is an ill-advised and dangerous policy. In 1978, there was a wonderful spirit of both international and ecumenical cooperation. Both of these bridges have been seriously weakened by the recent events in Turin.

Learning that there was much negative concern among the international Shroud community who had been totally excluded and kept in the dark about the 'restoration', Turin diplomatically invited a chosen few – some of whom had not been present at the conclave in March of 2000 – to a special conclave and display of the altered cloth and the ensuing press conference on Saturday, September 21, 2002. ... many of those attending that September weekend believe that Turin cannot and should not be allowed to be the sole authority responsible for access to and determination of future testing of the Holy Shroud. Either the Pontifical Academy of Sciences or some newly-created International Scientific Commission which will insure adequate international peer review of any and all proposals prior to allowing same to be performed is in the best interest of the Shroud itself.

Paul Maloney, Archaeologist and Shroud Researcher – I know that many technicians working on their object detest wearing latex gloves and even cavalierly dismiss such criticisms as irrelevant. Emphatically, they are not! There are several reasons why the use of such gloves is important in this case ...

I was horrified to learn that after removal of the burned fabric the borders of the burn holes were treated to the tweezer/scraping technique ... If this often subtle evidence is altered, or erased through our own ignorance, then we have destroyed something extremely important and a part of the whole that ought to have been considered for conservation. This part of the operation has clearly and irretrievably destroyed precious pieces of the history of the Shroud in their original context and of material important for science.

Behind the latest efforts to conserve the Shroud lies a basic philosophy that appears to this writer to be inimical not only to the future of Shroud research but even to its preservation. My fear is that by the very practices applied to the Shroud we do damage to its longevity ...

I am 99.999 percent convinced that this operation need not have been done in the very first place – at least not for the reason given by the commission. And certainly it need not have been acted upon with the speed they did.

Emanuela and Maurizio Marinelli, Shroud Researchers, Educators and Authors – From the historical point of view, the loss of the folds, which could testify to the way the Shroud was kept in more ancient ages, is feared. The 16th century restoration itself, which has been destroyed, was an historical testimony, now irretrievably gone.

The intervention has raised remarkable perplexities: in fact, such a drastic intervention did not appear necessary and urgent. The decision to carry out such an operation has been taken by a very narrow group of people, without a wider consultation among the scientists and the historians, who have been interested in this Relic for many years. In fact, nobody had proposed any intervention of the sort at any of the eight international conferences held in the last four years (Turin 1998, Richmond 1999, Rio de Janeiro 1999, Turin 2000, Orvieto 2000, Dallas 2001, Paris 2002, Rio de Janeiro 2002). Not even those convened by the Turin International Center of Sindonology (Turin 1998) and by the Archbishop of Turin (Turin 2000) included such a proposal.

Joseph G. Marino and M. Sue Benford, Shroud Researchers – It is clear from comments made from experts who have seen the restoration that much significant historical and scientific information has probably been lost due to the restoration, including the possibility of using material from beneath the patches for new C-14 datings.

Serge N. Mouraviev, Shroud Researcher – Except for a few minor points I entirely share the views expressed here by Paul C. Maloney, William

Meacham and Emanuela and Maurizio Marinelli and I am in good agreement (with some reservations) with the statements by the Rev. Albert 'Kim' Dreisbach, Jr., and Giulio Fanti.

Those [in the Church] who believed that the relic had to be saved qua relic, i. e. taken away from the scientists and placed under the sole control of the Church, took the upper hand. The Shroud is the property of the Holy See, so there was no legal obstacle. The only problem was to choose the way to stage this coup de théâtre in order to make it look as resolute as possible on the one hand, as little shocking as possible on the other, and to dismiss the scientists without having to openly dismiss sindonology as such. They chose to take secretly unannounced measures of conservation.

Raymond Rogers, Retired Chemist (Los Alamos National Laboratory) and Former STURP Member – The important fact is that, before the restoration, we could look at the chemistry of specific locations on the Shroud where scorches intersected image, blood, serum, and water stains. The restoration totally destroyed any chemical information at those intersections.

A huge amount of chemical information existed in the scorches ... Such information was important for suggesting the chemical composition of the image. Most possibilities for studying the effects of the fire on image materials were destroyed by the restoration of 2002.

We might have been able to identify the actual chemical processes that produced the color of the image. Since the surface of the entire Shroud has now been disturbed, such an approach is unlikely to succeed. This is a terrible, discouraging loss for Shroud chemists.

Prof. Daniel Scavone, Emeritus Professor of History, University of Southern Indiana – I must take my stand, as a historian, on the side of those who regret the possible loss of much historical information as a result of the unfortunate intervention in 2002. As a result of the stretching of the Shroud so as to deliberately remove its historical fold-marks, the fairly clear raking light photographic evidence of its folding in eight layers may be nullified.

I read in the words of other Shroud scholars about other failings, about loss of other valuable information, and about unnecessary contaminations as a result of the intervention. Many scholars, therefore, have found it outrageous that a small group of well-intentioned persons who had the attention of the official curator of the Shroud should have used his influence at the papal court to gain permission to perform such radical and invasive surgery on the cloth. They did so with absolutely no discussion with experts and knowledgeable scholars who are also vitally concerned about all matters relating to the precious Shroud – but who were taken by surprise by the announcements only when the operation was a fait accompli. Whatever could have been the unspoken motives of the interventionists that moved them to such secrecy, haste, and the consequent carelessness?

Finally, permit me to add that, although burnt particles removed from the Shroud may have been carefully and properly kept separate as to their original location on the cloth, their value when used in any future carbon dating of the Shroud is much diminished or even negated. If any material or charred portions of the Shroud should be carbon-dated in the first century, sindonoclastic opponents of the Shroud's authenticity who were not present witnesses at their removal and storage during the intervention may still reject the new date as faked or manipulated.

Bryan Walsh, Statistician and Shroud Researcher – The listing that follows is one attempt to identify some of the broad areas of concern that result from the recent intervention.

Possible Data Issues: provenance, light exposure, exogenous biological contamination, nature of new 'Holland' cloth, problematic techniques.

Procedural Issues: open access, lack of protective clothing, consultation.

The intervention that just occurred most likely lost valuable data as a result of the experimental design utilized. This data loss did not have to occur.

Frederick T. Zugibe, M.D., Ph.D., Medical Examiner and Professor of Pathology – ... for obvious reasons, serious Shroud researchers in the various disciplines should have been consulted for their input prior to embarking on such an irrevocable project since these manipulations could have a serious effect on future Shroud research. I then expressed my chagrin that both Lemberg and Tomedi were not wearing surgical gloves and apparently were not wearing dust free garments as the numerous movements of the hands in contact with the Shroud during the laborious sewing operations as shown on the video presentation, would cause skin oils and numerous epithelial cells to slough off onto the cloth.

This type of contamination onto the Shroud could seriously influence DNA and other determinations. The garments they were wearing may also have released fine particulates onto the cloth adding to further contamination.

* * *

There has been no official reaction to these highly critical comments. In an Italian newspaper article, Ghiberti repeated his allegation that critics were angry at being excluded from the project. Poletto made the outrageous and stupid comment that "a small squad was making war on the Turin Group." Apart from my correspondence with Poletto, there seemed to be little direct communication between the two camps. It was clear that this "Turin Group" under Poletto was content to ignore the international criticism until it melted away, confirming some of the comments above that the clique in Turin did not particularly care what the international community thought. They had firm control. As one of the sycophants at the unveiling had put it so succinctly, Poletto and the Centro held all the cards, they were the only game in town, and one could either cooperate with them or be left out in the cold. Like voices crying in the wilderness! But sometimes the wilderness is the only moral place to be.

PART IV – WHAT NEXT FOR THE TURIN SHROUD?

14. New Research Proposals

The Villa Gualino Conference In Turin of March 2000 appeared to be a glorious new beginning in Shroud research. Following on from it there was going to be a coordination of research proposals, an international dialogue about those proposals and research directions in general, and discussion of a process to evaluate them. What was not decided at Villa Gualino was how a final decision would be made. Of course the standard refrain from the "authorities" in Turin is that the final decision rests with the Pope, but this is scarcely more than a smokescreen behind which to operate and make the real decisions. This screen will not work any longer, after the "restoration" has shown so dramatically how the current Vatican leadership has delegated responsibility for decisions about the Shroud to Poletto and his chosen advisers. Referral to the Vatican seems to be little more than rubber-stamping.

It is unclear how many proposals or other submissions were submitted before the original deadline of October 30, 2000, but as we have seen, a few days after that deadline a week-long study of the underside was started by personnel from the Centro. Clearly this particular research proposal (apparently from Soardo and Zaccone) had been approved long before the October 30 deadline, that seems in retrospect to have been a façade for concealing the real plans. Of course, there may have been a darker purpose involved in this farce, as some have suggested, namely to examine the contents of all the international scientific proposals and borrow any useful bits. Cynical, yes, but it gives sense to otherwise inexplicable behavior.

When the "final call" for proposals was made in April 2002, a list of 24 submitters was sent out for confirmation and any others not on the list were invited to make their submissions. A few additional proposals were made before the new deadline that was set for May 5. The two co-chairmen of the Villa Gualino conference later affirmed in their press statement at the unveiling that all proposals received by them were handed over to Poletto on July 18. The "restoration" had begun one month before and would finish on July 23. One can only wonder at the timing. Assuming that they were not involved in a deliberate deception, what on earth could the honorable chairmen have been thinking or doing? Was it an entirely empty performance that was being carried through to a conclusion devoid of meaning? It is remarkable that it seemed to be a re-run of the first "deadline" that was followed immediately by Soardo's scanning project. The formal submission of research proposals to Cardinal Poletto took place on July 18, whilst in the next room the new backing cloth was being sewn onto the Shroud, to seal the underside away "for who knows how long" in Ghiberti's ironic words. And another research proposal had just been carried out. According to Flury-Lemberg: "The sites to be investigated were identified on the basis of a proposal by Prof. Baima Bollone. This proposal identified ten sites with precise characteristics ..."

It is clear that Baima's proposal, like Soardo's in 2000, was also not included in the batch that arose from Villa Gualino, since no one except the ten (or eleven) Commission members knew that the underside of the Shroud was going to be available for research. One might well ask if there was any peer or independent review of Baima's proposal, but the answer is obvious. The same applies to all the measurements done by the "experts called in by Piero Savarino" – all seemingly from Turin. How fortunate that all of the possible testing that should be done on the underside of the Shroud, during its brief availability, could be decided upon by one person, and lo and behold, all the necessary expertise was available right there in Turin and its suburbs!

Apparently there were two streams of research proposals, with very different characteristics. One stream consisted of international research and conservation proposals whose originators were totally in the dark about what was being planned for or done to the Shroud. This stream after inspection was diverted out into the labyrinthine swamps of bureaucracy, and perhaps, after many moons of stagnation therein, some tiny part of it might reach its goal. The other stream consisted of proposals from the ten (or eleven) members of the Commission, involving entirely Turinese personnel for all measurements and data collection. This stream was fast-tracked, under the cover of secrecy, to lead right to the Shroud.

In a letter to me, Poletto mentioned that research proposals were still being accepted up to the end of 2002. He stated further that the proposals will be reviewed by a jury of international scientists, and in an email Ghiberti implied that they have already been sent to the jury. How was this jury selected? Who is on it? Does it consist of a few international scientists plus a bunch of cronies of Ghiberti, Savarino, Baima, etc? What criteria have they been given to weigh the proposals against? Do they know anything at all about the Shroud, and especially the huge mass of work that has already been done on it? There are no answers at present; it is a black box operation and subject to manipulation. It is possible that there are one or two scientists of international standing who know little to nothing about the Shroud, and a few more hand-picked by the Centro who are knowledgeable about the Shroud, but of little or no international standing. In other words, a composition wide open for manipulation, especially as it is operating completely in secret and anonymously.

What is even worse than the procedural arrangements is the fact that many of the proposals have been rendered out of date or irrelevant by the "restoration." An entirely new situation exists now, but most of the proposals were submitted long before the "restoration." Those that deal with conservation issues would clearly need to be revised, or withdrawn; others need to be revised to take into account the changes on the relic, the new data, and/or the available samples.

The people who were involved with the "restoration" should be excluded from the process, since they obviously have inside information and could make a proposal that took advantage of such. For example, Baima took sticky tape samples from the underside, and he should not be allowed to make a research proposal involving those tapes, as he has insider information on their location, context and strategic meaning. Similarly Dietz made video photomicrographs and could easily use the knowledge acquired during the recording to make a research proposal precisely fitting the data that only he and one or two others have seen.

Quite a lot of scientific data and many samples were obtained during the "restoration" but nothing has been offered to those who made proposals that hinge on or would make use of this data. The samples taken included the carbon dust, the brittle fibers that were scraped off, the sticky tape and aspirated samples from selected spots on the underside, and the weft ends protruding from the cloth on the underside that were clipped off. There is however no list of these samples, except for the skimpy information in Flury-Lemberg's book (no list of aspirated samples, no list of sticky tape samples, a list of threads removed with locations, but without lengths or weights of the threads). If someone was proposing to study for example the blood stains, and there are blood-stained fibrils amongst the dust, then it is senseless to judge their proposal made in 2000 on the basis of the current situation. They may be proposing to lift sticky tape samples and individual blood microshards from the Shroud, and their research proposal may be rejected on the basis of intrusiveness or destructiveness (which of course would be an enormous irony considering the destruction wrought by the "restoration"). It is unknown whether the "jury" is even aware of the nature of samples that are now removed from the Shroud.

In addition to the materials taken from the cloth, a range of scientific measurements (Raman, reflectance and fluorescence spectra) was made, as well as video photomicrographs and an assortment of other photography. None of this data has been made available to any of the international submitters, despite the fact that a number of proposals contained similar study elements, and there have been modest requests for release of data.

In sum, the situation regarding the proposals from international scientists is one gigantic mess. Turin may not be aware of the many contradictions and inconsistencies, or it may not care about them, and it has been suggested by some that Turin's intention may be to drag out the process for years, until the proponents have lost interest and moved on to other endeavors. This is precisely what happened to STURP's proposals for a second round of testing. Submitted in 1984, pushed aside by the C-14 dating in 1988, they finally died away in the early 1990s with scarcely a whimper, followed by STURP itself. This also happened to the "call for new research proposals" made by the Vatican in 1990. Six years later, Cardinal Saldarini urged researchers "to be patient until a clear and systematically planned research program may be arranged." This was the last anyone heard of that. Years go by with no progress. Some people console themselves with the notion that the Church moves very slowly, and this is most often true for things it does not really want to deal with. For pet projects and whims of the powerful, it can move with lightning and even ungodly speed, as seen in the "restoration."

Clearly what needs to happen now is for all the previous proposals to be scrapped. A new phase of study should be centered on the analysis of samples and digestion of data made available by the "restoration," including of course C-14 dating. Only after this phase has been conducted should proposals be invited for direct access study of the Shroud. This new phase need not be a long and drawn out affair. One or two years would suffice if the procedure for gaining access to the materials is not cumbersome and bureaucratic. Since the samples are less than ideal for certain studies, having been taken without proper regard to sampling strategy, their usefulness for other studies could be assessed rather quickly. Qualified researchers with knowledge of the Shroud should be given priority. It is doubtful of course that any of this will happen, and the international scientific study of the Shroud may be in the doldrums until a new archbishop is appointed to Turin. Poletto is due to retire in 2008.

NEW RESEARCH PROPOSALS 241

Reviewing the situation at the end of 2003 regarding further scientific testing of the Shroud, a prominent American scientist and member of STURP circulated the following comments by email:

> Neither Poletto nor his scientific advisor will communicate or study the evidence on the subject. I have to assume that the textile experts are trying to suppress any negative observations. For example, Flury-Lemberg has issued her 'expert opinion' [but] I do not have any faith in 'looks-like' evidence, and I have no opinions on reweaving or other textile subjects. I look at the characteristics of the linen, and I see chemical and physical differences. Scientists look at all of the evidence. Evidently, Flury-Lemberg is not a scientist. Are there any I can communicate with?
>
> If the cardinal or his advisors can prove me wrong, that is the way science is pursued. I would be happy to look at their evidence. It might even help me in my studies. Are they willing to take the risk of having to modify their beliefs? If they close their minds, they may lose knowledge that is to their advantage.
>
> I firmly believe that the arrogant failure to communicate is detrimental to both truth and the world's perception of the Shroud of Turin. Most people around the world now are certain that the Shroud is a hoax. Even *National Geographic* magazine published a large article saying that. Are the authorities of Torino willing to have what could very well be a material connection between Jesus and the modern world remain degraded in the eyes of the world?
>
> I cannot honestly and rigorously prove something like the resurrection through science. I think I can prove one of the original questions, that the Shroud is a real shroud. What do the authorities want from me? Is all of my work being ignored out of personal dislike for scientists or Americans?
>
> Those of us who are trying to obtain the truth can not fight against arrogant ignorance. Can anything be done to improve the situation? [...]
>
> I got the impression from Fr. Rinaldi that many people have sufficient faith such that they do not need evidence. Why did we do the STURP study? I have heard the following quotation: 'Faith is the God given ability to pull the wool over our own eyes.' While the wool is over the Torino authorities eyes, the world views the Shroud as a joke.
>
> Torino has all of the samples they need to observe the fine structures and chemical properties of the Shroud. Has anything like that been done? Is Baima the only person who does any chemistry?

The Shroud needs objective, honest study by many qualified, different, independent investigators.

I am disgusted. Maybe it is acceptable to let the world see the Shroud as a piece of dirty, damaged cloth of no significance. I know that if I write to Savarino or Poletto I will get no response. I have tried that. I am just wasting my time on a futile effort to help people who either don't care or don't understand.

Very strong words, but shared by quite a few frustrated researchers around the world. It appears that a long stay in purgatory will be required before any research proposals from those outside the "Turin Group" will be approved, if it even happens in this decade.

A new proposal for C-14

Without great hope of success, I decided to make an attempt to move on from the disaster of the "restoration" and to try to persuade Poletto to allow another carbon dating of the cloth. The material removed from the Shroud during the restoration could provide dozens of new C-14 dates from ten different sites on the cloth. As discussed above, the fact that the charred material was scraped from the edges of the burnholes rendered the material "virtually" useless for C-14 dating, because it has been reduced to fluff. There are two serious consequences of not keeping the fabric intact, even in a tiny segment: 1) the pretreatment is much more difficult and questionable; 2) the fabric can no longer be verified as coming from the Shroud. All seven of the labs involved in the 1986 conference in Turin on dating the Shroud stated their strong view that the samples should not even be unraveled, as this would make pretreatment more of a problem.

Meanwhile, there had been dramatic developments regarding the C-14 dating issue, mentioned at the end of my last letter to Poletto. It will be recalled that two American researchers, Sue Benford and Joe Marino, had presented a paper at the Orvieto conference in 2000 arguing that the sample taken in 1988 came from an area of reweaving, an "invisible patch" as they called it. Citing rather unorthodox sources (tailors, reweaving companies), they pointed to a shift in thread diameters and also to the slight differences between the three dates obtained by the C-14 labs, suggesting that there was a difference of material in the sample vis-à-vis the main cloth. As discussed earlier, the C-14 sample was taken from an area right next to the strange side strip and its seam. On the other hand, the area had been examined by the two textile experts present at the sample-taking in 1988, and they reported no anomalies or irregularities.

Ray Rogers was highly sceptical of the Benford-Marino hypothesis, and set about to disprove it. He wrote in 2001:

> Their claims seemed unlikely; therefore, I reviewed the samples and data I had archived after STURP disbanded. I thought that it would be simple to refute their claims. For the first time in my career as a scientist, I found that I had to support something that was based on subjective observations. Honesty and Scientific Method demanded that I release my observations, and I sent information to Benford and Marino. The next thing I knew, that information appeared in an unrefereed publication. I had no opportunity to edit or approve it, and it made it impossible for me to publish the data in an ethical journal.

A brief summary of his findings and the current C-14 situation was translated and sent to Poletto. These observations are compelling:

> Since the C-14 dating of the Shroud was announced in 1988, there have been doubts expressed as to the nature and reliability of the sample taken. Garza-Valdes, supported by the microbiologist Mattingly, claimed that there was a substantial 'bioplastic coating' on Shroud fibers that constituted contamination and skewed the C-14 date. Marino and Benford, supported by weaving specialists, claimed that the area of the C-14 sample had been partially re-woven.
>
> Prof. Adler had begun to study these claims. In a paper published in 1998, he noted that '... a great deal of variability was evidenced in the radiocarbon samples. Some of the patchy encrustations were so thick as to mask the underlying carbon of fibers ...'
>
> Over the last two years, [Rogers] examined the claims of Garza-Valdes/Mattingly and Marino/Benford, at first with considerable skepticism, but he found that fibers of the 'Raes sample' adjacent to the C-14 sample did indeed have a coating of some kind, and did indeed have quite different chemical characteristics to fibers from other parts of the cloth.
>
> After a considerable number of tests on samples taken by STURP, Rogers found that no sample from the main part of the Shroud showed any feature even remotely similar to the coating in the anomalous Raes/C-14 area. These findings have been published

in detail on the web. In summary Rogers found that the area of the Raes and radiocarbon samples was anomalous.

All of the above observations lead inevitably and outstandingly to a single conclusion: the Raes/C-14 area is quite different from the rest of the cloth. The combined evidence from chemistry, cotton content, technology, fluorescence photography, and residual lignin proves that the material of the main part of the Shroud is significantly different from the Raes and radiocarbon sampling area. The radiocarbon sample was not representative of the main part of the cloth. The radiocarbon date was invalid; it was run on a spurious sample. A rigorous application of Scientific Method would demand a confirmation of the date with a better selection of samples.

Discussions with Ray forced me to re-consider the value of dating the material removed during the "restoration." The first consideration was that this material was no longer part of the relic and its use did not require access to the relic. In theory it should be much easier to obtain than fresh samples from the Shroud. And there was a lot of it, not only the loose carbon dust, but many square centimeters of charred cloth reduced to bits of charred fiber. C-14 dates from different points on the cloth could be obtained with only a small portion of the material removed.

But there were problems with the use of that material. A major consideration was authenticating the samples. My first reaction to the suggestion to use the carbon dust and fiber bits removed in 2002 was that one is open to the possibility (and more importantly, the allegation) that the samples could have been substituted, especially if the date really did come back as first century. There are certain safeguards against this, however. Ray was confident that the chemical and physical signature of the Shroud would not be easy to duplicate, and with fragments of thread even as small as 1mm, a non-Shroud sample could probably be identified. There are several areas from which a substantial amount of material was scraped away; it consists not only of completely carbonized cloth in the form of carbon powder, but also of brown lightly scorched fiber bits. A close scrutiny of this material would allow for a fairly probabilistic identification of the sample as Shroud.

When we put the idea out for wider discussion, several people raised the possibility that someone in Turin might substitute first century carbon or fiber bits. It was even suggested that some ranking Church official might be content with the medieval C-14 date on the Shroud to the point of providing false samples. It has been a constant source of amazement that conspiracy theories about the C-14 dating of the Shroud continue to have such a following in Shroud circles. These ideas are right up there with

Elvis-is-alive, I-was-abducted-by-aliens, men-never-landed-on-the-moon, and other nutty ideas that are floated from time to time. They cannot be disproved, as it is impossible to prove a negative, but they do not deserve serious consideration.

But in view of the ever-present possibility in the public mind of some subterfuge having taken place, we concluded that if the new dates on the removed material came back significantly earlier than the 13th century this would require testing of fresh samples removed from the Shroud, and this should be written into the proposal. So even if there was a substitution of the sample by a misguided Shroud-sympathizer in the inner sanctum of the Turin "Archbishopric", and even it was so cleverly done that it mimicked the linen of the Shroud in physical properties and chemistry, it would not, in the end, have the desired effect. A first century date or any other variant date would have to be corroborated by fresh samples taken directly from the cloth.

On reflection, I decided all these conspiracy fantasies were not worth bothering about. They will always be around, no matter what safeguards are instituted. What truly did merit consideration was the opportunity and availability as presented by the dust and fibers now sitting in glass vials. Even though created by an unnecessary act of aggression on the Shroud (the "restoration"), the material was now removed and stored away. In the past, protecting the Shroud from "destructive" sampling or intrusive operations was often cited as a reason to avoid further C-14 testing. Whether this was a real concern or simply an excuse for doing nothing (more likely), it applies no longer for these samples, and the time should be ripe to obtain another C-14 measurement on at least two or three different areas of the Shroud, preferably more.

The second major reservation about using the vial samples was the fact that they are no longer intact cloth fragments. The carbon dust was scraped away from the charred edges of the burnholes, or it was already loose under the patches. The fiber bits were brittle and/or weak cloth scraped away from near the burnholes. These constitute two sample types that could be dated separately, providing a check of sorts on the other. The realization of this fact helped me to overcome the initial reservation.

The basic problem with fluff of this kind is that it cannot be subjected to the same rigorous pretreatment that intact samples can. Most C-14 labs advise against any handling or pretreatment prior to submission to the laboratory, since it is important to examine the material intact to be able to separate what is intrusive from what is original. In the case of completely carbonized cloth reduced to powder by abrasion, this concern is much reduced. Recent particulate contaminants such as bits of wax, plant and insect debris, plus other various residues (e.g. salts and skin oils from touching) would be easily removed in pretreatment, first by visual separation and then by chemical action, leaving only the carbon.

There are other concerns about the use of charred material from the Shroud in general. In particular, there are two categories of potential contaminants that would pose difficulties. The first is carbonized bits of cloth or wood from the interior lining of the reliquary that might have been deposited on the Shroud during the 1532 fire. The second is contaminants (especially starch) that might have been on the Shroud itself in 1532, and were carbonized along with the linen. And finally there is the possibility, which admittedly is slim, of a heat-induced isotope exchange. There are ways of dealing with these potential problems, but they are not entirely satisfactory. The charred fiber bits however would not be affected by the first of the above contamination possibilities, as they could be definitively identified as linen rather than other textile or wood.

By dating the vial samples, we can quite definitively rule out two of the three main scenarios that have been proposed to explain the medieval date – repair on the edge and bioplastic coating – even with the other contamination possibilities described above. What is important to remember is that first, contamination of the two serious intrusive types from transfer of charred material described above is unlikely. Second, such contamination would be much reduced through handling, rolling and unrolling, after such a long period of time, as intrusive carbon would be the first to drop away. Third, whatever the contamination possibilities of the charred area, they would be markedly different from the edge where the C-14 sample came from. And fourth, any intrusive contamination in one area would probably result in a quite different dating from another's.

If the cloth is really 2000 years old and the C-14 area is anomalous, the anomaly will be crystal clear. Most probably the new date would come back as first century. Even if the date on the carbon dust comes back as 300 A.D. or 600 A.D. or 900 A.D., these results would tell us that the 1988 dating does not represent the entire cloth, and that there is variation between that sample and the charred samples. Eh voila! That is all we need to know to re-open the case and move forward to a proper direct sampling and definitive dating program.

Surprisingly, on the Shroud internet forum, there was only limited support for the proposal to use the vial samples for another C-14 dating. All sorts of issues were raised, some valid such as the contamination possibilities mentioned above, some rather bizarre. One concern that had seemed a potential problem was the idea that the nozzle of the vacuum could retain particles from one area and these could then wind up in the vial for another area. On further reflection this did not seem to a cause for worry, because the amount of material would have been very small and it would have almost certainly been from the same source (i.e. the Shroud).

Another concern was that burning wood or silk might have fallen onto the Shroud during the 1532 fire. Even if this did happen, there would probably not be any fusion transfer of that carbonized material onto the Shroud. And even if there was, it would probably be a very small amount relative to the carbonized cloth. Let us say for the sake of argument that 50% (an extremely unlikely amount) of the charcoal dust comes from something other than the burnt Shroud cloth. Would the true radiocarbon age of the cloth still be indicated or strongly hinted at by the resultant data?

Assume that the contaminant carbon is from material of 1500 A.D., and the cloth is 10 A.D. With an uneven distribution of the contaminant through the 15 mg of carbon dust, one might expect a scatter of dates something like:

620, 1310, 790, 1090, 970, 310 (all A.D.)

Two things would be clear from this: something is very strange with the samples, and there is some quite old material, especially as compared with the official Shroud C-14 date of 1260-1390 A.D.

In addition to the carbon dust, there would be the other two 15 mg lots of material – the slightly charred fiber bits. Even though there are contamination possibilities for these also, such as the bioplastic, it is virtually impossible that it would produce similar dates to those from any contamination of the carbon dust. If the Shroud is really 2000 years old, this round of dating would give a strong indication of that fact – that it comes from near the time of Christ. And the relic would be resurrected in the eyes of the world.

Having become convinced that the vial samples could provide either a reliable indication that the 1988 date on the Shroud was wrong, or conversely corroborative evidence that it was right, I drafted a formal proposal to submit to Poletto. Ray Rogers made a few alterations, and it was sent in August 2003:

> Dear Cardinal Poletto,
> In the light of the removal last summer of material from the Shroud, we are writing to you to request that a small portion of that material be released to us for C-14 measurement. This is intended only as a data measurement to confirm, or otherwise, the previous C-14 dating of the Shroud conducted in 1988.
>
> From the reports that have been published about the intervention last summer, we learned that data and measurements of various kinds were obtained at that time. The material that was removed can

serve the very basic yet highly important purpose of corroborating or contradicting the 1988 C-14 result.

Re-testing and replicating results is an important part of science. It is not necessary to have a full understanding of all factors that could be involved or that could conceivably have had an influence on the previous C-14 result. The evidence does very strongly indicate, however, that the sample taken in 1988 was not representative of the cloth as a whole.

We believe that it is extremely important to move forward with this very simple and basic measurement, as the previous C-14 dating of the Shroud has generated much debate, dispute and consternation over the last 15 years. It led to the Shroud being universally considered a medieval fake. However, there are very good reasons to believe that the result of 1988 does **not** indicate the true radiocarbon age of the cloth. Continued discussion of this issue on any level, popular or scientific, is useless, whereas testing of a very small amount of material will settle the basic question – was the sample taken in 1988 representative of the cloth as a whole? It will put an end to the debate that has raged in Shroud circles for years over the reliability of the 1988 sample.

We note that Mons. Ghiberti in the publication *Sindone le imagine 2002 Shroud images* stated the following: "...an unexpected amount of material for future examination was collected when the patches were removed and the burnholes cleaned." A very small portion of this material, chiefly consisting of carbon dust and tiny fragments of burnt fiber, will be sufficient for this very important measurement. As no new access to the Shroud itself is required, and the proposed C-14 measurement is quite straightforward, we do not see any need for peer review of this proposal. The measurement we are proposing is similar to other measurements that were made without peer review during the intervention last summer.

The following assumptions are made:

1. that the requested material has been kept under tight security and that its provenance from the Shroud can be assured;

2. that it was collected with due diligence to avoid mixing with any fragments of stitches from the 1534 repairs.

The Shroud has languished under an almost universal cloud of dismissal ever since the C-14 results were announced in 1988. Most people wrongly believe that science has now proven the precious relic to be a medieval forgery. The measurement that we are proposing could have an enormous and positive impact on the public perception of the Turin Shroud around the world, if it contradicts the earlier date. In that case, a more thorough and comprehensive program of study and testing of fresh samples, as proposed already in the paper submitted by Meacham, Cardamone, Haas, Rogers and Schwalbe, will be required before any firm conclusion can be drawn about the radiocarbon age of the cloth.

Alternatively, if the result is the same as that of 1988, it will have virtually no impact in the public arena; for scientists and Shroud researchers it would eliminate the possibility of an anomaly or aberration in the original C-14 sample, and focus attention instead on theoretical issues.

Cardinal Poletto, we trust that this proposal will gain your support, and that we may soon take a very important step in discovering the truth about the age of the Shroud.

Sincerely,

William Meacham and Raymond N. Rogers
cc: Prof. Savarino, Scientific Advisor to the Archbishop

Attached were the scientific observations on the anomalies and unrepresentativeness of the C-14 sample dated in 1988. This letter was sent in the middle of August, which is national holiday month in Italy. I was not expecting a reply until one or two months later. But a letter from Poletto arrived on September 10, having been posted on September 2. This was an extremely short turn-around time. I had also sent emails to Ghiberti, Savarino and people in the Centro seeking their support for the proposal, and received a short email note from Ghiberti a few days before Poletto's letter. It said much the same thing, and some words were identical. This suggested that Ghiberti handles Shroud correspondence for the cardinal, and is *primus inter pares* amongst his advisers. Poletto's reply was not encouraging:

> Esteemed Dr Meacham,
>
> I received your letter of 5 Aug. 2003 and am happy to know that the world of scientists appreciates the fact that the works carried out for the restoration of the Shroud in 2002 can offer material useful for sindonological research.
>
> As to the request of yourself and Dr Rogers, I must tell you that I am not in a position to grant it. As you know, a process of study and valuation has started for an organic program of sindonological research. All the requests that the scientists (you included) presented in 2000 (but we accepted also those that arrived up to the end of 2002) are under study by a jury of scientists, from whom we await a judgement. When we have received and evaluated it, I will prepare a

report to the Pope and we will do what he says. If the Holy Father decides to go ahead with another C-14 test, we will take into consideration all that you have written me.

I take the occasion to send you my cordial greeting and invite you to extend it also to Dr Rogers, with a particular wish for your/his health.

Severino Card. Poletto

This seemed to be another "definitive" statement ex cathedra, but the real authority has spoken already. The Pope had stated publicly more than once that he favored continuing research on the Shroud. Of course he was at that time very frail and suffering from Parkinson's; it was known that much of his workload is handled by others. Poletto may have been playing a little shell game here, setting up a procedure whereby he makes a "recommendation" to the Vatican, then arranges, through his Vatican contacts, for the appropriate decision to be made in the name of the Pope. The process is basically a rubber stamp of what he had already decided.

We seemed to have reached a dead end, with nothing further that could be done to push the subject forward. From a source close to Turin I learned of serious reasons to doubt that an international jury had really been appointed, or rather that it was all a façade and the real decisions would be made in the same manner as the "restoration" was decided. This was disturbing, but not really surprising, considering all that had transpired since the betrayal of the "spirit of Villa Gualino."

15. A Final Effort

In Late 2003, The Media Was Full of Talk about the new movie Mel Gibson had made, and was showing to preview audiences, entitled "The Passion of the Christ." It was said by many to be the most violent and most moving depiction of the Crucifixion events ever made. It was scheduled for general release on Ash Wednesday, in early March 2004. I decided to try one more time to reason with Poletto, and to appeal to his vanity and ambition as well. This latter approach might succeed where all the scientific reasoning in the world would fail. There had been the occasional rumor in the Italian press that some prelates considered Poletto to be *papabile*, a possible candidate for the papacy. This was of course very far-fetched, and to my mind outrageous, as Poletto speaks only Italian, is not well educated, and as we have seen, has a very nasty temper.

Still trying to move on from the disastrous "restoration," in October 2003 I sent Poletto this letter, with copies to Ghiberti and Savarino:

> Dear Cardinal Poletto,
> Thank you for your letter of Sept. 2. I appreciate your sense of humor and irony, noting that the world of scientists have acknowledged that the "restoration" has provided samples that could be useful to scientists. You must know, however, that scientists will always seek to take advantage of any disaster, natural or man-made, in order to advance knowledge.
> It is my fervent hope that you will consider granting us the samples that we seek for C-14 dating. The dust samples are no longer part of the Shroud, and it is surely within your power to decide what is done with them. The intervention of last summer created a new situation, and the opportunity is now at hand to obtain new C-14 measurements without requiring access to the Shroud. The results of these measurements would certainly have an impact on any future organic program of research, and they should be

obtained first. I would hope you would, with the assistance of your advisers, determine that the proposal put forward by Ray Rogers and myself is a legitimate proposal, that we are bona fide researchers, and that it is supported by other researchers. A rigorous peer review should not be necessary for testing of the dust samples, just as there was no peer review of the measurements made during the "restoration."

The C-14 testing we propose could have very important benefits for the Church. There is growing interest worldwide in the suffering and crucifixion of Jesus, due largely to the movie soon to be released by Mel Gibson. God willing, this could be an important time for the Church to strengthen, and the Shroud might have a crucial role to play in this. But we will never know, unless the truth is revealed. For 15 years the small group of Shroud researchers who retain their belief in the relic has waited to see if the C-14 dating can be corroborated. All that is required is a tiny amount of material, about the size of two beans; a comparatively large amount has already been removed from the Shroud. It seems most illogical to continue to refuse permission for the use of such a tiny amount of material for such an important purpose.

When we met at Villa Gualino in 2000, I (along with quite a few others) had high hopes that a new era was dawning for Shroud studies. But these hopes were soon dashed. The so-called "restoration" was a terrible mistake and a disaster for the Shroud. A great majority of Shroud researchers believe so. Nevertheless, I continue steadfastly to pray that you as archbishop of Turin will do something positive for the Shroud – something that the whole world will appreciate.

Months went by without any response, and it became clear that there would be none. I was annoyed at this, but Emanuela told me that of all the Italians who had written to Poletto about the "restoration," only one leading academic had received a reply directly from the esteemed cardinal. I had had three, but somehow it did not seem like any great honor. Whatever bridge I might have had to Poletto and his inner circle was clearly not working now. I would soon set it ablaze.

Meanwhile, "The Passion of the Christ" was released, and began breaking box office records in the US. Discussion of the tortures and crucifixion of Christ appeared in newspapers, magazines and internet sites around the world, yet there was barely a mention of the Shroud. After seeing and being very moved by the film myself, I was propelled to write

A FINAL EFFORT 253

Poletto for what I said to myself would be the last time. All the stops were pulled out. I sent this by email on March 7, 2004:

> Dear Cardinal Poletto,
> I feel compelled to write to you one final time, in view of the tremendous opportunity that now presents itself. A quite amazing situation has been created by the movie "The Passion of the Christ." It has achieved spectacular success in moving people deeply through visual contemplation of the sufferings of Christ.
> There is now a grand and wonderful opportunity for the Church, and the Shroud could have a major role to play at this moment in time. The truth about the age of the Shroud can be known quite easily from 60mg of carbon and bits of fiber. Or, the Shroud can remain as it is – universally dismissed as a medieval fake, because of the single C-14 date done 16 years ago.
> As you know, Ray Rogers and I requested a tiny amount of the material already removed, so that this C-14 dating can be confirmed or refuted. If a new C-14 date indicated an age significantly older, even say 800 or 900 A.D., the impact around the world would be extraordinary. Such a result would confirm that the C-14 dating of the Shroud is problematic, that it is clearly older than 13th century, and that the Shroud might actually have the true image and the blood of Christ. If on the other hand, the new result turned out to be similar to what was obtained in 1988, this could be published quietly in a scientific journal, and hardly anyone would notice.
> The impact of an older C-14 date would be greatly magnified at this time when the attention of the entire western world is focused on the torture and crucifixion of Christ. You, Cardinal Poletto, could announce this result on Easter Sunday in Turin. If you can act swiftly to obtain Vatican approval, and if the samples can be released [soon], the results can be known by April 9. I would personally carry the samples to Ray Rogers for preliminary screening, and then to the C-14 laboratory for the analysis.
> From two tiny samples of 30 mg each (two small spoonfuls of fairly useless material), a wonderful and earth-shaking revelation could come. There is a fantastic opportunity here, and I hope you will seize it. If the Shroud does provide an older date, you would go down in history as the cardinal who brought the image of Christ back into the collective mind of the 21st century.

There was nothing but silence from Turin, even with this blatant appeal to Poletto's ambition and vanity. Easter came and went, the passion that had been stirred by "The Passion" began to die away. I was left to wonder once again what could explain such stubbornness and resistance to such a simple and attractive idea. Perhaps another sample really had been dated already, and the result was known to the inner sanctum of the Turin "Archbishopric." What else could explain such a seeming lack of intellectual and spiritual curiosity about the age of this extraordinary relic? I had heard from some of the Italians that Poletto does not believe in the Shroud, but still wishes to make use of it to promote himself and the Turin archdiocese while he is head. Perhaps this could explain why he lends support to the Centro and to the cult of the Shroud, but is not interested in finding out the truth about its dating. On the other hand, perhaps he does believe that the Shroud might be authentic, but is biding his time in order that people of his choosing (i.e. Turinese) are the ones who will make this discovery. God only knows what is in his mind.

The final straw

In April 2004 an article by my friend Giulio Fanti and his colleague Roberto Maggiolo at the University of Padova was published in the scientific journal *Pure and Applied Optics*. Working with photographs published in Ghiberti's 2002 book, they claim to have detected very faint traces of a facial image on the underside of the cloth. If it can be confirmed, this is a quite interesting and important phenomenon, suggesting that whatever mechanism produced the body imprint acted on both sides of the cloth to produce a "double superficial" image. It was known from the STURP examination that blood seeped through to the underside, but no body image had been seen there. Fanti told me he had been unable to obtain any original photographs or documents from Turin. These included already published color photographs, as well as microscope video that had been made of slow scans over selected parts of both sides. There were approximately 154 minutes of such video, at magnifications of between 80X and 450X. In addition there were the high resolution digital scans of the underside that had been done in 2000. Refusal to allow access to these materials struck me as highly objectionable and absurd, a new peak even for the Turin clique.

But still more infuriating was this paragraph in the April issue of *Sindon News*, an email newsletter of the Turin Archdiocese Commission:

> Prof. Balossino, Teacher of Image Processing at the University of Turin also lingered over the latest news regarding the presence of a

A FINAL EFFORT

mark also on the back of the Shroud, declaring that 'as far as the hidden side of the Holy Shroud is concerned, looking directly at the Sheet, it comes out the full lack of marks attributable to body contribution and particularly to that of the face. On the face, on the contrary, spots due to the spread of blood both on the forehead and on the hair, are present. The possible illusion to notice, even if not distinctly, the structure of a face can be due to the psychophysiology of the vision. The spots of blood which surround the face behave exactly as focusing points that create, at cortical level, the formation of the image of the face on the basis of that one well-known of the frontal side, stored in the memory for long time. From the objective point of view, the methodology of picture processing connected with the recognition of shapes, enabled us to exclude that there is a body print on the back of the sheet. The news coming out in these days on the presumed demonstration of the presence of the print of the face also on the back has to be considered unfounded for two basic remarks [reasons?]. First of all, researchers who spread it, have never seen the Holy Shroud directly, and so they lack the essential component of the visual interpretation. In second place, the prints analysed are not split into the two main components, that is the one due to hematic material and those of another nature, among which also the possible body contribution. It follows that the processings are free interpretation of the blood spots, of the folds and of the chromatic variation due to the weaving and to pollution'.

This merited some sort of protest, I thought, and I began to draft a letter to object to two things: the denial of access to original documents and photographs, coupled with the use of insider knowledge by Balossino to dispute the conclusions of Fanti and Maggiolo. As I wrote, all the frustrations of the last few years boiled up to the surface and the draft became more and more a vehement protest against all that had gone wrong since 2000. It was strong, it was blunt, and it called a spade a bloody spade. I considered long and hard about whether to send it, as it would probably mean banishment from the Turin archdiocese for as long as Poletto and his clique remain in power. But these things needed to be said. I sent it.

The Turin Diocesan Commission for the Shroud

Dear Commission members,

I have just read the English version of *Sindon News* No. 15 of April 2004, that contains remarks that I consider to be extremely inappropriate and infuriating.

There is a long passage citing Prof. Balossino's arguments against the new claim published recently by two Shroud researchers that there are faint traces of a facial imprint on the underside of the cloth. Of course Prof. Balossino is free to hold and argue whatever view he wishes, but what is objectionable is the remark that the recent claim 'has to be considered unfounded' because, among other things, 'the researchers who spread it, have never seen the Holy Shroud directly, and so they lack the essential component of the visual interpretation.' One of the researchers in question **has** seen the Holy Shroud directly, but neither he nor anyone else in the world has seen the underside, apart from members of the so-called 'Conservation Commission' and a few Turinese technicians selected by them.

This happened because the Conservation Commission decided to remove the backing cloth of 1534 and immediately affix a new one. This latter action can only be described as colossal stupidity. The reason given was that a new one was required to provide support when the Holy Shroud is publicly exhibited. The next such exhibit is planned for 2025. Why could the cloth not have remained with the underside accessible for scientific study for a few years, before a new backing cloth was affixed (if indeed there was even a need for one)? The underside had not been seen since 1534. It is now hidden again, 'for who knows how long' as Don Ghiberti put it, seemingly without remorse.

To make matters worse, the two researchers mentioned above were denied access to any of the measurement data, photographs or microscope video recorded in 2002. In these circumstances, it is totally improper for members of the Conservation Commission, or members of the small clique around Cardinal Poletto that has been called '*Il Gruppo di Torino*' (The Turin Group), to make use of their insider knowledge to challenge the interpretations of others. And it is highly regrettable that the Turin authorities have rejected all legitimate requests from scholars for documents such as photographs and videos, or for minute quantities of material removed from the cloth in 2002.

It is doubly regrettable that during the last few months, when huge public interest around the world was focused on the Crucifixion, there was hardly a mention of the Turin Shroud. I am not alone in believing that the situation regarding the Shroud is now at an all-time low since its modern study began in 1898. The carbon dating of a single sample from a bad location led to the Shroud being universally dismissed as a medieval fake. And for some unfathomable reason, the Church has refused for more than 15 years (!) to allow even a single piece the size of a fingernail to be tested to confirm or refute the C-14 result, even though it has everything to gain and nothing to lose. This attitude simply defies logic and belief. As does the so-called 'restoration' of 2002 – a terrible and inexcusable tragedy in which valuable scientific data was destroyed, and great opportunities for proper scientific investigation were lost.

International research on the Shroud remains in a state of limbo because of these anti-scientific and ill-considered postures. In contrast, over the last three years, three coffee table books have been published by members of the Conservation Commission, using data and photographs obtained during the interventions carried out in 2000 and 2002, and apparently more such books are in preparation. How is it that only 'The Turin Group' can have access to all these materials, publishing one book after another? What can justify such a double standard?

Meanwhile, the rest of the world still waits for some vague 'peer review process' for the testing and conservation proposals from all other scholars – incredibly, four years after proposals for research were invited. Many colleagues now believe that this invitation to submit proposals was a deception. Some say it was a device to conceal what was really being planned. Others feel it may have been intended to attract ideas that could then be considered for use by 'The Turin Group.' It may have been both. What is certain is that, **only a few days** after the deadline of October 30, 2000 for submission of proposals, an elaborate project was carried out in secret to study and scan the underside of the Shroud; there was no prior peer review or consultation with independent experts. How could this project be selected, clearly well before the deadline, without going through the same review process as all the others? How can such a deliberate, flagrant violation of the process possibly be justified?

I blame myself and others for not protesting against it in the strongest terms at the time. Only one person that I know of dared to speak out – Barrie Schwortz, in an editorial on his website in June 2001. He did so in clear and compelling terms; his was however 'a voice crying in the wilderness.' We outsiders who had attended the Villa Gualino congress said nothing, failing to understand what was really going on. Our eyes would be brutally opened in August 2002.

Recalling the 'spirit of Villa Gualino' now is very painful. For a brief moment in March 2000, it seemed as though a new era of real international cooperation and collaborative academic/scientific quest for the truth about the Shroud had dawned. Cardinal Poletto seemed like a dynamic church official who would re-ignite Shroud research. There was much idealistic rhetoric spouted at the conference, especially from the two conference co-presidents and from officials of the Centro. Shortly afterwards, all participants received from Don Ghiberti a warm fraternal greeting that was effusive in its description of the wonderful and fruitful time that colleagues had spent together. A line from Psalm 132 (Vulgate version) was cited: *ecce quam bonum et quam jucumdum habitare frates in unum* (How good, how delightful it is to live as brothers all together.)

This memory is now a bitter, mocking irony. A more appropriate citation would be from Seneca: *fallaces sunt rerum species* (The appearances of things are deceptive.) Only now do we realize that all the high-sounding talk at Villa Gualino was empty, worthless. Now we see that there was never to be real international cooperation, or a true spirit of scientific inquiry. Instead we see all sorts of insider dealings and hoarding of data and opportunists taking advantage of their standing within the clique. Whilst on the outside we have the sad spectacle of a few individuals and organizations in the role of sycophants and lackeys hopeful of obtaining favor. Cardinal Poletto has indeed brought in a new era for the Holy Shroud, but it is the opposite of what began with such promise. Being extremely badly advised, and failing to seek independent expert opinion, he authorized the most grievous and deplorable damage to the relic in its entire history, worse even than the fire of 1532, since that event was an accident.

Tragic as it was, the effects of the fire on the cloth provided much useful information to 20th century researchers regarding the nature of the image. After the shock of the 'restoration,' some researchers dared to hope that this new tragedy might at least provide some useful advance in knowledge, that something positive could come out of it, and that everyone might move on. Alas, this was not to be; all requests for information or samples have been flatly refused. The 'peer review process' that is supposedly underway (for all study proposals from the rest of the world) has not been defined, the reviewers not named, the entire operation is secretive and subject to manipulation and outright rigging. Of course, the process was devised by the same people who decided on the abominable 'restoration,' and it is being executed in the same machiavellian manner.

Furthermore, most proposals from 2000-2002 have been overtaken by events. There is now a significant amount of data collected and material removed from the Shroud that should be made available for study by bona fide researchers **immediately**. All the former research proposals need to be reconsidered in the light of this new body of off-cloth evidence. After the newly acquired information and material has been thoroughly studied, fresh proposals for direct testing of the relic should be drawn up. An open, transparent and fair process of peer review, by prominent scholars nominated by the international community, should then be initiated.

The present situation regarding the study of the Shroud is a huge mess, with a horrid admixture of incompetence, cronyism, double dealing, and backroom decision-making. This is unworthy of Turin and of the Holy Shroud. Is the Diocesan Commission for the Shroud willing to re-consider the process, and most importantly, to get independent professional advice? Is there anyone on the Commission who has a clue ... that things are terribly wrong with the current situation?

Daring to hope that there is,

As might be predicted, there was no reply. Even the internet discussion group was stunned by this letter, and no one offered any comment. Privately, I received quite a few commendations for having the courage (polite way of saying the foolhardiness) to "tell it like it is" for the record, and being willing to accept the consequences. These will almost certainly mean *Arrivederci Torino* for the immediate future. As I mentioned previously, sometimes the only moral place to be is in the wilderness, crying with the other voices. It is not lonely out here; in fact, more and more Shroud researchers are finding that they too cannot stomach the absurdities and incompetence and cronyism of the current "Turin Group" any longer. One can only hope that someone somewhere in the ecclesiastical corridors of power will hear this collective wail, and institute serious reforms.

Epilogue

In Late January Of 2005 Ray Rogers published a paper on his analysis of the Raes and radiocarbon samples. He had been trying for two years to get the paper published in a peer-reviewed scientific journal, and it finally appeared in *Thermochimica Acta*. This paper grew out of his study of the Marino-Benford hypothesis of an invisible patch, and his analysis first of threads from the Raes sample that Gonella had provided to STURP in 1978, and then of two threads from the "reserve" piece that AMSTAR had obtained via Adler. Rogers concluded that the sample dated in 1988 was invalid because it was not part of the original Shroud.

Somewhat surprisingly, AMSTAR decided to jump in and publicize the appearance of this scientific paper, but oddly its press release trumpeted itself as much as Rogers and his findings. It sat largely ignored on the Yahoo news site for a week. I decided that this needed a push and wrote the *New York Times* science editor. Two days later the story ran in that paper and concurrently on the BBC website. It then received wide play in the press around the world, and deservedly so, for here was a widely respected scientist stating in a peer-reviewed journal that the much ballyhooed C-14 dating on the Shroud was dead wrong.

It was a blessing that Ray lived to see this article published in a proper scientific journal, and the beginnings of a new public attitude toward the Shroud. His last weeks were spent dealing with press inquiries, answering critics and debating the finer points with members of an internet forum for Shroud science. He passed away on March 8, much mourned by those who knew him, or had the privilege (as I did) of speaking with him by telephone on occasion and corresponding by email.

The reaction from Turin to his paper was negative at first. Ever the henchman, Ghiberti commented to the Catholic newspaper *Avvenire* that there was no evidence of a repair or reweave, citing Flury-Lemberg. He even ventured into the scientific debate, declaring himself "astonished that an expert like Rogers could fall into so many inaccuracies in his article."

However, a softer tone was adopted later in *Sindon News*; it was stated that Rogers' findings of inhomogeneity were worthy of further research.

Pope John Paul II died in April 2005, and his successor Benedict XVI is said to have a special interest in the Shroud. For a few days after his election there was among some Shroud researchers a feeling of guarded optimism that things might change. Then the former Secretary of State for the Vatican, Cardinal Sodano, was re-appointed, and that brief wisp of optimism evaporated. Poletto is rumored to be a good friend of Sodano's, and to have made use of his close connections with the highest echelon in the Vatican to have the "restoration" approved. The only hope now for a change in the status quo is for Poletto to be moved to another position, or, what seems very much less likely, for the Pope to give a directive regarding research on the Shroud. At present (November 2005) there is no sign of any movement, and the Vatican seems content to let Poletto manage the Shroud in whatever manner he chooses, regardless of the travesty perpetrated on the relic under his watch.

The last straw in the pile of frustrations and bitterness generated by the "restoration" and the arrogance of the "Turin Group" was the AMSTAR conference in Dallas on September 8-11, 2005. It was heralded as a chance to discuss all the major issues confronting the Shroud, and to recover a sense of harmony amongst researchers. In the weeks leading up to the conference it became painfully clear that the conference was going to be a show and a farce. It exceeded these expectations; it was a disgrace. Communications from Cardinals Sodano and Poletto stated their hopes for dialogue at this meeting, but the three members of AMSTAR decided that there would be no discussion, no comments or even questions from the floor! Questions had to be submitted in writing, were read out by Minor in a special session on the last day, and answered by the Turin delegation. This was a blatant form of censorship, unheard of at academic and scientific conferences, and served only to allow the Turin delegation (Ghiberti, Flury-Lemberg, Baima, and Dietz) to pontificate without being challenged, somewhat like an old-fashioned catechism class.

The only opportunity for discussion was at an evening session devoted to a video interview with Ray Rogers prepared by Barrie Schwortz. In it Rogers was scathing in his criticism of the "ignorant" Turin authorities and the "terrible tragedy" of the restoration. Only Ghiberti and Dietz attended this evening session, and at the end of the video, when it was clear that free discussion was going to take place, Ghiberti and Dietz walked out. In his paper presented the day before, Ghiberti had stated: "Discussion and exchange of ideas is good; polemics and personal attacks are not." Even worse, however, were the measures that the AMSTAR organizers deemed necessary to enforce order and silence. An armed guard, member of the

Texas Highway Patrol, was stationed at the door. When an unscheduled speech by Flury-Lemberg was suddenly inserted into the schedule the day after the Ray Rogers video, the guard came inside the conference room and took up at position about mid-way along one wall. He kept glancing at me and I just smiled, shaking my head in disbelief. At the final session, incorrectly titled "Discussion Period," when one delegate was going on in some detail to answer a question put to him, Minor said, "Give me the mike, please." As if on cue, the guard moved from the back of the hall towards the podium. Someone said it was "fascism, Texas-style." One can only reflect on the sad state of affairs that Shroud studies had come to, when an armed guard is employed to impose silence on researchers seeking the truth about a relic possibly associated with Jesus.

There was hardly anything new from the Turin delegation: Flury-Lemberg repeated statements from her book, and even showed video clips of the horrors of scraping away deposits around the "pokerholes" and of the lamp shining unattended at close range on the Shroud while Ghiberti nattered on about the measures being taken to preserve it. It was as if the Turin clique did not know about, or care about, the range of serious criticisms that had been made of the 2002 intervention. The conference also had a grand anti-climax. Ghiberti was going to make "an important announcement" in the keynote speech and there were all sorts of speculations as to what this might be. It turned out to be nothing more than the fact that the so-called "peer-review" of research proposals had been completed, and a recommendation would be forwarded to the Vatican "in a few months." There was no information at all as to which proposals were supported, or what the recommendation from Poletto would be. The process remains highly suspect, wide open for manipulation by cronies, much akin to the process that gave birth to the monstrous "restoration."

One day, perhaps by the grace of God within in our lifetime, the truth will be discovered about the radiocarbon age of the Shroud. As discussed in Part Two, it may be that the result obtained in 1988 will be confirmed by further testing. This would pose a huge and irresolvable dilemma. The cloth would have to be either a freak of history (the imprint of a corpse bearing all the marks of crucifixion long after the practice had disappeared, and the only such body imprint known, somehow created by a medieval forger of unimaginable genius), or it is a freak of nature (a cloth dating back at least 1600 years to the era of crucifixion but with a C-14 content enriched through some unknown process and indicating an age of only about 700 years). If new C-14 dating confirms the age of 700 years, scientific attention would then have to re-visit all the evidence concerning the blood and the image, and new research would focus on how such an unlikely artifact could have been created.

EPILOGUE

Whatever the radiocarbon age, the Shroud image poses a great enigma, and there is no good hypothesis to explain it. At our present state of knowledge, one can conclude that a forger simply could not have done it, and one can equally conclude that a body also could not have produced it. Clearly the image needs much deeper investigation, and the only solution to these dilemmas lies in new and improved scientific testing.

In the article that comprises chapter 1 of this book, I wrote that the Turin Shroud is probably the most intensively studied object in the world. This may have changed recently, because research on "Oetzi the Iceman" (the frozen corpse of a Bronze Age man found in the Alps) has been proceeding by leaps and bounds in recent years. It has also seen major errors, most notably the X-rays that showed a fuzzy area in the shoulder but was not noticed by the specialists. Later it was found to be an arrowhead! The difference is that research on Oetzi has been vigorous, it has been encouraged by the relevant authorities, and it has thus made remarkable progress every year, while Shroud research languishes in the doldrums, with old data constantly re-hashed. The responsibility for this lies squarely on the shoulders of the clique in Turin who unfortunately seem to have unfettered control at present and a possessive, unscientific attitude. This would be a sad enough state of affairs if the Shroud was safe and locked away; it is dreadful and tragic when one considers the vandalism (however unintentional) it was subjected to 2002.

And if a new C-14 date gives an age in the range of 1500-2000 years? Surely this would have to open a new and re-invigorated worldwide interest in the cloth, and the most sophisticated 21st century technology and scientific knowledge could be brought to bear on the inexplicable image. We would need to satisfy a multitude of questions, and doubts, and even then an answer to the image mechanism may still not be forthcoming. It may belong to a future generation to discover, or unbearable as it is to consider, it may never be known.

The great Al Adler was fond of saying that "there is no laboratory test for Christness," and thus the identity of the man whose image is on the cloth cannot ever be known with scientific certainty. As discussed in Part I, historical facts are established by a different method. But in the future, when the human genome is mapped back into the past, DNA from the Shroud could perhaps assign the image to the body of a Jew in first century Palestine. That would suffice for a very secure historical judgment. The mystery of the image may continue. But as Fr. Rinaldi always pointed out, behind this cloth and its image, beyond the reach of scholarly historical or scientific methods, lies the greatest mystery of all, and the turning point of human history.

References

Accetta, J. S., and J. S. Baumgart. 1980. Infrared reflectance spectroscopy and thermographic investigations of the Shroud of Turin. *Applied Optics* 19:1920-26.

Adler, Alan. 1984. The Turin Shroud. Lecture given at the Dept of Chemistry, Queen Mary College, London, July 20 (tape recording)
----- 1991. Conservation and preservation of the Shroud of Turin. *Shroud Spectrum International*. No. 40.
----- 2002. Chemical and Physical Aspects of the Sindonic Images. *The Orphaned Manuscript*. Turin: Effata.

Angier, Natalie. 1982. Unraveling the Shroud of Turin. *Discover*, October, pp. 54-60.

Antonacci, Mark. 2000. *The Resurrection of the Shroud*. New York: M. Evans

Anon. 2002. *Shroud Images 2000*. Turin: ODPF

Avis, C. D., and   J. Lynn, J. Lorre, S. Lavoie, J. Clark, E. Armstrong, J. Addington. 1982. Image processing of the Shroud of Turin. *Proceedings of the 1982 IEEE Conference on Cybernetics and Society*, pp. 554-58.

Baima Bollone, Pierluigi, and Maria Jorio, Anna Lucia Massaro. 1981. La dimostrazione della presenza di tracce di sangue umano sulla Sindone. *Sindon* 30:5-8.

Barbet, Pierre. 1963. *A Doctor at Calvary*. New York: Image.

Bender, A. P. 1895. Beliefs, rites, and customs of the Jews connected with death, burial, and mourning. *Jewish Quarterly Review* 7:101-3.

Benford, M. Sue, and Joseph G. Marino. [see also Marino and Benford]
----- 2002a. Textile evidence supports skewed radiocarbon date of Shroud of Turin.   http://www.shroud.com/pdfs/textevid.pdf
----- 2002b. Historical Support of a 16th Century Restoration in the Shroud C-14 Sample Area. 2002. http://www.shroud.com/pdfs/histsupt.pdf

REFERENCES

Bortin, Virginia. 1980. Science and the Shroud of Turin. *Biblical Archaeologist*, Spring, pp. 109-17.

Brandone, Alberto, and P. A. Borroni. 1978. L'analisi per attivazione neutronica nello studio della Sindone di Torino. [in] *La Sindone e la Scienza.* Edited by Piero Coero Borga, pp. 205-15. Turin: Paoline.

Bucklin, Robert. 1961. The medical aspects of the crucifixion of Christ. *Sindon*, December, pp. 5-11.
----- 1970. The legal and medical aspects of the trial and death of Christ. *Medicine, Science, and the Law* 10:14-26.
----- 1981a. Afterword. [in] *Verdict on the Shroud*, by Kenneth E. Stevenson and Gary R. Habermas, pp. 189-90. Ann Arbor: Servant.
----- 1981b. The Shroud of Turin: A pathologist's viewpoint. *Legal Medicine Annual* 1981.
----- 1982. The Shroud of Turin: Viewpoint of a forensic pathologist. *Shroud Spectrum International* 1(5):3-10.

Bulst, Werner. 1957. *The Shroud of Turin*. Milwaukee: Bruce.

Burleigh, Richard, and Morven Leese, Michael Tite. 1985. An intercomparison of some AMS and small gas counter labs. Paper presented at the International Radiocarbon Conference; Trondheim, Norway.

Cameron, Averil. 1980. The sceptic and the Shroud. Inaugural lecture in the Department of Classics and History, King's College, London, April 29.

Cameron, Malcom. 1978. A pathologist looks at the Shroud. [in] *Face to Face with the Turin Shroud.* Edited by Peter Jennings, pp. 57-59. Oxford: Mowbray.

Caselli, Giuseppe. 1950. Le constatazioni della medicina moderna sulle impronte della S. Sindone. [in] *La S. Sindone nelle Ricerche Moderne.* Turin: Lice.

Chevalier, Ulisse. 1900. *Etude critique sur l'origine du Saint Suaire de Lirey-Chambèry-Turin.* Paris: Picard.

Codegone, Cesare. 1976. Sulla datazione di antichi tessuti mediante isotopi radioattivi. [in] *La S. Sindone.* Turin: Diocesi Torinese.

Culliton, Barbara J. 1978. The mystery of the Shroud challenges 20th century science. *Science* 201:235-39.

Curto, Silvio. 1976. La Sindone di Torino: Osservazioni archeologiche circa il tessuto e l'immagine. [in] *La S. Sindone*. Turin: Diocesi Torinese.

De Clary, Robert. 1936. *The Conquest of Constantinople*. Translated by E. H. McNeal. New York: Columbia University Press.

Delage, Yves. 1902. Le Linceul de Turin. *Revue Scientifique* 22:683-87.

DeSalvo, John A. 1983. The image formation of the Shroud of Turin and its similarities to Volckringer patterns. *Shroud Spectrum International* 2(6):7-15.

Devan, D., and V. Miller. 1982. Quantitative photography of the Shroud of Turin. *Proceedings of the 1982 IEEE Conference on Cybernetics and Society*, pp. 548-53.

Dinegar, Robert H. 1982. The 1978 scientific study of the Shroud of Turin. *Shroud Spectrum International* 1(4):3-12.

Donovan, Vincent J. 1980. The Shroud and the laws of probability. *The Catholic Digest*, April, pp. 49-52.

Ercoline, W. R., and R. C. Downs, J. P. Jackson. 1982. Examination of the Turin Shroud for image distortions. *Proceedings of the 1982 IEEE Conference on Cybernetics and Society*, pp. 576-79.

Fanti, Giulio, and Roberto Maggiolo. 2004. The double superficiality of the frontal image of the Turin Shroud. *Journal of Optics A: Pure and Applied Optics*, 6:491-503

Filas, Francis. 1980. *The dating of the Shroud of Turin from coins of Pontius Pilate*. Privately printed.
----- 1981. *The dating of the Shroud of Turin from coins of Pontius Pilate*. Youngtown, Ariz.: Cogan Productions.

Filogamo, Guido, and Alberto Zina. 1976. Esami microscopici sulla tela sindonica. [in] *La S. Sindone*. Turin: Diocesi Torinese.

REFERENCES

Fleming, Stuart J. 1978. The Shroud: further scientific investigation. [in] *Face to Face with the Turin Shroud*. Edited by Peter Jennings, pp. 61-68. Oxford: Mowbray.

Flury-Lemberg, Mechthild. 2003. *Sindone 2002 – L'intervento conservativo – Preservation – Konservierung*. Turin: ODPF.

Foley, Rev. Charles. 1982. Carbon dating and the Holy Shroud. *Shroud Spectrum International* 1(1):25-27

Frache, Giorgio, and Eugenia Mari Rizzatti, Emilio Mari. 1976. Relazione conclusive sulle indagini d'origine ematologico praticate su materiale prelevato dalla Sindone. [in] *La S. Sindone*. Turin: Diocesi Torinese.

Francez, J. 1935. *Un Pseudo Linceul du Christ*. Paris.

Frei, Max. 1978. Il passato della Sindone alla luce della palinologia. [in] *La Sindone e La Scienza*. Edited by Piero Coero Borga, pp. 191-200. Turin: Paoline.
----- 1982. Nine years of palynological studies on the Shroud. *Shroud Spectrum International* 1(3):3-7.

Gabrielli, Noemi. 1976. La sindone nella storia dell'arte [in] *La S. Sindone*. Turin: Diocesi Torinese.

Garza-Valdes, Leoncio. 1999. *The DNA of God?* New York: Doubleday.

Ghiberti, Giuseppe. 2002. *Sindone le Immagini 2002 Shroud Images*. Turin: ODPF.

Gilbert, Roger, and Marion M. Gilbert. 1980. Ultra-violet visible reflectance and fluorescence spectra of the Shroud of Turin. *Applied Optics* 19:1930-36.

Goude, Andrew. 1977. *Environmental Change*. Oxford: Clarendon

Gove, Harry E. 1996. *Relic, Icon or Hoax? Carbon Dating the Turin Shroud*. Bristol and Philadelphia: Institute of Physics Publishing.

Gove, Harry E., and S.J. Mattingly, A.R. David, L.A. Garza-Valdes. 1997. A problematic source of organic contamination in linen. *Nuclear Instruments and Methods in Physics Research*.

Green, Marus. 1969. Enshrouded in silence. *Ampleforth Journal* 74:319-45.

Haas, Nicu. 1970. Anthropological observations on the skeletal remains from Giv'at ha-Mivtar. *Israel Exploration Journal* 20:38-59.

Hachlili, Rachel. 1979. Ancient burial customs preserved in Jericho Hills. *Biblical Archaeology Review*, July/August, pp. 28-35.

Heizer, Robert F. and John A. Graham. 1967. *A Guide to Field Methods in Archaeology.* Palo Alto: National.

Heller, John H. 1983. *Report on the Shroud of Turin.* Boston: Houghton Mifflin

Heller, J. H. and A. D. Adler. 1980. Blood on the Shroud of Turin. *Applied Optics* 19:2742-44.
-----1981. A chemical investigation of the Shroud of Turin. *Journal of the Canadian Society of Forensic Science* 14(3):81-103

Hengel, Martin. 1977. *Crucifixion.* London: SCM.

Hofenk de Graaff, J.H. 1994. Research into the cause of browning of paper mounted in mats. [in] *Contribution of the Central Research Laboratory to the Field of Conservation and Preservation.* Amsterdam: Central Research Laboratory.

Hynek, R. W. 1936. *Science and the Holy Shroud.* Chicago: Benedictine.

Jackson, J. P., and   E. J. Jumper, W. R. Ercoline. 1982. Three dimensional characteristics of the Shroud image. *Proceedings of the 1982 IEEE Conference on Cybernetics and Society*, pp. 559-75.

Jackson, John P., and Eric J. Jumper, Bill Mottern, Kenneth E. Stevenson. 1977. The three-dimensional image of Jesus' burial cloth. *Proceedings of the 1977 U.S. Conference of Research on the Shroud of Turin.* Edited by Kenneth Stevenson, pp. 74-94. Bronx: Holy Shroud Guild.

Johnson, R.A. and J.J. Stipp, M.A. Tamers, G. Bonani, M. Suter, W. Woelfli. 1985. Archaeological sherd dating: comparison of thermo-luminescence dates with radiocarbon dates by Beta counting and accelerator techniques. Paper presented at the Int'l Radiocarbon Conference; Trondheim, Norway.

Judica-Cordiglia, G. 1961. *La Sindone*. Padua: Lice.

Jumper, E. 1982. An overview of the testing performed by the Shroud of Turin Research Project with a summary of results. *Proceedings of the 1982 IEEE Conference on Cybernetics and Society*, pp. 535-37

Jumper, E.J., and A.D. Adler, J.P. Jackson, S.F. Pellicori, J.H. Heller, J.R. Druzik. 1984. A comprehensive examination of various stains and images on the Shroud of Turin. *Archaeological Chemistry II, ACS Advances in Chemistry*, 205:446-476

Jumper, Eric J., and Robert W. Mottern. 1980. A scientific investigation of the Shroud of Turin. *Applied Optics* 19:1909-12.

Kanael, Baruch. 1963. Ancient Jewish coins and their historical importance. *Biblical Archaeologist* 26(2):38-62.

Kerr, Amanda. 1896. *Life of Blessed Sebastian Valfre*. London.

Kouznetsov, Dimitri A., and Andrei A. Ivanov, Pavel R. Veletsky. 1996. Effects of fires and biofractionation of carbon isotopes on results of radiocarbon dating of old textiles: the Shroud of Turin. *Journal of Archaeological Science* 23:109-121.

Kraus, S. 1910-11. *Talmudische Archäologie*. Leizpig.

La Cava, Francesco. 1953. *La passione e la morte di N. S. Gesù Cristo illustrata dalla scienza medica*. Naples: D'Auria.

Lavoie, Bonnie B., and Gilbert R. Lavoie, Daniel Klutstein, John Regan. 1981. The body of Jesus was not washed according to the Jewish burial custom. *Sindon* 30:19-30.

Marano, Ettore. 1978. Aspetti ultrastrutturali al microscopio elletronico a scansione di fibre della Sindone di Torino [in] *La Sindone e la Scienza*. Turin: Paoline.

Marino, Joseph, and M. Sue Benford. 2000. Evidence for the skewing of the ^{14}C dating of the Shroud of Turin due to repairs. [in] *Proceedings of the Worldwide Congress Sindone 2000*. Emanuella Marinelli, Ed. On CD.

McCrone, Walter C.   1978.   A current look at carbon dating. [in] *La Sindone e la Scienza*. Turin: Paoline
----- 1980. Light microscopical study of the Turin "Shroud" 2. *The Microscope* 28:115-28.
----- 1981. Microscopical study of the Turin "Shroud" 3. *The Microscope* 29(1):19-39.
----- 1983. Comment. *Current Anthropology* 24(3):298

McNair, Philip. 1978. "The Shroud and history: Fantasy, fake, or fact?" [in] *Face to Face with the Turin Shroud*. Edited by Peter Jennings, pp. 21-40. Oxford: Mowbray.

Meacham, William. 1983. The authentication of the Turin Shroud: an issue in archaeological epistemology. *Current Anthropology* 24(3):283-295 and Reply 305-309.
----- 1986a. On carbon dating the Turin Shroud. *Shroud Spectrum International*. 19:15-25
----- 1986b. Radiocarbon measurement and the age of the Turin Shroud: possibilities and uncertainties. [in] *Turin Shroud – Image of Christ? Proceedings of a Symposium held in Hong Kong, March, 1986*. Hong Kong: Organizing Committee.

Miller, V D., and S. F. Pellicori. 1981. Ultraviolet fluorescence photography of the Shroud of Turin. *Journal of Biological Photography* 49(3):71-85

Miller, V., and D. Lynn. 1981. De Lijkwade van Turijn. *Natuur en Techniek*. February, pp. 102-25.

Moedder, Hermann. 1949. Die Todesurache dei der Kreuzigung. *Stimmen der Zeit* 144:50-59.

Moran, Kevin E.   2000. Optically terminated image pixels observed on Frei 1978 samples. [in] *Proceedings of the 1999 Shroud of Turin International Research Conference, Richmond, Virginia*. Edited by Bryan J. Walsh. Richmond: Magisterium

REFERENCES

Moroni, Mario, and Francesco Barbesino, Maurizio Bettinelli. 2000. Possible rejuventation modalities of the rdiocarbon age of the Shroud of Turin. [in] *Proceedings of the 1999 Shroud of Turin International Research Conference, Richmond, Virginia.* Richmond: Magisterium

Morris, R. A., and L. A. Schwalbe, J. R. London. 1980. X-ray fluorescence investigation of the Shroud of Turin. *X-ray Spectrometry* 9(2): 40-47

Mottern, R. W., and R. J. London, R. A. Morris.1979. Radiographic examination of the Shroud of Turin: A preliminary report. *Materials Evaluation* 38(12):39-44

Mueller, Marvin M. 1982. The Shroud of Turin: A critical appraisal. *The Skeptical Inquirer* 6(3): 15-34

Münnich, K.O. 1957. Heidelberg natural radiocarbon measurements—I. *Science* 126:194-199.

Murphy, Cullen. 1981. Shreds of evidence. *Harper's.* November, pp. 42-65.

Nickell, Joe. 1978. The Shroud of Turin – solved! *The Humanist* 38(6): 30-32.
----- 1979. The Turin Shroud: Fake? Fact? Photograph? *Popular Photography* 85(5):97-99, 146-47.
----- 1981. New evidence: The Shroud of Turin is a forgery. *Free Inquiry* 1(3):28-30.
----- 1983. *Inquest on the Shroud of Turin.* Buffalo: Prometheus Press.

O'Rahilly, Alfred. 1941. The burial of Christ. *Irish Ecclesiastical Record* 59.

Orlofsky, Patsy, and Deborah Lee Trupin. 1993. The role of connoisseurship in determining the textile conservator's treatment options. *Journal of the American Institute of Conservation* 32 (2): 109-118

Papini, Carlo. 1982. *Sindone: Un mistero che si svela.* Turin: Claudiana.

Peacock, B. A. V. 1979. The later prehistory of the Malay peninsula. [in] *Early South East Asia.* Edited by R. B. Smith and W. Watson. Oxford: Oxford University Press.

Pellicori, S. F. 1980. Spectral properties of the Shroud of Turin. *Applied Optics* 19:1913-20.

Pellicori, S. F., and R. A. Chandos. 1981. Portable unit permits UV/Vis study of "Shroud." *Industrial Research and Development*, February, pp. 186-89

Pellicori, Samuel, and Mark S. Evans. 1981. The Shroud of Turin through the microscope. *Archaeology* 34:34-43.

Raaen, Vernon F., and Gus A. Ropp, Helen P. Raaen. 1968. *Carbon-14.* New York: McGraw-Hill

Raes, G. 1976. Rapprt d'analyse du tissu, [in] *La S. Sindone*, pp. 79-84. Turin: Diocesi Torinese.

Ricci, Giulio. 1977. Historical, medical, and physical study of the Holy Shroud. *Proceedings of the U.S. Conference of Research on the Shroud of Turin.* Edited by Kenneth Stevenson, pp. 58-73. Bronx: Holy Shroud Guild.

Riggi, Giovanni. 1981. Electronic scanning microscopy and microanalysis of dust taken from burial fabrics of Egyptian mummies, in relation to dust taken from the Shroud of Turin. Paper read at the STURP conference, New London, Conn., October 9.
----- 1982. *Rapporto Sindone 1978-1982.* Turin: Il Piccolo

Rinaldi, Peter M. 1972. *It is the Lord.* New York: Vantage.
----- 1979. *When Millions Saw the Shroud.* New York: Don Bosco.

Robinson, John A. T. 1978. The Shroud and the New Testament. [in] *Face to Face with the Turin Shroud.* Edited by Peter Jennings pp. 69-80. Oxford: Mowbray.

Rodante, Sebastiano. 1982. The coronation of thorn in the light of the Shroud. *Shroud Spectrum International* 1(1): 5-24.

Rogers, R. N. 1977. Chemical considerations concerning the Shroud of Turin. *Proceedings of the U.S. Conference of Research on the Shroud of Turin.* Edited by Kenneth Stevenson, pp. 131-135. Bronx: Holy Shroud Guild.

----- 2001. Supportive comments on the Benford-Marino '16th century repairs' hypothesis. *British Society for the Turin Shroud Newsletter* 54, 28-33.
----- 2002a. The chemistry of autocatalytic processes in the context of the Shroud of Turin. http://www.shroud.com/pdfs/rogers3.pdf
----- 2002b. Pyrolysis/mass spectrometry applied to the Shroud of Turin. http://www.shroud.com/pdfs/rogers4.pdf
----- 2002c. Scientific method applied to the Shroud of Turin. (with Anna Arnoldi) http://www.shroud.com/pdfs/rogers2.pdf
----- 2005. Studies on the radiocarbon sample from the shroud of Turin. *Thermochimica Acta* 425:189-194

Sava, Anthony F. 1957. The wounds of Christ. *Catholic Biblical Quarterly* 16:438-43.

Scavone, Daniel. 1983. Review of William Meacham, 'The Authentication of the Turin Shroud: An Issue in Archaeological Epistemology.' *Shroud Spectrum International* 2 (8): 43-45.

Schafersman, Steven D. 1982a. Science, the public, and the Shroud of Turin. *The Skeptical Inquirer* 6(3):37-56.
----- 1982b. Are the STURP scientists pseudoscientists? *The Microscope* 30(3):232-34.
----- 1982c. Letter. *The Microscope* 30(4):344-52.

Schwalbe, L. A., and R. N. Rogers. 1982. Physics and chemistry of the Shroud of Turin. *Analytica Chimica Acta* 135:3-49.

Schwortz, B. 1982. Mapping of research test point areas on the Shroud of Turin. *Proceedings of the 1982 IEEE Conference on Cybernetics and Society*, pp. 538-47.

Segal, J. B. 1970. *Edessa the Blessed City*. Oxford.

Sox, H. David. 1978. Bringing the Shroud to the test. [in] *Face to Face with the Turin Shroud*. Edited by Peter Jennings, pp. 41-56. Oxford: Mowbray.
----- 1981. *The Image on the Shroud: Is the Turin Shroud a Forgery?* London: Unwin.
----- 1988. *The Shroud Unmasked – Uncovering the Greatest Forgery of All Time*. Hampshire: Lamp Press.

Stacpoole, Alberic J. 1978. The Shroud of Jesus: icon and relic. [in] *Face to Face with the Turin Shroud*. Edited by Peter Jennings, pp. 81-85. Oxford: Mowbray.

Stevenson, Kenneth E., and Gary R. Habermas. 1981. *Verdict on the Shroud*. Ann Arbor: Servant.

Stuckenrath, Robert, Jr. 1965. On the care and feeding of radiocarbon dates. *Archaeology* 18:277-81.

Tamburelli, G. 1979. La Sindone dopo l'elaborazione tridimensionale. *L'Osservatore Romano*, November 7.
----- 1981. The results in the processing of the Holy Shroud of Turin. *IEEE Transactions on Pattern Analysis and Machine Intelligence* 3(6):670-76.
----- 1982. Reading the Shroud, called the fifth Gospel, with the aid of the computer. *Shroud Spectrum International* 1(2):3-11.

Thurston, Herbert. 1903. The Holy Shroud and the verdict of history. *The Month* 101:17-29.

Turin Commission. 1976. *La S. Sindone: Ricerche e studi della commissione di esperti nominata dall'arcivescovo di Torino, card. Michele Pellegrino*. Rivista Diocesana Torinese, Supplement.

Tyrer, John. 1983. Looking at the Turin Shroud as a textile. *Shroud Spectrum International* no. 6

Tzaferis, Vasilius. 1970. Jewish tombs at and near Giv'at ha-Mivtar. *Israel Exploration Journal* 20:18-32.

Van Haelst, Remi. 2000. The Shroud of Turin and the reliability of the 95% error confidence interval. [in] *Proceedings of the 1999 Shroud of Turin International Research Conference, Richmond, Virginia*. Edited by Bryan J. Walsh. Richmond: Magisterium

Vignon, Paul. 1937. The problem of the Holy Shroud. *Scientific American* 156:162-64.
----- 1939. *Le Saint Suaire devant la science, l'archéologie, l'histoire, l'iconographie, la logique*. Paris.

Volckringer, J. 1942. *Le problème des empreints devant la science*. Paris: Carmel.

REFERENCES

Walsh, Bryan. 2000. The 1988 Shroud of Turin radiocarbon tests reconsidered. [in] *Proceedings of the 1999 Shroud of Turin International Research Conference, Richmond, Virginia*. Edited by Bryan J. Walsh. Richmond: Magisterium

Walsh, John. 1963. *The Shroud*. New York: Random House.

Weaver, Kenneth F. 1980. The mystery of the Shroud. *National Geographic* 157:730-53.

Weitzmann, K. 1976. *The Monastery of Saint Catherine at Mount Sinai: The Icons*. Vol. 1 Princeton University Press.

Wilcox, Robert K. 1977. *Shroud*. New York: Bantam.

Wilson, Edmund. 1955. *The Scrolls from the Dead Sea*. London: Allen.

Wilson, Ian. 1978. *The Turin Shroud*. Middlesex: Penguin.
----- 1979. *The Shroud of Turin*. New York: Image Books.
----- 1981. New findings on the Turin Shroud. Unpublished manuscript.
----- 1998. *The Blood and the Shroud*. London: Orion.

Wormington, H. Marie. 1983. Early man in the New World: 1970-1980 [in] *Early Man in the New World*. Edited by Richard Shutler, Jr. Beverly Hills: Sage.

Wuenschel, Edward A. 1945a. The Shroud of Turin and the burial of Christ. *Catholic Biblical Quarterly* 7:405-37.
----- 1945b. John's account of the burial. *Catholic Biblical Quarterly* 8:135-78
----- 1953. The truth about the Holy Shroud. *American Ecclesiastical Review* 129:170-87.

Zaccone, G. M. (Ed.). 2002. *The Two Faces of the Shroud*. Turin: ODPF.

Zeuner, Frederick E. 1970. *Dating the Past*. Darien (Conn.): Hafner.

Zugibe, F. T. 1981. *The Cross and the Shroud*. Cresskill: J.McDonagh.
----- 1982. *The Cross and the Shroud*. Garnerville, N.Y.: Angelus Books.

Index

Adler, Alan 14, 15, 35, 41, 43, 45, 46, 49, 50, 51, 58, 60, 67, 71, 72, 74, 75, 90, 96, 111, 116, 122, 131, 134, 136, 140, 149, 153, 155-159, 161, 173, 176-181, 197, 205, 224-227, 243, 260, 262, 263
Alcock, James 32, 43, 48, 54
AMSTAR (American Shroud of Turin Association for Research) 175, 184, 186, 192, 193, 260-261
ASSIST (Association of Scholars International for the Shroud of Turin) 59, 67-69, 108
Baima Bollone, Pierluigi 44, 69, 126, 127, 153, 154, 171, 188, 212, 238, 239, 241, 261
Ballestrero, Anastasio Cardinal 62, 64, 66- 70, 72, 76, 84, 87, 91, 93, 98, 99, 103, 108-110, 113, 117, 118, 126, 150
Baden, Michael 36, 41, 44
Barberis, Bruno 153-154, 160, 171
Barbet, Pierre 3-6, 17, 23, 26, 45
Benford, Sue 131-133, 138, 233, 242, 243, 260
British Museum 71, 76, 83, 84, 87, 93, 94-96, 101, 103, 117
British Society for the Turin Shroud 67, 68, 103, 108-110, 122, 175
Bucklin, Robert 3, 4, 6, 30, 32, 41, 44, 50, 51
Burridge, K. 33, 49
Cameron, James 3, 9, 29, 42, 45
Canuto, Vittorio 64, 65, 67, 71, 72, 75, 79, 83, 84, 87
Cardamone, Jan 150, 151, 153, 155, 175, 176, 181, 184, 196, 210, 216, 249

Chagas, Carlos 64, 66, 67, 70, 71, 74-77, 79-83, 88
Cole, John 33, 39, 40, 41, 44, 48, 49
Commission for Conservation (Turin Archdiocese) 153-158, 161, 163, 166-168, 171-172, 176-178, 181-183, 188, 191, 193, 197-199, 202-208, 210, 213-214, 217, 222-230, 233, 238, 254, 256-257
Current Anthropology ii, 32, 40, 54, 58
d'Muhala, Tom 60, 192
Damon, Paul 71, 84, 92, 129
Dardozzi, Renato 80
Delage, Yves 3, 6, 29, 39, 45
Dent, Richard 33, 39, 40
Dietz, Karlheinz 153, 171, 176, 181, 187, 191, 211, 219, 225, 239, 261
Dinegar, Bob 41, 55, 61, 63, 65, 67, 71, 72, 74, 103, 122, 265
Donahue, Douglas 71, 72, 77, 84, 92, 122, 129
Dreisbach, Albert R. "Kim" 110, 232, 233
Evin, Jacques 67, 71, 72, 143-145, 158
Fanti, Giulio 198, 199, 233, 254, 255
Fleming, Stuart 28, 41, 45, 94, 107, 132
Flury-Lemberg, Mechthild 71, 74, 76, 82, 138, 151, 153, 154, 157, 159, 166, 171, 173, 176, 181, 189, 190, 193, 201-207, 209, 210, 213-222, 224-226, 238, 239, 241, 260-262
Frei, Max 12, 15, 37, 41, 44
Garza-Valdes, Leoncio 120-127, 135, 136, 138, 139, 143, 243

INDEX

Ghiberti, Giuseppe   126, 127, 152, 153, 154, 160-163, 166-171, 173, 184, 187, 190-192, 195, 199, 207, 209, 210-215, 217, 220-222, 225, 235, 238, 248, 249, 251, 254, 256, 258, 260-262
Gonella, Luigi   iii, 58-60, 64-69, 71-75, 77, 81-84, 86-91, 93-96, 98, 99, 102, 103, 109, 110, 114, 118, 120, 126, 133, 138, 141, 147, 148, 150, 260
Gove, Harry   56, 57, 62-68, 71, 72, 74-77, 79-96, 112, 113, 120, 122- 125, 129, 135, 144
Hall, Teddy   65, 71, 72, 77, 84, 92, 97, 98, 111
Harbottle, Garman   56, 61, 62, 65, 70, 71, 73, 77, 82, 84, 85, 87, 116, 144
Hedges, Robert   71, 73, 92, 113, 119
Heller, John   14, 15, 35, 41, 43, 45, 46, 49-51, 58-61, 67, 111
Holy Shroud Guild   36, 57, 93, 108, 109, 122, 268, 271
Jackson, John   13, 34, 48, 50, 51, 60, 61, 127, 130, 131, 133, 140, 142, 159, 174, 181, 184, 187, 191, 194-196, 216
Jumper, Eric   14, 42, 44, 50, 51, 55, 103
Kouznetsov, Dimitri   127-131, 140
Landi, Sheila   150, 153, 155, 157, 175, 176, 225
Lukasik, Stephen   71, 72, 74, 88, 89
Maloney, Paul   35, 42, 44, 48, 54, 69, 195, 232, 233
Marinelli, Emanuela   155, 169, 173-175, 184, 186, 187, 191, 192, 198, 199, 233, 252
Marino, Joe   131-133, 138, 233, 242, 243, 260

Mattingly, Stephen   120-125, 128, 135, 140, 143, 157, 243
McCrone, Walter   15, 20, 34, 38, 41, 43, 45, 46, 51, 54, 56, 103, 122, 202
McNair, Philip   10, 17, 22, 47
Miller, Vernon   50, 96, 115, 165
Minor, Mike   192-193, 261-262
Mueller, Marvin   16, 35, 39, 40, 41, 44, 45, 46
Nature   89, 110, 113
Nickell, Joe   16, 20, 36, 39, 41, 43- 47
Oetzi   263
Otlet, Bob   62, 71, 72, 74, 143, 144, 145, 161, 181
Otterbein, Adam   36, 48, 62, 93, 110
Pellicori, Sam   14, 15, 37, 42, 44, 46-48, 50, 96, 181, 219, 268, 269
Petrosillo, Orazio   173, 192, 196, 199
Pfeiffer, Heinrich   176, 181, 185, 186, 191, 198, 199
Piczek, Isabel   175, 190-192
Poletto, Severino Cardinal   iii, 127, 133, 135, 146, 156-159, 161-163, 167, 168, 170, 172, 177, 179-184, 187-192, 194, 196, 197, 199, 204, 208, 210, 212, 228-231, 235, 237, 238, 240-243, 247, 249-253, 255, 256, 258, 261-262
Pontifical Academy of Sciences   ii, 57, 64-66, 71, 79, 80, 82, 85, 88, 94, 107, 168, 210, 218, 231, 232
Pope John Paul II   65, 74, 84, 105, 155, 174, 183-184, 211, 229-231, 237, 250, 261
Raes, Gilbert   12, 56, 69, 90, 92, 134, 144
Riggi, Giovanni   15, 44, 45, 46, 51, 71, 73, 74, 82, 83, 90, 91, 94,

118, 120, 121, 122, 123, 125, 126, 139, 147, 148, 164
Rinaldi, Peter M.   8, 25, 51, 57, 60, 62, 67, 70-72, 76, 83, 87, 93, 98, 99, 103, 106, 107, 110, 241, 263
Rogers, Ray   2, 12, 15, 35, 46, 50, 96, 133, 138-140, 148, 202, 207, 214, 229, 230, 234, 243, 247, 249, 250, 252, 253, 260, 262
Saldarini, Giovanni Cardinal   111, 112, 120, 126, 135, 150-152, 240
Savarino, Piero   141, 142, 153, 162, 170-172, 179, 180, 187, 189, 192, 196, 198, 207, 211-215, 222, 225, 238, 239, 242, 249, 251
Scannerini, Silvano   153, 156, 160, 162, 170, 171, 179, 180, 196, 197, 211
Scavone, Dan   114, 122, 124, 168, 196, 234
Schafersman, Steve   28, 37, 40, 41, 43, 45, 47, 55
Schwortz, Barrie   50, 96, 133, 164, 166, 221, 228, 257, 261
Sindon News   254, 256, 261
Soardo, Paolo   153, 164, 171, 172, 237, 238
Sodano, Angelo Cardinal   167, 261
Sox, David   19, 29, 55, 56, 103, 193

STURP (Shroud of Turin Research Project)   i, ii, 13-15, 20, 22, 25, 30, 34-38, 41, 42, 44-46, 49, 51, 54, 55, 57, 58, 60-72, 75, 76, 78, 81-83, 88, 89, 91-93, 96, 98, 99, 101, 103, 108, 109, 127, 133, 134, 139, 144, 150, 153, 159, 164, 172, 195, 196, 202, 207, 214, 216, 219, 224, 225, 234, 240, 241, 243, 254
Tamburelli, Giovanni   13, 38, 42, 47
Testore, Franco   90, 138, 148, 178
Tite, Michael   71, 83, 87, 91, 95, 97, 110, 117, 118, 218
Tyrer, John   114, 208
Vignon, Paul   3, 6, 20, 23, 42
Walsh, Bryan   119, 132, 141, 147, 196, 235
Whanger, Alan   13, 20, 37, 39, 41, 42, 47, 181
Wilson, Ian   2-4, 7, 9, 15, 18, 19, 42, 55, 67, 89, 97, 109, 130, 135, 142, 157, 175, 186, 193, 196, 216,
Woelfli, Willi   71, 84, 92, 101, 116, 128
Zaccone, Gian Maria   154, 158, 160, 163, 171, 219, 237, 274
Zugibe, Fred   3, 47, 174, 181, 185, 190, 223, 235